Praise for *Delivering Alpha*

Ochoa-Brillembourg's 30-year record—140 basis points above a portfolio of benchmarks, with 75 percent of rolling three-year periods yielding above-market returns—creates all the credibility necessary to make her book a primer for every serious investor. However, the real greatness of *Delivering Alpha* is how Ochoa-Brillembourg helps investors navigate the 25 percent of rolling three-year periods when they feel like failures. "There is no worse professional pain than underperforming your benchmarks." For Ochoa-Brillembourg this is where that battle for superior performance is won with philosophical vision and disciplined organization.

> —PETER ACKERMAN, former head of special projects in the
> high yield and convertible bond department and head of
> international capital markets, Drexel Burnham Lambert

What a marvelous book! Smart, informative, intelligently wrought, and beautifully written. I've been in management for my entire career, running offices and divisions for two New York publishers as well as the *Washington Post* and the Library of Congress, and I have never read as engaging and illuminating a business book as Hilda Ochoa-Brillembourg's *Delivering Alpha*. Punctuated throughout with entertaining asides, from Albert Einstein to Oscar Wilde—as well as lessons from her personal experiences—this is a primer for anyone who wishes to understand leadership practices, investment markets, the building of prosperity, the economy as a whole, and the human component that underlies all these.

> —MARIE ARANA, prizewinning author, most recently of
> *Bolivar: American Liberator*, and literary director,
> Library of Congress

Those of us who know her from her Venezuelan Quinceañera years know her as Mañanita: an unusually thoughtful girl. Now Hilda has become an unusually thoughtful and experienced portfolio manager, gifting us an unusually charming and expert account of what it takes to add value to life and portfolios alike. She teaches us it's more important over the long run to master the right piñata culture than to take home the most candies. A great lesson for the UN Security Council members. An admirable life and book.

> —AMBASSADOR DIEGO ARRIA of Venezuela,
> former president of the UN Security Council

In the sea of life, while many drift with the current, a brilliant few become the force of waves that crash the status quo and carry us forward. Hilda Ochoa-Brillembourg is one such force. *Delivering Alpha* captures the energy that imagined, developed, and nurtured an entity marked by integrity, innovation, and excellence in the pursuit of alpha. No matter one's investment acuity, readers will appreciate the illumination of ideas and the manifold skills needed to amplify that genius into practical and positive results.

> —CAROL GREFENSTETTE BATES, cofounder and
> former managing director, Strategic Investment Group

I never see this. Ever. As if penning the last letter to her heirs, one of the great minds in global investing sets out everything she has learned in 40 years. Strategy, tactics, rules of thumb, avoidable mistakes, and the talent, psychology, and governance of great investment cultures. Hilda Ochoa-Brillembourg writes for experts and professionals. But there is enough here to make anyone, in the words of the English proverb, "healthy, wealthy, and wise."

> —DAVID G. BRADLEY, chairman, Atlantic Media Group

Hilda Ochoa-Brillembourg has written a compelling insider's tour through professional, sophisticated investing. With wisdom, clarity, and the charming relief of personal stories—from childhood piñata theory to boardroom strategy—she unpacks how the best investors achieve strong, stable returns over time. *Delivering Alpha* allows all of us to learn from the very best.

> —KATHERINE BRADLEY, founding chairman, CityBridge Education

It is widely acknowledged that good governance is critical to an organization's long-term success. Actually implementing such governance, however, is another matter entirely. In *Delivering Alpha*, Hilda Ochoa-Brillembourg expertly demonstrates not only *why* good governance matters, but also *what* it looks like and *how* it can be achieved. Any manager wishing to secure a strong and stable future for his or her organization will benefit from reading this book and absorbing Ochoa-Brillembourg's wisdom.

> —ARTHUR C. BROOKS, president, American Enterprise Institute

The concepts and practices Hilda describes here were developed by bringing to the task of portfolio management the best analytical resources and experience-born judgment and insight we could find. It was exciting to be pioneering a new service model for large asset pools, and particularly satisfying to be doing so among respected, creative colleagues and friends. The only thing better than reading about it in this wonderful book was living it. Hilda offers the reader the opportunity to do both.

—MARY CHOKSI, cofounder and former managing director, Strategic Investment Group

Hilda Ochoa is one of the great investors of the last 30 years, and her book *Delivering Alpha* is a one-of-a-kind insightful journey into the facts, processes, and principles of delivering sustainable value-added in investing. And it's a pleasure to read.

—RAY DALIO, founder, co-CEO, and cochairman of Bridgewater Associates and author of the *New York Times* number one bestseller *Principles*

Delivering Alpha, like its author, Hilda, is a fountain of knowledge and wisdom. This book is a guide for institutional fiduciaries on how to create alpha over a generation time frame. Hilda's experience highlights how to combine the science of finance with pragmatic solutions to governance challenges that face institutional investors and how a culture of innovation renews the investment tools as well as renewing the governance relationships. The best reward is the enhanced wealth creation to the ultimate beneficiaries of our joint efforts.

—MICHAEL DUFFY, cofounder and former managing director, Strategic Investment Group

A one-of-a-kind book. Light on theory and serious on practice, *Delivering Alpha* is for any finance professional who wants to know how to add sustainable value to globally diversified institutional portfolios beyond what's learned in textbooks.

—RICARDO ERNST, Baratta Chair in Global Business, McDonough School of Business, Georgetown University

Over three decades, the ex-World Bank investment team led by Hilda Ochoa-Brillembourg has outperformed the market benchmark without generating any additional volatility. This well-constructed book lays out the thinking that underpinned this achievement. A mind-clearing and often mind-stretching read for investors.

—SEBASTIAN MALLABY, the Paul Volcker Senior Fellow in International Economics at the Council on Foreign Relations and author of *More Money Than God: Hedge Funds and the Making of a New Elite* and *The Man Who Knew: The Life and Times of Alan Greenspan*

Alpha is the holy grail of investment management. It is rare, difficult, elusive, and enormously valuable. Hilda is one of the very few managers who have delivered alpha consistently over a long period of time. Pay attention . . .

—JACK MEYER, former president and CEO of
the Harvard Management Company and founder CEO
of Convexity Capital Management

Hilda's book reflects both her investment acumen and creative instincts, which she translated into an enduring enterprise that continues to thrive years after her departure. As the investment environment evolves, the principles of analytical rigor, disciplined governance, innovation, and collaboration espoused in Hilda's book are her lasting legacy that guides us in the continuing pursuit of alpha for all of our clients.

—BRIAN A. MURDOCK, president and CEO
of Strategic Investment Group

Hilda Ochoa-Brillembourg's technical prowess as a finance professional is as impressive as her ability to combine the state-of-the-art techniques she masters with a deep understanding of human behavior. These pages are full of useful, actionable insights. A must-read.

—MOISÉS NAÍM, Distinguished Fellow, Carnegie Endowment,
and author of *The End of Power*

Every finance professional, portfolio manager, and individual investor should read this book. But so should everyone else who wants to know what it takes to build and run a successful organization focused on challenging problems in a highly competitive space. You will leave *Delivering Alpha* with new ways of thinking about investment risk and reward (pay special attention to "portfolio fit"!). But you'll also leave it with a rare wisdom—about managing organizations, recognizing and rewarding talent, decision making, and governance—that will serve anyone who aspires to build or lead a complex organization in a volatile world.

—DAVID NIRENBERG, executive vice provost,
Deborah R. and Edgar D. Jannotta Distinguished Service Professor,
Committee on Social Thought, The University of Chicago

The world is in the midst of a mutation. Changing times always create uncertainties and opportunities; geopolitically, socially, and, yes, for investment. The key is knowing how to sensibly approach an environment under transformation with both speed and depth. Through her exceptionally long and successful career, Hilda Ochoa-Brillembourg has navigated the shallow waters of a changing world using a particular approach based on principles tested and developed over time. *Delivering Alpha* is the product of that 30-year journey. It is an invaluable resource for investors during this time of global and societal transformation."

> —ANA PALACIO, former Spanish Minister of Foreign Affairs
> and former senior vice-president and general counsel
> of the World Bank Group

After a successful career in the highest stratospheres of global finance, Hilda Ochoa's gift to the world is *Delivering Alpha*. Her framework for managing funds and delivering results, including the innovative Fit Theory, will become a must-read for business students and the most sophisticated asset managers. But it's her humility, humor, and honesty that makes the work compelling. The added bonus is a set of practical and battlefield-tested tools for investment committees and boards to raise their game to the highest standards, which has been a hallmark of Hilda's entire career.

> —DOUGLAS PETERSON, president and CEO, S&P Global

In this insightful and psychologically astute book, a masterful investment strategist shows us, step by step, how to achieve a portfolio that is the right fit for the specific investor. Leavening complex theory with personal anecdotes, *Delivering Alpha* is like a rare feast that is both delicious and good for you.

> —NORMAN E. ROSENTHAL, M.D., clinical professor
> of psychiatry at Georgetown University Medical School
> and author of *Super Mind*

The Bible on risk management. Full of rich, juicy anecdotes from an industry insider. If you are a serious investor, run, don't walk, and buy a copy.

> —DAVID M. SMICK, CEO of Johnson Smick International, Inc.,
> and author of the *New York Times* bestseller *The World Is Curved*

Hilda Ochoa-Brillembourg pioneered the use of alternatives in institutional portfolios, adding a rich set of opportunities for forward-thinking investment professionals. Unlike Warren Buffett, who seems overly concerned with gross fees, Hilda recognizes that superior managers overcome the fee burden to produce excess returns for their partners. She further knows that great teams identify winners. In fact, her multidecade record of adding value for her clients proves the point. While her discussion of the nuts and bolts provides valuable background for portfolio management practitioners, the central takeaway from her book is that effective governance underpins success. Without a high-quality investment committee focused on the right issues and without a top-notch investment staff executing on the right plan, portfolio management will fail. *Delivering Alpha* belongs on the bedside table of every serious practitioner of asset management. Read it and learn!

—DAVID F. SWENSEN, chief investment officer, Yale University,
and author of *Pioneering Portfolio Management:
An Unconventional Approach to Institutional Investment*

Thirty-plus years—from my 90-plus years perspective not so long, but long enough to experience enormous changes in the world at large and in the financial world in particular: unbridled enthusiasm to corrosive doubts, the triumph of free markets to costly dependence on official rescues of shaky institutions; reasoned and successful investment strategies have never been more challenged. This book is a reassuring collection of ideas, unlike the sagas of greed, misplaced loyalties, and fraud that have characterized too much of "Wall Street" in recent years. *Delivering Alpha* highlights the value of being open to new approaches, adapting to perpetual, sometimes tumultuous changes. This is a good, thoughtful book.

—PAUL VOLCKER, former chairman, Federal Reserve

DELIVERING
ALPHA

DELIVERING ALPHA

Lessons from 30 Years of

Outperforming

Investment Benchmarks

HILDA OCHOA-BRILLEMBOURG

New York   Chicago   San Francisco   Athens   London   Madrid
Mexico City   Milan   New Delhi   Singapore   Sydney   Toronto

1 2 3 4 5 6 7 8 9   LCR   23 22 21 20 19 18

ISBN   978-1-260-44148-2
MHID   1-260-44148-2

ISBN   978-1-260-44149-9
MHID   1-260-44149-0

This publication is designed to provide accurate and authoritative information in regard to the subject matter covered. It is sold with the understanding that neither the author nor the publisher is engaged in rendering legal, accounting, securities trading, or other professional services. If legal advice or other expert assistance is required, the services of a competent professional person should be sought.

> —*From a Declaration of Principles Jointly Adopted by a Committee of the American Bar Association and a Committee of Publishers and Associations*

Library of Congress Cataloging-in-Publication Data

Names: Ochoa-Brillembourg, Hilda, author.
Title: Delivering alpha : lessons from 30 years of outperforming investment
    benchmarks / Hilda Ochoa-Brillembourg.
Description: 1 Edition. | New York : McGraw-Hill Education, 2018.
Identifiers: LCCN 2018030689| ISBN 9781260441482 (hardback) | ISBN 1260441482
Subjects: LCSH: Investments. | Portfolio management.
Classification: LCC HG4521 .O234 2018 | DDC 332.6—dc23
LC record available at https://lccn.loc.gov/2018030689

McGraw-Hill Education books are available at special quantity discounts to use as premiums and sales promotions or for use in corporate training programs. To contact a representative, please visit the Contact Us page at www.mhprofessional.com.

To life and freedom, to Arturo, and to our children
and grandchildren who make it all worthwhile.

Contents

PART III
Structuring the Asset Class

PART IV
Selecting and Terminating Managers

PART V
Measuring and Managing Risks

PART VI
Built to Last: Leadership Attributes, Creative Management, Succession Planning, and Transitions

Preface

THE FIRST QUESTION you are asked when you write a book is, "Who is it for?" This book is for any finance professional who wants to know how to add sustainable value to globally diversified institutional portfolios beyond what's learned in textbooks. It's for investment committees and board members who would like to be better fiduciaries by increasing their understanding of the impact of their actions on portfolio returns. It's for professionals who have already been exposed to the basic principles of portfolio management—valuation, expected returns, volatility, correlations, and diversification—and who want to learn the limits of modern portfolio theory and how experienced practitioners can profitably depart from standard academic theory.

The book is intended as a practical guide to building intelligent, sensible, and sensibly managed portfolios; to creating a decision-making governance structure and process that reduces errors and correctly assigns responsibilities and incentives; to selecting the most astute, competent, dedicated fiduciary boards and agents to help you manage your portfolio over time; and to terminating managers and reversing errors. It is light on theory and serious on practice. We hope it helps readers develop a better understanding of the process by which you can deliver *alpha*, risk-adjusted excess returns, fairly consistently over time. Over the long run, well-managed globally diversified portfolios can add sustainable value over a purely passively managed option, net of all costs and without significant increases in volatility—sometimes with lower volatility.

A Bit of History

My colleagues and I have managed assets for corporate, nonprofit, and family groups for over 40 years. That includes our time at the World Bank, whose pension fund we managed for 20 years, first inside (1976–1987) and then at Strategic Investment Group (1987–1995), the firm we founded in 1987. Over the 30 years through late 2017, Strategic outperformed its benchmarks for all major asset classes and for total balanced portfolios more than 75 percent of the time on a rolling three-year basis. The investment team underperformed the benchmarks in only 4 of 30 years. The value added has accrued with less volatility than the benchmarks exhibited. This outperformance was achieved under widely diverse client needs and circumstances and while dealing with differing, sometimes less than ideal, governance—that is, the organizational setup, the timing, and the manner and quality of the decision-making process in use by those responsible for approving policy and monitoring performance.

From Strategic's inception, its governance structure was designed to complement or supplement, and in all cases strengthen, our clients' governance. Optimal governance structures are rare and in my experience persist only in exceptional cases. Judging by its performance, Yale University seems to be one of those few cases. Yale's sustainable value added is a testament to its strong governance as well as to the skills and tenure of chief investment officer David F. Swensen's group. Optimal governance structures are robust and supportive of skilled service providers. They are long-term oriented while responsive to short-term needs, and they are committed to innovation and independent thinking.

Strategic was founded to provide focused, fact-based, comprehensive investment management services based on global asset allocation with multiple managers of assets and dynamic risk management. Our "open architecture" asset management structure—offering clients financial products from other firms as well as our own oversight—was rare at the time as an outsourcing option but is now the model most commonly used in the institutional world. Parts of certain chapters of this book describe specific services offered by Strategic as well as others. I do so only when I believe that is the most useful information I can offer in each case, and I try to include enough information for readers to make that judgment for themselves. I have an ethical duty to alert you that past performance should not be construed as an assurance of future success. The assumptions and tables throughout the book simply illustrate how the data might all come together into a strategic framework. They're not forecasts, recommendations, or samples of any particular investor portfolio. As the narrative makes abundantly clear, each investor and market brings a unique set of needs and opportunities.

Delivering Alpha reflects on what I believe have been the major contributors adding value and keeping a competitive advantage over time despite increasingly complex capital markets and competitive forces. I document some important concepts to help fiduciaries correct some of the less constructive habits of governance and financial theory I have observed. Innovation and independent thinking are central to this refinement and improvement. Decision-making tools and capital market knowledge should be continually refined and improved.

I want this to be a concise, useful book, to be snacked upon, depending on your particular interests and concerns. It is not a treatise on investment theory, of which there are so many, a few of which I list in the Bibliography. The knowledge I wish to share is nuanced and subtle. The right path has many ambiguous junctures where certainty is elusive. Nuanced knowledge based on experience and wisdom might turn off readers in search of black-and-white arguments. Those arguments are attractive to beginners in the field, who should stay away from any form of active management and go for minimum cost, broadest diversification, and passive management. Delivering alpha requires subtly timed and textured investment decisions. But even passive management requires some subtlety and wisdom, not always characteristics of rookies. Quite often, academically inclined amateurs, along with a few tenured academic theorists, opt for total indexing at the exactly worst possible time, after the markets have gone through a long, unsustainable rally and have become extremely overvalued. This is a case of a little knowledge being dangerous. This behavior happens regularly, particularly but not exclusively with retail investors who flock to equity or bond index mutual funds and exchange-traded funds (ETFs) after a couple of years of outstanding returns only to face significant losses when prices fall.

Convictions, particularly simple ones, are severely tested from time to time. Most people fail those tests! To paraphrase Josh Billings, certainty is much more dangerous than uncertainty.[1] Greed and fear more than wisdom guide the emotions of almost every human being when markets appear irresistibly alluring or frightening. Randomness, abundant in life, allows disciplined investors to take advantage of extreme valuation anomalies, banking on historic cycles that generally drive markets to revert to mean values.

The investment world sails on many myths—and many inspiring, motivating, big, and lasting lies. Here are three among those that we will challenge in these pages.

- **Myth number one: Markets are fairly valued.** Given the wide levels of volatility around "fair" price, that fair price is as fair as the chance that a reality TV star will stay married for more than seven years: 50–50? 80–20? Zero? How could prices be fair, when over 30-plus years we have found more than 100 active managers beating benchmarks pretty consistently, and we have done so ourselves? It must mean that experienced players get a very unfair, but well-deserved, advantage against impulsive or inexperienced investors.
- **Myth number two: Diversification is the only free lunch.** Diversification is a wise strategy, but whether it is a free lunch depends largely on whether the asset you are diversifying into is overvalued. Correlations are anything but stable, and they tend to go to 1 when we need diversification the most. The best free lunch is the meal left at the table by panicked investors. The profitable pickings come from actively focusing on purchasing cheap assets after a crash when bargains are abundant.
- **Myth number three: The coming decades of predicted slow growth and high volatility do not bode well for equity markets.** In fact, there is little correlation between economic growth and equity returns, because growth expectations are priced pretty quickly into multiples. There is no better place to add value than a no-growth, politically charged, opinionated, volatile marketplace. You get many chances at the roulette table to

buy low and sell high because quarterly volatility is high and the markets keep adjusting prices to compensate for the volatility. I look forward to the next 20 years with tempered enthusiasm.

I'm keenly aware that the future is for those who live in it; they will develop their own theories in response to market and world events as well as to their own professional development and needs. Every generation is entitled to repeat past mistakes and learn anew from its own. Governments and regulations will change and affect investment opportunities. But I have learned four timeless lessons: *Timing, market awareness, price,* and *relative value to the investor (goodness of fit)* are critical drivers of effective investment decisions. Investors will rediscover them and dispute them at their own peril.

My experience has been enriched by the work of a highly trained and experienced global investment team with access to the most talented external managers in all asset classes. Responsibilities have been actively transferred to the team by the firm's founding partners over many years, but particularly since 2002. I gradually ceded management and research responsibilities until my retirement as CEO in 2014. Keen awareness of the inexorable passage of time and the force of retirement needs, as well as the intellectual growth and readiness of our successors, guided an explicit effort to transfer knowledge and culture. We fully expected the founders would be bested by their successors. This has clearly been the case. Technological and cognitive advances are the renewable and expanding real wealth of the human species.

The added value delivered over many years for long-term clients, past and present, didn't depend on good or bad luck, though we experienced both. I feel emboldened to summarize our experience because there is now strong evidence of repeatable skill, beyond 30 years, including the time during which we initiated the process at the World Bank pension fund and the intervening years of refinement and improvement. The process reflects the knowledge and expertise accumulated over the professional lifetimes of many smart and dedicated investors, during a period in which we have enjoyed free, highly competitive, and globally traded security markets. We have lived at a time in which world capital markets increased fivefold in less than 25 years. I believe many elements of our approach will succeed in less conducive times ahead, as they happily did during and after multiple market crises including the crash of 2008. But be warned: this approach has not been tested in extraordinarily extended market disruptions such as the ones experienced in world wars. Holding large amounts of well-diversified cash to invest sporadically in uniquely mispriced opportunities might be the way to handle periods of extended market dysfunction.

The growth in financial assets and increasingly sophisticated products supporting their development allowed us to take advantage of market inefficiencies where we found them, mostly in newly securitized assets, emerging management styles, and orphaned assets with bright prospects. But we have been just as driven to make use of inexpensive, passively managed market products where there have been few inefficiencies to exploit.

Importantly, the investment process has been tested with clients possessing impeccably robust investment governance *and* some with flawed governance. Flawed governance can take many forms, but most commonly it shows in impulsive decision making, reward systems that discourage measured risk taking, slow responses to improved policy choices, and behavior driven by fear and greed. We learned from both kinds of governance. Surprisingly and quite counterintuitively, I have found bad governance tends to persevere, while great governance can come to an abrupt halt. After a period of good followed by bad governance, there is some hope of returning to good governance. As suggested by the historian Barbara Tuchman, it's much easier to reconstruct a society destroyed by war than to build one from scratch; but in the case of weakened business governance structures, the right glue may be lost for a long time. That's why good governance should be furiously defended and preserved. Like virtue, it can withstand a lot, but once lost it is hard to fully regain.

The Piñata Strategy

The strategies we develop to accomplish our objectives, including building and managing portfolios that will meet investment goals, arise from many forces: heredity, opportunities, experience, and chance. Some memories are particularly telling. For me, none is as poignant as my recollection of piñatas and the strategy I developed to cope successfully with their challenge.

I was born and raised in Caracas, Venezuela, in a middle-class family. My father was a pilot who evolved into an airline executive. My mother stayed at home, vocally disappointed by not having been allowed to become a physician. When I was about six, piñata parties were not necessarily fun, at least not for me. Mother would dress me up in itchy, cumbersome dresses, while the boys wore comfortable pants. They could hit the piñata and make a run for the candies that spilled out. The girls with their pretty dresses were at a serious disadvantage.

So what was a girl to do? Was it to be first at the bat and watch the following action comfortably from a safe place (it was easy to get hit randomly by the bat)? Was it to break the piñata and feel like a hero? Was it to get the most candies? I tried all three strategies and concluded that getting the most candies should, indeed, be the benchmark by which I judged my own success. Knowing my objective made the experience fun and worth pursuing.

Developing the best strategy to get the most candies became clear by observing piñata dynamics. I determined to be among the three to five last players to hit the piñata. It was important not to be the one to break it open: The last one to break it, the hero, lost valuable time getting to the candies. Being second or third from the last meant one could break it a bit, satisfying the lust of the crowd, but still have time to get to the optimal position to capture the most candy when the piñata broke. As it broke, I would run quickly to where the candies were falling and squat on the ground with my puffy skirt spread widely. I would scoop as many candies I could get under the skirt, wait for all the kids to move away, and bring all the candies from under my skirt into the pouch of my gathered skirt, now transformed into a generous sack. Thus I turned the major disadvantage of a large, puffy dress into an effective candy-gathering weapon.

At the party, a couple of kids would always end up crying because they didn't have enough candies, which gave me the opportunity to share my winnings with them. Whether these were the sentiments of a budding philanthropist or just a sense of fairness, it gave me great pleasure to share the wealth. For me, success meant not how many candies I could take home but rather that I could win the piñata game! Years later at Harvard Business School, I learned that the Piñata Strategy was an early use of SWOT analysis—an approach to corporate planning based on an analysis of strengths, weaknesses, opportunities, and threats.[2]

As I grew up, it became clear that life was a bit more complex than a piñata. But the core elements of those early findings have remained with me to this day: clarity of mission and clarity of strategy in an uncertain world are critical to success.

Key among my findings is the distinction between decisions that are reversible and those that are not. Incremental decisions, such as my trying out different approaches to the piñata until I found the one that best accomplished my mission, are highly reversible. With many piñatas a month, I could try different strategies. Small, reversible decisions should not be feared. Revolutionary changes—such as having kids or dramatically changing your portfolio policy—are expensive or impossible to reverse and should be pondered carefully.

Introduction

The Incredible Ride

ANY COMPILATION OF lessons ought to be read in the context in which they were learned. Any investment strategy ought to be designed to fit the prevailing macroeconomic and market environment. Our experiences are no exception.

It has been quite a ride for investors since the oil crisis of the seventies. That shock brought the U.S. economy to its knees and, along with amazing competition from Japan, forced a restructuring of corporate America. The restructuring was facilitated by Michael Milken and his team at Drexel Burnham Lambert and their innovative use of junk (aka high yield) bonds. Through high-yield financing, it became surprisingly easy to acquire and break up the inefficiently managed conglomerate structures that had come to dominate corporate strategy in the previous decades. The expense of high-yield debt motivated acquirers to control costs and capital budgets and focus on earnings growth for the individual component companies. CEOs were forced to be less imperial portfolio managers and more focused company managers.

While not wholly constructive—the upheaval led to Milken's conviction for illegal stock parking and Drexel's bankruptcy—ousters and replacements of managements financed by high-yield debt ended the American era of uncompetitive management complacency. Now, when complacency reappears, it can often be corrected (again, not always constructively) by activist investors with access to ample financing to displace boards and management. Sometimes just the threat of corporate activism can be enough to force more efficient behavior from management.

As the microeconomic picture was improving, on the macroeconomic front growth prospects were transformed by the passage of ERISA (the Employee Retirement Income Security Act of 1974) and a burst of human capital formation as the baby boomers, professional women, and increased numbers of immigrants joined the labor force. ERISA forced corporations to fund their defined benefit pension plans, sharply boosting long-term institutional savings and investment in the United States. That provided additional sources of growth capital and financial innovation in traditional and less traditional markets. The rewards to capital investment were endangered, however, by inflationary pressures dating back to the oil crisis and excessive government spending during the Vietnam War, bringing about the political and economic need to appoint a determined inflation buster and one of the most virtuous U.S. public servants, Paul Volcker, to a revolutionary stewardship at the Federal Reserve from 1979 to 1987. The U.S. and world inflationary spirals were controlled rapidly (and violently for Latin American debt holders). The shift in monetary policy was accompanied in 1981 by record bond yields and therefore record low bond prices, allowing us to tilt our portfolios in favor of long-term bonds and capture extraordinary returns when inflation was subdued.

Restructuring corporate America, controlling inflation through tight monetary policy, increasing competition through deregulation, breaking up major monopolies, and getting past the costs of the Vietnam War created years of noninflationary growth that showcased the vitality of free markets. (No wonder Ronald Reagan's presidency is regarded with such admiration by friends and not a few foes.) Along with the sustainable military superiority of the developed democracies, resurgent Western economies eventually helped bring down the totalitarian USSR, opening world markets to almost unprecedented increases in growth, trade, and financial assets.

When markets show sustained growth and development, new opportunities for profitable investments appear. Private assets are securitized and become easily tradable. We took advantage of newly securitized assets, including real estate, private equity, international equities, emerging markets, high-yield bonds, and hedge funds, because they tended to be attractively priced. However, in time, as assets like these become more liquid and popular, market efficiency cuts down opportunities to add value through active management. That can increase the impact of management selection for each asset class. Choosing asset managers well requires observing pricing inefficiencies, identifying new management styles, and understanding the environment in which active managers are operating. The process by which a decision maker for a pension fund, endowment, or family assets may seek new asset classes and control the manager mix is covered in Parts II, III, and IV.

Recent decades have been a period of extremely active securitization. More than 100 stock and bond markets emerged, and derivative securities exploded in number and size to become household names among large institutional investors. Investable assets including bank deposits increased fivefold in a quarter century, from $48 trillion in 1990 to $252 trillion in 2015.[1] Since the fall of the Berlin Wall, world GDP has almost tripled from around $28 trillion to $78 trillion in 1990 constant international dollars, while world trade has quadrupled. Its share of world GDP has grown from 39 to 60 percent.[2] This was a singularly exciting period to be an investor. But competition also became increasingly fierce, with some of the world's sharpest competitive minds entering the lucrative and growing investment field.

Without such growth in trade, GDP, and investable assets, it would have been harder to achieve attractive absolute returns. And even though value added—alpha—is more critical when returns are low, alpha might have been more volatile. Along the way we experienced bull and bear markets, bubbles and crashes in the United States and abroad that tested every conviction of seasoned investors.

It was a period of relative world peace and historically unprecedented expansion of wealth, with the attendant set of market abuses and regulatory backlash. It was also a period in which extreme poverty collapsed from 37 percent of the world's population in 1990 to under 10 percent in 2015,[3] underscoring the value of free trade, competition, and investments in health and education as incomparable sources of wealth creation and poverty reduction. Reduced poverty and rising wealth increase competition for the management of savings pools. Competition, an extreme quality of liquid financial markets, forces finance professionals to remain technically savvy and innovative. Qualitative experience and quantitative tools need constant updating.

While its benefits are obvious, high growth also increases income inequality and may give rise to political and financial instability. Understanding the sources of inequality and potential political and financial volatility may be more critical in managing portfolios over the next 10 to 20 years than it was from the 1990s to 2008. Let's first try to understand why high growth brings inequality. As Albert-László Barabási documented in his book *Linked: The New Science of Networks*,[4] the higher the growth rate, the more all of us benefit, but the larger will be the spread between those closest to the growth vectors (absolute and relative winners) and those farther from the action (relative losers). The clearest example of this phenomenon is the internet. In a perfectly equal internet world, traffic would be equally distributed. In fact, despite no barriers to entry, 10 percent of the websites soon attracted more than 90 percent of the traffic.

An increase in social envy, workforce displacement and unemployment, political unrest, populism, and extremism may be the price we pay for rapid innovation and high growth, particularly when the growth slows down. That's been the environment since 2008 and the one we may continue to experience over the next decade or two; much will depend on whether the millennial generation, those born between 1980 and 2000, gets to enjoy its own demographic dividend—the increase of income over expenses that baby boomers enjoyed in their forties and fifties. Much will depend as well on how we manage global human resources and migration policies. Managing through political and capital market uncertainty is covered in Part V.

Inequality and how societies deal with it aren't the only potential risks. Faced by increasing radical, populist, or just outright destructive views of Western free market systems after the 2008 global market collapse, central banks moved to defend growth and democracy by flooding developed economies with liquidity. Gushing liquidity reduced interest rates to encourage investment, consumption, growth, and employment. The massive injection has, however, dramatically increased the government's role in the economy and significantly decreased expected returns on bonds and equities. Unwinding nearly zero interest rate monetary policies around the world puts us in unknown territory.

Our expectations for investment returns, volatilities, and correlations might now be for lower returns and erratic volatility of returns, rather than simply using long-term historical figures and projecting more of the same. This is a subject elaborated in Part II.

No Tree Grows to Heaven: Threats to Growth

The 2008 crash proved that too much leverage can be lethal to investors, borrowers, and lenders alike. Financial intermediaries and U.S. homebuyers had borrowed too much. Excessive leverage sparked the backlash of increased regulations and controls over financial intermediaries, now likely to be reviewed. Thankfully, nonfinancial corporations weren't overleveraged. They retained the productive capacity to maintain slow but steady growth despite the collapse of a few financial intermediaries.

The threat of social radicalization and authoritarian regimes is the highest we have observed in the last 50 years. It presents a real challenge to the well-being of humanity and investment portfolios. The challenge comes in the form of so-called Knightian uncertainty (outcomes for which we cannot measure the odds—unlike risks, which are situations where we can't know the outcome but can predict the odds).[5] Unpredictability will accentuate a need to identify fairly priced assets that "fit" particular global uncertainties and our own existing portfolios and that add insulation against political shocks. We develop these concepts in Parts I and III.

The deceleration of the fast, overleveraged global economic growth experienced through mid-2007 has disillusioned many and created both anarchical populist movements and extreme liberal and conservative responses. The pendulum seems to have swung not completely but certainly against the free-market-driven world equilibrium of the 1990s and early 2000s. The resulting macroeconomic and political developments will create price and valuation swings—and opportunities to take advantage of price corrections. Importantly, these opportunities can only be seized if investors carry sufficient liquidity in their portfolios and have diversified risks well. This subject is covered in Part V.

Major economies face other significant challenges not yet properly addressed: aging populations in the developed world, India, and China; the need to design wise immigration and training policies to help rebalance those age demographics in the United States, Europe, and Japan; employment disruptions from technological breakthroughs; insufficient savings for health and retirement needs; increasing terrorist threats; nuclear proliferation; an eruption of rogue political leaders not seen since the mid-twentieth century; slow growth and possible deflation—or inflation if we overcorrect for deflationary threats—and the longer-term challenges of climate uncertainty.

All these factors point to a world of lower returns, larger migrations, and volatility shocks. It is a world in which asset diversification is most critical, and yet there are now few reasonably priced diversifying assets. The silver lining in the market corrections certain to come is that they will create opportunities to diversify risks at reasonable and even attractive valuations. In this likely scenario of diminished returns, higher volatility, and Knightian uncertainty, every building block covered in the six sections of the book is critical to achieving an outcome in which you add to rather than detract from market returns. The quality of governance covered in Part VI is a central ingredient for sustaining returns in an era of increased uncertainty.

Clearly, we may not have seen the end of this phase of history. These cycles take 20 to 30 years, a generation, before we learn from and correct our generational mistakes. Barring world wars, societies should find their path to growth, social connectedness, and freedom over time. That's how human beings iteratively move toward social equilibrium and growth after they have tried and failed with extreme alternatives. But first we must grapple with a time in which Knightian *uncertainty* is as high as or higher than measurable *risks*. The way to look at the shape and management of measurable risks and unmeasurable uncertainty is taken up in Part V.

Initial Proof of Concept

We learned our initial skills at the World Bank pension fund and developed some of our first tools and lasting beliefs there. Some of the methods we developed while at the World Bank may still be in use, with increasing levels of precision and subtlety honed by experiential wisdom. Most of the tools have been developed by our talented successors, and we are proud of that intergenerational accomplishment.

Our strong World Bank returns were based on three major concepts:

- Expected alpha from placing certain assets with small, specialized external investment management boutiques, which could effectively compete with large money center banks. Surprisingly, boutiques temporarily hurt our equity segments in the three years through 1986. Smaller active-management firms tended to equal-weight their investments, favoring small-capitalization stocks rather than the larger-cap stocks that make up broad market indexes. That experience taught us that every investment style has its cycle, and the best predictor of a cycle may be the relative valuation of the style (undervalued styles offer better prospects) and the popularity of the segment (the less the better).
- The search for significantly undervalued *newly securitized* assets, such as hedge funds, high-yield bonds, and international equities including emerging markets. These investments not only increased returns but also helped reduce total portfolio volatility.
- Efficiently diversifying into cheaper assets and managing market risks. We bet heavily on bonds in 1981–1982 when long-term yields reached 15 percent. This bet worked wonderfully in less than a year. And in the mid-eighties we took an extreme bet to underweight Japan. The Japan decision decimated our relative non-U.S. equity returns for several years but paid off significantly in 1989. A more granular and nuanced scaling of risks based on these experiences helped us deliver less volatile returns since.

For the 11-plus years I worked at the World Bank, the application of these three concepts required new analytical tools, a strong, trustworthy

governance structure, and attention to recruiting and developing insightful colleagues with diverse educational and cultural backgrounds. The outcome, as reported in the World Bank Staff Retirement Plan annual report
for 1986, was 330 to 560 basis points per year of value added relative to
the median performance of the 100 largest pension funds in the United
States.[6] This performance often placed the World Bank pension fund in
the top percentile of that universe. We continued to develop and employ
strategies, analytical tools, and decision-making processes that delivered
sustained value added for our clients. Identifying and developing human
capital have been central. Part VI adds color to aspects of cultural development and human capital management that can contribute greatly to better
governance and decision making.

Sources of Value Added, Net of Fees

The ability to generate value added continued as the firm's founders transferred knowledge and responsibilities to the successor teams. As Figure I.1
shows, rolling three-year total balanced-portfolio returns exceeded benchmarks more than 76 percent of the time. Underperformance was concentrated in periods of high market returns; these tend to coincide with periods
of overvaluation such as 1998–1999, when we reduced valuation risks prior
to market corrections.

Figure I.2 shows that one can add value with lower volatility and a better
Sharpe ratio. Sharpe ratios compare returns with units of risk (volatility).

Seemingly small amounts of yearly value added, compounding over time,
are significant to wealth creation. Strategic's risk-adjusted returns were 35
percent higher than the benchmarks (0.65 versus 0.49). Thanks to the magic
of compound returns, this outperformance has big consequences. An investment of $100 over 30 years would yield a terminal value of $1,402 versus
$952 invested in the policy benchmark, a 46 percent increase in terminal
wealth. Even 1 percent makes a really big difference over time. A single point
of compound value added to an 8 percent benchmark return adds 20 percent
to terminal wealth in 10 years.

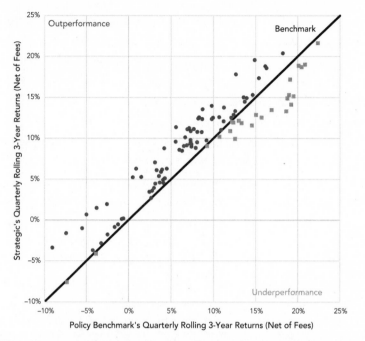

FIGURE I.1   Strategic's quarterly returns versus benchmarks, 1991–2017

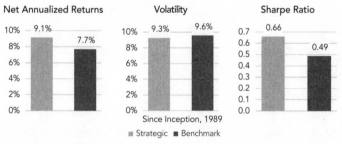

FIGURE I.2   Decades of excess returns without added volatility.

Strategic Investment Group's composite global balanced portfolio generated 1.4 percent of net-of-fee value added per year from 1989 through March 2018, without raising portfolio volatility. The net value added was not just at the total portfolio level but also across individual asset classes. Returns are net of all fees for balanced portfolios. The portfolios include an efficiently diversified mix of U.S. and international equities, fixed income, hedge funds, private equities, venture capital, real estate, and commodities, measured against broadly accepted market indexes and client-approved dollar-weighted benchmarks.

*Unless otherwise noted, the sources of all performance and market benchmark estimates in this book are Strategic Investment Group and/or client-approved benchmark index providers.

Strategic's staff has included diverse economists, engineers, statisticians, actuaries, modelers, financial analysts, and portfolio theorists, educated at some of the world's most demanding, respected, and diverse universities. As a group, the staff has read most of the relevant literature and research papers by academics and practitioners. To do well, you need to understand the analytical tools that have been developed by the greatest minds over the last 300 years, ranging from statistical and probability theory to macroeconomic policy, and you need to understand portfolio theory from classical to Keynesian to behavioral economics. Wisdom and insight can come from the most unexpected places. We have spent thousands of hours reading and listening to knowledgeable and sometimes obscure experts, from the halls of academia to the corridors of journalists and practitioners, analyzing premortem and postmortem daily market events. If 10,000 hours marks the threshold of expertise in any field, many of the senior investment principals have booked multiples of those threshold hours of focused attention to the topic of adding value to investment portfolios. Insightful expertise beats data mining and any theoretical construct over time. Hours of expertise increase the sample size and statistical relevance of your conclusions. And at all times one should keep an open mind, a certain amount of intellectual innocence and curiosity to nurture informed intuition and creativity. Be open to surprises and new opportunities. *Don't allow expertise to blind you to innovation and creativity.*

Experience teaches us what we know and what we don't or can't know. Most importantly it has taught me that expertise and fact-based analysis are critical in controlling the human and sometimes destructive impulses that drive many of our actions. Impulses should first trigger thought and analysis, including a deep, unbiased search for facts and insight, and subsequently drive focused, disciplined action.

I now reflect from the vantage point of having worked in a highly experienced, disciplined investment organization that uses passive and active external managers to compete in one of the most competitive arenas: global capital markets. We haven't been alone in our portfolio management journey. As arguably the first dedicated outsourcer for complex, competitively robust global portfolios, we have been surrounded by some of the best minds in the business, including the hundreds of outstanding specialist external managers we hired over time to help us manage our clients' portfolios. Creating a culture of trust that fosters acquiring and sharing insights is a critical component of good governance.

In the past 40 years we have met and discussed investments in every asset class with thousands of managers. We have seen dozens of asset classes and many more investment approaches emerge and decline. Markets destroyed by wars and revolution were rebuilt and opened after the fall of the Soviet Union in the late eighties and in dozens of emerging markets in Asia, Eastern Europe, the Middle East, Africa, and Latin America.

Our willingness to serve on corporate and nonprofit boards has been valuable in developing lasting governance qualities. We have observed how decisions are made by some of the best and best-intentioned decision makers, along with unfortunately some poor ones.

As I reflect on four decades of experience, I feel much gratitude to those I have worked with and for, and I feel I owe my colleagues, peers, clients, future clients, and newcomers to the investment field a well-reasoned summary of what I have learned. I'll also try to sum up the things we may never know.

What I Have Learned

Here are 10 lessons I have learned and around which I have organized the six sections of this book.

1. Price Is Not Value

The value of an asset to any particular investor may be lower or higher than the price (or fair value) of the asset in the marketplace, depending on the correlation of that asset to the investor's legacy (existing) portfolio and needs. This is true even if the investor agrees with market forecasts. Many portfolios contain legacy assets or structures (and reflect client needs) that cannot be easily or cost-effectively changed. Financial theory is insufficient to understand the relationship between market prices and investors' utility curves, which lead to different "fair values" (multiple equilibrium pricing) for the same asset depending on the investor. Assets have a *market price* available to all buyers but have a different relative *value* to different buyers. Part I offers a shortcut formula I have found useful to begin identifying assets that fit your legacy portfolio better than other assets.

There is a brilliant moral assessment of flawed characters we encounter in life in Oscar Wilde's swipe at people who know "the price of everything and the value of nothing." In investing as in life, theory may teach you how the market sets the *price* of assets, but it will not fully tell you whether that price equals the *value* of that asset when added to *your* existing portfolio. In the world of efficient-market believers, this first lesson is probably the most controversial of my findings and possibly the most relevant. The difference between market value and value to an investor might help explain the gap between multiple equilibriums in efficient and inefficient markets—those conditions where different investors are willing to pay different prices for similar assets at the same time.

The value of an investment to a particular buyer will be determined by the *market price*, the *expected return and risks*, and the *correlation of that marginal investment to your legacy portfolio*. Few institutional portfolios start with cash. And even if one does, once you have built an optimal portfolio structure from cash, you have a legacy portfolio to contend with. Every new asset added to the legacy portfolio may have a different value to your portfolio than it has to the market at large. The largest factor influencing such value, other than price, expected return, and risk, is the *correlation* of the asset to the rest of your portfolio. When a certain type of investor (e.g., a corporate buyer) is crowding into an asset to the point of overpricing it for other classes of investors (e.g., an endowment), the investor with no strategic interest in it should give it a pass. The asset fits one investor better than the other investor.

2. But Watch the Price

The price you pay for an asset is one of the most important determinants of the risk embedded in owning the asset. We don't ever know the perfect price for an asset, but we do know that an asset will likely be overpriced and more risky than average if its valuation is at a historic peak, or more than two standard deviations from historic fair value. Mean reversion for asset prices is a safe bet if you allow sufficient time for it to happen—except in times of war or extended market closures. Postmodern financial theory accepts that markets are not always fairly valued, as behavioral biases affect investors' rational choices and move markets away from fair value. Almost any management style works if the horizon is long enough, if you stick with the discipline, and if the timing of implementation isn't terrible. Put simply, almost any style works if you initiate it at a reasonable price and give it the requisite time to show its value.

There are some exceptions. Based on the valuable empirical finding that assets will tend to revert to a trending mean over time, we have found that pure *momentum* styles tend to create more extreme losses than gains over time. Momentum styles are those that invest more in securities whose prices are appreciating at a constant or increasing rate, hoping to detect when the trend is showing signs of reversing so as to pull out of the asset promptly. Momentum styles are generally used in fast-moving commodity-based investments, which don't lend themselves to fundamental price analysis (discounted cash flow) because they offer no cash flows to be discounted. One can employ a momentum technique if applied in combination with price-sensitive styles. In those cases, momentum is a valuable second filter.

If you pay a fair price, you will be fine over time. If you overpay, you may never fully recover your investment, and yet the best course of action may be to stay with the investment unless it is still grossly overvalued. Relative valuation should guide your decisions looking ahead. Much academic theory tries to prove that price-sensitive ("value") investing will pay off more frequently than momentum investing, because momentum investors will generally overpay for the assets they buy. But sometimes cheap assets remain cheap for a really long time (the so-called value trap). Identifying emerging momentum out of the value trap is important to avoid being caught for a long time in a cheap asset that isn't going anywhere.

According to Robert Shiller's analysis, cyclically adjusted P/E ratios (based on 10-year normalized real earnings) can help estimate the range of future long-term returns.[7] Starting with a relatively low P/E of 8, the expected return would hover around 15 percent per year over the next 10 to 15 years, within a range of 8 to 18 percent. As adjusted P/E ratios rise from 8 to 20, expected returns drop to a range of 0 to 12 percent, with a mean value slightly above 5 percent. At starting P/E ratios of 30 to 40, it's difficult to clear positive returns for the next 10 to 15 years. Risks in asset classes other than equity are also dependent on the level of overvaluation or undervaluation at the time of purchase.

3. Don't Bet the House

We can't be certain of anything, regardless of how strong the evidence. Our experience has validated academic uncertainty theories regarding tail events (extreme, unexpected occurrences). Such events happen very infrequently but can be devastating if your portfolio isn't prepared to survive them. Still, portfolios should not be managed around tail events, because they are not the most likely outcome; portfolios should be managed so that risks taken are not devastating in an extreme scenario. We have to manage for the probable, but make sure unlikely events won't destroy our ability to reinvest in the probable. To this end, in this book I expand on the academic understanding of the limits and optimal manner of risk taking and liquidity management. Liquidity generally is either greatly overvalued or undervalued; valuing it properly is critical to handling uncertainty properly. Uncertainty is taken up in most sections of the book dealing with optimal policy, risk and liquidity management, and asset-class structuring (Parts II, IV, and V).

4. Potholes Are Unavoidable

Intelligent diversification is the best way to control risk, even though the more you diversify, the more likely you are to step in a pothole. The mishap should have only a small impact on your portfolio but can embarrass and shame decision makers. Some perceptive recent academic theory on fragile and robust (resilient) structures, developed by observing biological evolution, deals properly with this issue. We need to be aware of the inherent but manageable weaknesses of robust structures. Attention to diversity and diversification of risks is central.[8] Despite what Warren Buffett might say, many small and good bets are the most important source of superior returns and portfolio robustness for institutional portfolio managers. Multiple bets allow you to add new assets, new styles, and volatile but diversifying risks without subjecting the portfolios to outsize volatility and fragile (highly uncertain) outcomes. Buffett's unique skills over more than 60 years are supported by the preferred pricing that his well-established brand can command on purchases. From time to time there may be opportunities to place a larger bet in an asset that is undervalued (big game hunting), or away from an asset that is expensive, but those large bets—5 to 10 percent of total multi-asset-class assets in a single bet—should have uniquely high certainty, evidenced by a two-plus standard deviation from fair value.

5. Fraud Is Also Unavoidable

Though probably less frequent in U.S. capital markets than in the markets of other countries, fraud is a peril everywhere. You have to protect against it. The best protection is through thorough due diligence and intelligent diversification of risk—limit the amount placed in any one asset (stock or bond issue) or manager.

6. We Need Guardrails Against Volatility

The impact of annual volatility on wealth creation compounds at geometric rates over time and tends to be grossly underestimated by the average investor. Portfolio volatility can be measured by calculating the standard deviation of annual returns. Volatility is caused by often reversible changes in market prices, as well as losses created by active trading or unrecoverable capital impairments. Not understanding compound interest and how to temper yearly volatility can be your greatest source of loss of principal over time. Managing volatility requires separating expected market returns and risks (returns to beta) from excess active returns and risks (alpha), an exercise that few investors engage in as thoroughly as they should. (See Parts IV and V.)

7. Adversity Can Be a Gift

Efficiently rebounding from a loss demands as much effort as managing risks efficiently. Many high-level decision makers freeze for longer than necessary after a loss or, worse, flee from well-conceived but now threatened investment beliefs and miss the opportunity to recover. Our experience confirms behavioral finance findings on "interrupted rationality" or prior rational decisions, superseded by "new rationality," and the relevance of governance structures in maintaining discipline. Recovering from a loss by rebalancing your portfolio to sustain the intended policy is critical to superior performance. Figure I.3 shows an example of the importance of rebalancing equal-weighted portfolios regularly to benefit from market volatility. The critical topic of risk management in containing as well as rebounding from loss is covered in Part V.

	Return	Standard Deviation	Valued Added
U.S. Capitalization Weighted	9.7%	15.3%	0.0%
Rebalanced Equal Weighted	11.5%	17.4%	1.8%

FIGURE I.3   Theoretical value added by rebalancing.

Roughly speaking, a rebalanced equal-weighted portfolio adds 1.8 percent a year over a market-weighted U.S. equity portfolio, both absolutely and risk adjusted. (Robert D. Arnott, Jason Hsu, Vitli Kalesnik, and Phil Tindall, "The Surprising Alpha from Malkiel's Monkey and Upside-Down Strategies," *Journal of Portfolio Management*, Summer 2013.)

8. It's Hard to Beat Markets, but Experts Can Do It

Active management can outperform passive management fairly consistently in expert hands. Passive management of marketable assets is appropriate for inexperienced and average players. But you have to be sensitive to valuations when initiating passive strategies to avoid paying peak prices. Active management can be particularly rewarding when you are dealing with segmented markets where competition is restricted by regulation or other drivers. *In certain markets, significant, lasting segmentation creates pricing anomalies* that can be exploited by the experienced, undogmatic investor who is unconstrained by inflexible governance rules or other limitations, some self-imposed.[9] The high-yield market is an example, but other markets too face fragmented supply and demand that fail to bring prices to equilibrium levels. The buyout market has experienced sustained fragmentation, as has the market for emerging technologies. Given the relative discount at which these assets can be purchased by the unconstrained investor, or by "preferred" intermediaries that offer a competitive advantage to the future of the asset (contacts, synergies, management expertise), these assets can provide a permanent or medium-term advantage to a class of investor. In addition to high yield and hedge funds, private equity and venture capital are fairly fragmented markets in which some preferred intermediaries capture pricing advantages. Part III discusses strategic and tactical tilts to take advantage of mispriced assets and different management styles.

9. Alpha Hides in Small Places

"Texturing" your exposure is another subtle but important component of adding alpha. For example, a manager's stock-picking skills might be hidden by her holding too much cash (which she might need to act promptly on opportunities). Offsetting the cash exposure without restricting the manager's ability to trade would call for increasing market exposure by use of equity futures. But some investors might wrongly pass on such a manager unless she can avoid holding any cash; that would hinder her ability to trade in a timely manner.

10. Watch Out for Bad Apples

Many times, poor governance inflicts more damage on portfolios than underperforming managers. Markets and managers recover from cyclical losses (mean reversion at work), but portfolios don't easily recover from permanent losses created by bad governance decisions. Common symptoms of poor governance by a board or investment committee are:

- High manager turnover.
- Frequent committee or staff turnover.

- A focus on what seems to have worked in the past three to five years.
- Persistently negative or zero value added over seven years.
- Managers fired after relatively brief but painful underperformance.
- Simplistic rules for hiring and firing managers.
- An episodic, beauty-contest process for hiring managers.
- A paint-by-the-numbers silo approach to asset-class structuring, which overlooks crossover opportunities. Bucketing styles—value, growth, small cap, etc.—is not a bad first cut, but you have to be alert to periods in which the opportunities are found between the buckets (investments that don't fit well in one or another bucket) or in different buckets.[10]
- High management costs relative to value added.
- Conflicts of interest among fiduciaries.

Portfolio theory and industry practice haven't sufficiently factored in the impact of poor governance, so prevalent in so many places, and remedial actions. The filters used in recruiting the committee members who approve policy and oversee governance are generally quite poor or inappropriate, frequently explaining the poor quality of decision making at the top. And the value added or detracted by investment committee decisions is seldom measured. Part VI offers suggestions for selecting and maintaining superior governance structures.

Essential as it is to sustainable returns, good-to-great governance is vulnerable to "bad actor'" actions by individual trustees, committee members, or staffers. Bad actions can stem from ignorance, big egos, bad faith, or hubris. While ignorance can become self-evident, big egos may be protected by authority or by their own dangerous, preclusive use of influence, which is much harder to protect against. Not enough work has been done in behavioral science to identify the reasons that even great institutions tragically retain bad actors for so long, and what might be done about it.

What We Do Not Know: Four Safety Tips

As important as it is to refine your knowledge of likely outcomes, it's also critical to know the limits of your knowledge. What you don't know can kill you. Sometimes improbable, extremely bad outcomes happen. Managing your risks around them is most challenging. Here are four cautions to keep in mind:

1. Don't Believe in Crystal Balls

We don't know the future with any certainty. We can only assign probabilities to various future scenarios. A highly overpriced or underpriced asset can remain so for many years. Markets and management style cycles don't have a predictable end; they might last two to seven or more years. That's why you should bet only at extremes and diversify the risks over many different types of bets with different uncertain investment horizons.

2. Count On the Unexpected—Black Swans and Fat Tails

We don't know if or when we will have another world war and what shape it might take. War is destructive of human and financial capital. Public stock and bond markets all but vanished during World War II in Europe. Cybersecurity risks appear to be an immediate threat, but we can't rule out physical, even nuclear, attacks. Wars erupt in surprising ways when "new rising powers challenge the ascendancy of established powers."[11] Chaotic natural events can destroy years of management success in a surprisingly short time. That's why you need many types of assets, hoping that when shocks come, one of them will offer a source of funds to readjust your portfolios to a new state of the world. A 5 percent allocation to a few "safe" assets (whatever they may be!) may offer enough leverage to fulfill adjustment needs, assuming that leveraging tools, such as futures, are trading at fair prices.

3. It's Risky to Kill a Snake

Committee members, institutional leaders, and others with egotistical agendas can create havoc. We don't know how to neutralize them effectively. The fate of whistle-blowers is generally unhappy. There is understandable reluctance to uncover bad actors in any organization. People observing bad actors tend to wait until the bad acts are evident to all and are stopped by "someone." This can take a very long time. If you are in a leadership position, you need to cut your losses as soon as you detect that a bad actor has taken control of a process. Either dilute the culprit's influence or find ways of moving him or her out of the way of good governance. If you're not in a leadership position, you may need to wait and see, and you may eventually need to resign your position if change is not possible and your fiduciary duty is compromised by staying.

4. Great Art Is Hard to Judge

We don't know the exact point where expertise beats theory. We suspect it has to do with assessing valuations looking forward and learning to build portfolios where risks are intelligently taken and diversified. Most modern portfolio theory echoes Hippocrates' oath to "first do no harm." It rightly starts with the concept that markets are relatively efficient and that it's hard if not impossible to add any value to a passively managed "market" portfolio, while it's easy to subtract value by active trading, paying management fees and brokerage commissions, and making mistakes. Charles D. Ellis gave us the holy book on passive management, *Winning the Loser's Game*,[12] and Jack Bogle at Vanguard gave us the first set of cost-efficient index fund vehicles with which to implement the concept. An investor who is not an expert in the art and science of investing should manage assets mostly by investing in market-indexed, passive portfolios. But even passive management requires discipline and foresight that the average investor may not have. As with yo-yo dieting, you end up worse off by being undisciplined and acting impulsively at moments of distress. Intelligent passive management requires the wisdom to interpret the right time for implementation.

There is no worse professional pain than underperforming your benchmarks. Losing the game makes you feel "broken, gut-shot," as Andre Agassi reflected after losing to Boris Becker.[13] That pain, though unavoidable, keeps alive the memory of what went wrong and why. In the six sections that follow, I will share the wisdom of many smart, experienced people, accumulated over many years of gains and a few painful losses. I will take on the challenge of questioning the tyranny of "perfect" markets. Once in a while, opportunities do arise to add value by tilting portfolios and, more often, selecting active managers with demonstrated skill.

Ours Is One of the Noblest Professions

Money and anything to do with it have been tainted throughout history as a necessary evil. In addition to serious, ethical service providers, it attracts certain unsavory, greedy characters and often seems to be unfairly distributed. But money is one of the surpassingly beneficent creations of the human race, and those managing it responsibly should be recognized for their contribution to human progress. Einstein is supposed to have said that compound interest is the most powerful force in the universe. *Understanding the power of compound interest is among the greatest human achievements,* because innovation depends on accumulating and compounding financial and human capital (knowledge). And without innovation, growth is limited.

I believe dedicated investment managers have contributed with their insight and service to a most noble professional endeavor. Managing personal and institutional savings is among the most important, sustainable ways to bring hope for the future, to grant people options in arranging their lives, and to build the economy, while reducing the substantial risks we all face in the span of our lives. Building the wealth that fuels economic and personal growth and opens up opportunities for all is critically important to secure our future.

In dozens of years of practice, I have, thankfully, found the profession reasonably clean of fraudulent or unethical behavior, despite the embarrassing scandals that appear from time to time. Because investment performance is reviewed monthly against challenging benchmarks, investment management tends to attract professionals who want to prove their ability to add measurable value over time. By contrast, other financial fields are more congenial to professionals who want to go for the rewards of "serial kills"—giant one-time deals. Their performance is not measured by clients that gave them the mandates over many years, and they are usually paid for each "kill" rather than for cumulative long-term performance. Serial killings attract more opportunistic players, and potentially more predatory behavior that is anything but noble.

Ethical behavior, however, does not guarantee good performance. It's hard to outperform market averages. Large, inexperienced institutional investors are handicapped relative to right-sized, experienced players. In most cases, performance failures stem from perceived pressure to serve clients' impulses and satisfy what clients *want*, even if it isn't what they *need*. Systemic risks are created by asset managers' increasing allocations to illiquid investments that don't match clients' redemption needs and by managers' adding undue leverage. These risk factors have been properly identified by the SEC in recent pronouncements.

The reality that half or more of all investors underperform market averages may not just be a mathematical truism (because the average is based on the sum of all investors' scores). Despite their hard work, a large number of mutual funds serving mostly retail investors—often more than half and seldom fewer than 40 percent—tend to underperform, and investors who chase top fund performers are not rewarded in the years after they have shown top results (see Figure I.4).

FIGURE I.4 Percentage of top-quartile funds remaining in the top quartile after one, two, three, and four years. Source: Standard & Poor's (as of 9/30/2015).

Looking at these results was an additional motivation to write this book. Throughout its six sections, in addition to touching on theory and practice, I compare and contrast what we did, sometimes behaving quite differently from the average fiduciary for the best of reasons: you can only outperform markets and peers if you behave intelligently and differently. Market averages can be outperformed through superior skills relative to those of inexperienced and emotional players; access to underpriced, newly securitized assets; efficiently managing risks and volatility through sensible portfolio construction and rebalancing; and, importantly, paying attention to how different assets fit your own legacy needs and portfolio.

What Comes Next

The chapters of this book follow the sequence of the elements of design and process that contribute to meeting investment objectives and adding value.

- **Part I. Portfolio Fit Theory: The Value of an Investment to *Your* Portfolio.** Understanding how different assets fit specific portfolio and investor needs, taking into consideration the investor's return requirements, risk tolerances, and competitive advantages
- **Part II. Building the Right Policy Portfolio.** Identifying the mix of assets that is most likely to meet investor objectives, given competitive pressures, market developments, and competitive strengths
- **Part III. Structuring the Asset Class.** Knowing how and when to slightly vary, or tilt, a policy portfolio's allocations to asset classes and manager styles, depending on your own and your service providers' skills and perceived market inefficiencies
- **Part IV. Selecting and Terminating Managers.** Retaining managers with best fit and expected value added
- **Part V. Measuring and Managing Risks.** Carefully assessing and scaling risks relative to expected returns and to your own ability to add value
- **Part VI. Built to Last: Leadership Attributes, Creative Management, Succession Planning, and Transitions.** Putting in place the appropriate governance structure and processes to increase the level of responsibility and rewards given to decision makers and improving the process by which human resources are managed

DELIVERING
ALPHA

PART I

Portfolio Fit Theory: The Value of an Investment to *Your* Portfolio

$$\alpha$$

Great truths begin as blasphemies.

—GEORGE BERNARD SHAW

1

Fit Theory

MANY IF NOT most times in life, the choices we make are not solely dependent on price and absolute attractiveness, but also on how well they fit our own needs and circumstances. The most attractive, intelligent cheerleader might not be the best fit as your father's new wife, although she might be for someone else. That's the way we choose spouses, careers, jobs, houses, and stocks and bonds.

None of the great philosophers and psychologists can explain the often crazy calls of the human heart. The best they can do is warn you that feelings of romantic love don't last more than 18 months. In my younger days, after a premature divorce, I was not about to succumb once more to the chemistry of love before I had focused on the fundamental qualities of the man I should marry.

I had made a list of qualities I was looking for: He had to be intelligent, highly educated, an independent thinker, kind, patient, well mannered, a good dancer, with a sense of humor and a good welcoming family. Looks were not that important; to witness, my first platonic crush at 15 had been an older bald man (go figure). For me, it was most important to make sure I was not infatuated by the chemistry of the man. My theory was that one would fall in love two or three times a year (I was much younger then). I wanted to make sure that when my time came to fall in love, the way one catches the flu, the right guy would be next to me. I would discuss this agenda with every date I had: a separation between good fit and romantic love, and a test period of no more than a year for the heart to meet the mind. Only a few of the dates, two to be precise, found it reasonable. One was a married man, who was prepared to live together for a while (the rascal!) until we could find out if we were a good fit. I did not think he should be eligible for the test. The other was Arturo, a single man.

During the test period, I could tell that Arturo was kind and patient, because he would brush his cat Max's fur every day after work. I could tell he was an independent thinker, because he and I seldom agreed on anything. He was highly educated, as certified by degrees from both Harvard and University of Chicago. He was not always well mannered; when his back itched, he would subtly scratch it with a fork! (Yes, he was creative and resourceful.) He would dress elegantly with a bow tie but wear Birkenstocks with socks. He had no sense of humor, and his dancing did not meet my benchmarks. Despite my disdain for looks, he was very good looking (that and a roving eye had me a bit worried).

Along the way and six months into the experiment, I fell in instant love with someone else I did not know much about. All he had done was to look deeply into my eyes while having coffee at the World Bank. A while back, the *New York Times* had an article certifying that a few minutes of keen attention into someone else's eyes can make the other fall in love![1] I told Arturo what had happened and that he shouldn't give up: Now that I was in romantic love, I could transfer the feeling to anyone, including him.

This theory sounded interesting if implausible, but Arturo thought it was probably correct. And that's exactly what happened. By objective measures, the other guy may have had a leg up on Arturo: he was successful, wealthy, and charming and had a mischievous sense of humor. But Arturo was a much better fit for the legacy I was bringing into the relationship: I was determined to succeed as a professional woman. Arturo would give me the space to do that. I had a young child. Arturo would take loving care of him. I wanted a larger family. Arturo had a most interesting, large, idiosyncratic family. Arturo had rare intellectual curiosity that would challenge me the way I wanted to be challenged in life. It would stretch my knowledge and imagination in unpredictable but gentle ways. In March 2018 Arturo and I celebrated our forty-first wedding anniversary. He was a most worthy asset to add to my portfolio. Regardless of how he may have been assessed by others, he is the best fit to my life as a professional, a mother, and a woman.

That lesson should resonate strongly if unromantically for investors. Rationally assessing the goodness of fit of any asset in an existing portfolio, independent of the value of that asset to the aggregate of all investors—the market—is critically important to success. Some seemingly wretched assets might have a perfect fit in your portfolio, and some great asset might have a wretched fit. This is where efficient-market price theory, although a great starting point for a portfolio construction process, might not be the best guide to analyzing the marginal attractiveness of a particular asset to a legacy portfolio.

I still recall an article from the 1970s about the then-nascent modern portfolio theory (MPT). It praised efficient-market theorists like William Sharpe, Eugene Fama, and John Lintner, my teacher at Harvard Business School, for having sensibly debunked the prevailing concept among broker-dealers that each investor deserved a different portfolio. That was referred to as the "interior decorator" approach to portfolio management, in which brokers or investment advisors would give each client a customized portfolio matching individual needs and stock name preferences. By contrast, MPT asserted that the "market" portfolio—a portfolio consisting of a weighted sum of every investable asset in the market—was most efficient. It was the portfolio that should be held by all investors, particularly institutional investors, regardless of needs, age, or any other circumstances. It was the portfolio that would provide the highest level of return per unit of risk. Efficient-market theory establishes that the price of risk is determined and expressed by the collective knowledge and wisdom of the market participants.

In MPT, the prices of all tradable assets are determined by the market price of risk (the price of the undiversifiable unit of risk of a global and efficiently diversified portfolio) and the risk of the particular asset, expressed as the regression coefficient (beta) of the price of the asset to the market, which theoretically consists of that globally diversified portfolio.[2] Nonmarket risks do not deserve an expected return—they would be diversified away by buying the market portfolio. Efficient combinations of all assets, delivering the highest rate of return for each unit of risk and for each risk level, create the so-called efficient frontier. As illustrated in simplified form in Figure 1.1, if an investor needs a higher rate of return than the one given by the optimal market portfolio—*P*(market)—he or she would have to borrow (leverage) and increase the return and the risk.

The investor needing higher return could augment the optimal portfolio with leverage, borrowing to reach the desired level of return and attendant risk—say, *P*(with borrowing) in the figure. If the investor wanted a lower-risk portfolio than the optimal portfolio to meet a given investment horizon or risk tolerance, he or she would have to blend the optimal portfolio with a risk-free asset, such as short-term Treasury bills, to lower the risk—say,

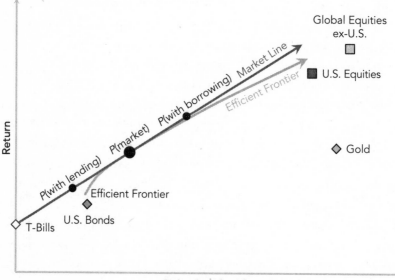

FIGURE 1.1 Sample asset allocation and returns at different levels of risk.

According to modern portfolio theory, the optimal portfolio would provide the highest return per unit of risk—shown in the figure as *P*(market) where the two lines intersect. The market line shows choices of market risks moving up from the "riskless" T-bill rate. The most efficient trade-offs between risk and return are along the efficient frontier curve. Various investments that might become components of the portfolio are scattered according to their approximate risk-return profiles.

P(with lending). Along with the lower risk, the investor would have to accept a lower return over time.

MPT contends that markets are always fairly valued, as they efficiently process all information available at a particular time and reflect it in the price. New information follows a random pattern, and therefore returns are randomly and "normally" or "lognormally" distributed around a mean. So the efficient portfolio should be the market portfolio of stocks, bonds, and other assets, as broadly and efficiently diversified as possible. Any deviations from the optimal portfolio, with borrowing or lending to adjust to desired return and risk objectives, would yield a less desirable portfolio, one that would compound at lower rates of return per level of risk over time. In our theoretical sample chart, *P*(with borrowing) would be a combination of the optimal market portfolio *P*(market) plus leverage to the level at which you would expect a higher real return than for *P*(market) and about double the volatility. *P*(with lending) would include a combination of *P*(market) and fixed income (lending) to reduce the risk and the return.

I have learned that despite the many merits of this theoretical construct, in practice there is significant slippage between the practical lip and the theoretical cup. Principally, the optimal portfolio will change dramatically over time with the volatility of the assets it contains and the return and risk preference of investors and securities issuers. Market variables are unstable, and most investors have significant risk and return constraints, forcing them to engage in exercises of "constrained optimization" that will move away from the most elegant MPT concepts. Life is messy and hard, and so are optimal investment choices.

Perhaps I should have chosen the "Hilda uncertainty principle" as the appropriate name for what I think is an optimal portfolio construction theory, developed from the insight that portfolio-optimization exercises have to consider both market circumstances and more subtle investor needs and constraints.[3] But portfolio fit theory seems more appropriate to give the theory and practice the recognition it deserves. Contrary to first appearances, it's not a rebirth of the interior designer theory of portfolio management, though it provides some support for it. The old interior designer portfolios were often inefficient and badly constructed, with market and active-management risks poorly measured and diversified. But the approach was correct in trying to fit the needs of the investor. Today, given the uncertainty around what may be the one and only "optimal" portfolio, it's relevant to look at other risks in the portfolio construction process, such as *peer risk* (the risk of underperforming institutions or managers that compete for the same type of clientele), and the *optimal fit* to legacy assets and the investor's competitive advantage. In fact, institutional investors tend to choose "optimal" policy portfolios that are quite different from the mythical "market" portfolio (see Figure 1.2).

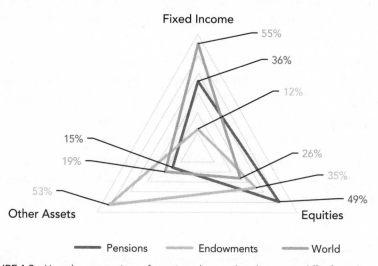

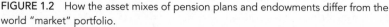

FIGURE 1.2 How the asset mixes of pension plans and endowments differ from the world "market" portfolio.

This graphic depicts the median allocation of corporate defined benefit pension plans relative to endowments and the world capital markets. The world capital markets have significantly more fixed income investments, largely issued by governments and held by central banks and insurance companies. Pension funds still hold on average a larger allocation to marketable equities, and endowments are tilted to other assets such as private equities and hedge funds.

The "Market" Portfolio

Let's see what the theory says and why the theory might not properly reflect reality or truly optimal portfolio choices. For a start, the "market" on which a true global market portfolio could be patterned turns out to be much broader and more changeable than may first appear.

Supply and demand for capital is broadly distributed around the world, and the relative weights can change quite dramatically, as they have in the last 40 years. The prices at which supply and demand for investable capital meet are called "equilibrium" prices. Those prices change continuously with GDP growth, new information, and the perceptions and needs of investors and securities issuers. By some estimates U.S. debt was about 56 percent of total world debt in 1980 and is now less than a third; Japan's debt was about a third in 1980 and is now about 10 percent of total debt; China's debt appeared negligible in 1980 and is now above 10 percent.[4] U.S. equities were nearly half of total world equities in 1980 and, according to Bloomberg, 36.3 percent in 2016, while Japanese equities were below 20 percent in 1980, rose to about a third in 1990, and declined to less than 10 percent in 2017; Chinese equities rose from nothing in 1980 to about 7 percent in 2017. According to multiple public sources, as of 2016 total investable capital markets (including real estate and private equities and excluding bank deposits) amounted to about $170 trillion. The United States was still the largest and most liquid at $70 trillion ($22 trillion equities and $37 trillion debt), followed by Europe at $45 trillion ($8 trillion equity and $26 trillion debt) and Japan at $20 trillion ($3 trillion equity and $14 trillion debt).[5] It is most likely those relative weights will change substantially in the next 5 to 10 years, as they have in the past.

In theory, the market clears the supply and demand for assets by pricing assets at equilibrium prices where all available assets are willingly held by market participants. In practice, the market's price setting is continuous and dynamic, reflecting the immediate environment and participants' needs and expectations. Many "willing" participants are subject to multiple regulatory and other constraints that impel them to buy certain types of assets over others even if the others are more attractively priced.

Theorists feel strongly that markets are *efficient* in the sense that there is no profitable, risk-free strategy to arbitrage between assets. In fact, investors have different investment objectives, horizons, skills, preferences, fears, taxes, regulatory constraints, and legacy portfolios that change over time. Some investors will face psychological and objective hurdles in adding leverage to their portfolios. If their minimum targeted return is, say, 5 percent real annual compounded, it's highly unlikely that they will hold the global market portfolio—which is heavily skewed to fixed income instruments yielding less than 3 percent real—and leverage it to the point where it delivers 5 percent. For most U.S. investors it would simply require too much explicit leverage and not enough diversification. Explicit leverage, segregating a portion of your portfolio as collateral for a loan, carries with it asymmetrical risk: more risk than potential. The lender can recall the loan for repayment and force you to liquidate your investment at inappropriate times or prices.

Instead, investors have preferred to hold much more equity than fixed income. Equities carry *implicit* leverage for the investor (the debt of the companies themselves). One or several companies may go bankrupt but not all companies, significantly reducing asymmetrical risk. Some investors also prefer to hold some of their equity exposure in higher-risk, higher-return illiquid private equities, and some of what would otherwise be fixed income investments in hedge fund strategies with low correlations to equities and fixed income. Figure 1.2 shows that, as of 2015–2016, the median defined benefit pension plans and endowments held portfolios with very different asset allocations from that of the world market portfolio.

Dealing with Legacy Portfolios

Some legacy assets already held by investors may be inefficient, may carry low levels of expected return in relation to their expected volatility, and may be inferior to the optimal market portfolio or the most desirable policy portfolio; these should certainly be restructured into a more efficient lineup. Other legacy assets may just be in need of adding assets that make them more efficient and closer to optimal. Liquidating all legacy portfolios to end up holding the market portfolio (with or without leverage) or the optimal policy portfolio (with implicit or explicit leverage) could be inefficient and costly, and the result might itself be a portfolio that becomes somewhat obsolete relative to market realities and expectations within a few years. The legacy portfolios may have significant unrealized alpha potential or a low tax basis, so continuing to defer taxes may be the most efficient choice. Even if tax free and tradable, institutional legacy portfolios may have some active managers with positions that appear undervalued and worthy of retention rather than wholesale liquidation, or active managers with restricted mandates and high potential for value added that should be retained. Some portfolios have significant exposure to illiquid assets with long lives ahead of them that would be inefficient to liquidate at deep price discounts. Legacy portfolios have made up a significant portion of all institutional and individual portfolios in our practice. Legacy portfolios worth preserving for tax or other investment reasons need to be considered when bringing new assets and strategies to build an optimal total portfolio that can be efficiently and dynamically adjusted to investor needs and market conditions over time. (See Figure 1.3.)

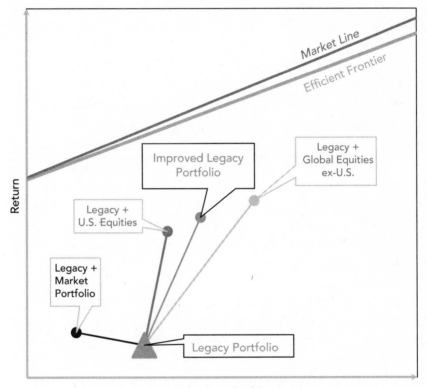

FIGURE 1.3   Mending, not ending, a legacy portfolio.

A legacy portfolio with suboptimal risk-return characteristics need not be abandoned. Using fit theory, by moving only 10 percent of the assets into certain other assets (a market portfolio, U.S. equity, and non-U.S. global equity in the example charted), the portfolio's risk-return profile is moved significantly closer to the optimal efficient frontier—even though some of the assets added may appear less desirable on their own. The critical quality of best-fit assets is their low correlation with the legacy portfolio.

Once you determine that certain assets in a portfolio are worth preserving or inefficient to liquidate, the portfolio construction process has to consider all other portfolio choices as marginal assets to be added to round up the optimal ratio of expected return to risk for the total portfolio. In this framework, the *value* of an asset needs to be assessed on the basis of its *price*, its *expected return*, its *volatility of return*—and, most important, its *correlation with the legacy portfolio*, not solely its correlation with the market portfolio.

With modern portfolio management tools, it's a simple exercise to find what set of assets best improves a legacy portfolio. But before going through this optimization exercise, I have found a back-of-the-envelope procedure useful. I developed a simple, quick fit ratio formula to test some unlikely assets that could fit well in legacy portfolios. The formula is the expected rate of return on the assets divided by the product of the volatility of the asset times the square of the correlation of the asset to the legacy portfolio. This fit ratio formula is marginally useful as an adjunct to an optimizing model when comparing different assets with no more than market volatility. The critical quality of a good-fit asset, other things equal, is a low and stable correlation with the legacy portfolio. I have found the fit ratio formula particularly useful in testing potential fits when there are no historical correlations to rely on because of the absence of reported performance data.

The assets to be added, whether replacing or complementing legacy assets, are like the stabilizers on a motorboat. They dampen the volatility of rough market seas so you get to port most efficiently and comfortably. By reducing the volatility of the legacy portfolio, you are increasing its rate of compounding wealth. Alternatively, you may be accelerating the rate at which you can compete with peers. Ideally you both improve risk-adjusted returns and reduce peer risk.

Value Really Can Be Personal

Certain assets may have a higher value to particular investors than their market price, and some assets can improve a legacy portfolio's return-to-risk ratio and compound rate of return despite apparently suboptimal characteristics on a stand-alone basis. The fit of an asset may also explain why some investors, such as corporate strategic buyers, are willing to pay a much higher price for an asset than the market at large, given how well that asset fits with the rest of their assets in lowering earnings volatility and with their competitive needs.

As you decouple an asset from the market portfolio in assessing its value as an efficient stabilizer to a legacy portfolio, you can arrive at a total portfolio that is more efficiently diversified. *In the process you will find assets that would be valued differently by different investors even if all investors were to agree on the return and risk characteristics of the asset.* In other words, the fair market price does not equal the value to a particular investor. This shouldn't surprise anybody. The value of a company is different to a portfolio manager than to a private equity financial buyer or a strategic corporate buyer; the asset serves different functions to the different buyers and complements their existing legacy portfolios differently. Not all acquisitions are triggered by conflicted CEOs seeking to increase their tenure and annual compensation, as some critics aver. There are legitimate reasons to protect and improve a corporate legacy portfolio.

Long-duration bond futures and high-yield bonds are examples of assets that may not look attractive by themselves (their return per unit of volatility doesn't compare well with alternatives) but that may fit well into total portfolios. More on this in later sections.

When assigning new managers to a legacy portfolio, alternative managers' alphas can be considered as potential stabilizers, assuming the managers' characteristics are stable over time. Once you have identified a few assets or portfolios that seem to improve the characteristics of your legacy portfolio and have calculated the initial fit ratios, the next step is to use an optimizer—analytical software that trades off returns, volatility, and *correlations* to identify optimal solutions for policy portfolios. This provides a higher degree of accuracy in selecting alternatives and allows you to assess the impact of increasing allocations of the best-fitting assets to the existing portfolio. The same process can be used to identify low-fit assets that could be sold and replaced by assets with better fits.

How to Use the Fit Ratio as a Sketching Tool

A metaphor that comes to mind in describing the fit ratio as a sketching tool is architectural sketches relative to final architectural plans. Extending the metaphor to understand the concept of optimal versus legacy portfolios, one can think of building a house from scratch as optimal and remodeling as the way we handle legacy portfolios. A house built from scratch, like a newly invested portfolio, might seem optimal when completed, but most likely never again. It needs to be remodeled from time to time, to be kept efficient relative to current needs and changing expectations.

The fit ratio is a useful first cut at identifying assets that improve the characteristics of the *policy portfolio* (the target asset allocation percentages approved by the oversight committee) in multiple legacy scenarios:

- Illiquid assets that need to be held because transaction costs are too high to take for the additional returns of new assets
- Strategic asset allocation choices to hedge "fat tail" events: regional or world wars, commodity shocks, and unique future scenarios that cannot be modeled from the past
- As an explicit explanation for why a seemingly underperforming asset or manager should be kept or added to the portfolio, given its unique fit ratio to the rest of the portfolio

Some assets' fit ratios should be tested regularly for potential sale or purchase.

The Fit Theory at Work

Many years ago I faced a great surprise. While analyzing optimal policies for taxable portfolios, I discovered that on an after-tax, after-inflation basis, U.S. government bonds (or even tax-free municipal bonds) yielded *negative* returns for high-net-worth investors. That wasn't the big surprise. What startled me was that despite their negative real after-tax returns, when you optimized the after-tax portfolios, the optimizer would still pick a certain amount of government bonds for certain risk levels. There was no mistake in the calculation. The fit theory ruled the day.

We faced a similar result when looking at international nondollar-denominated bonds prior to the creation of the euro. Their dollar return was about the same as U.S. dollar bond returns, as you would expect for similar risks to local currency investors. But they were less liquid and more volatile than U.S. bonds, including and excluding the currency effect. Given their currency-induced volatility, it didn't seem attractive to hold nondollar bonds in a dollar-denominated portfolio. However, if you looked at them relative to broadly diversified portfolios of stocks and bonds, the optimizer software would pick nondollar bonds, fully hedged, in about equal weights to the U.S. dollar bonds, and you would end up with a portfolio with lower volatility for the same targeted return. The reason for such a counterintuitive outcome is that the correlation of non-U.S. dollar bonds in local currency to the total portfolio was much lower than that of U.S. dollar bonds. That more than compensated for their higher volatility and hedging costs. Once more the magic of diversification contributed the fairy dust of low correlation to your total portfolio.

A more common example of the unexpected outcome of fit analysis may be found in the use of long-duration bonds in lieu of shorter-duration bonds in policy portfolios. If analyzed on a stand-alone basis, long-duration (say, 20-year) bonds are inferior assets to shorter-duration (say, 6- to 8-year) bonds. Their expected long-term returns in normal bond markets, a little higher than shorter-duration instruments, seldom if ever compensate for their much higher—more than double—volatility. And yet when brought into a broadly diversified portfolio of stocks and bonds, the lower correlation to stocks, particularly in recessionary environments, allows you to reduce total portfolio risk by much more than the impact on returns. The lowering of the total risk gives you a chance to increase your returns by transferring some of the allocations from fixed income to higher-risk, higher-return assets without increasing the initial risk levels of the total portfolio. Depending on the level of interest rates, a 5 to 10 percent allocation to a 20-year-duration bond future may roughly match the risk diversification impact of a 20 percent allocation to a 6- to 8-year-duration bond market index fund, letting you invest a larger portion of your portfolio in a well-diversified set of higher-return assets. Depending on yield curves and correlations, the ending portfolio would have a higher return per unit of risk than the initial one, assuming all assets were fairly valued.

The fit theory may let you take a new, more insightful look at assets that don't appear to offer an attractive return-to-risk ratio on a stand-alone basis but that can greatly improve your policy portfolio. Using the goodness of fit rather than the inherent goodness of an asset can add risk-adjusted returns to your portfolio by alerting you to asset classes and manager styles that may not appear competitive on their own but may contribute greatly to total portfolio return per unit of risk. Among other examples covered in Parts III, IV, V, and even VI (human resources), this explains how fit can be a more important criterion than best in class in making investment selections.

PART II

Building the Right Policy Portfolio

Luck is the residue of design.

—BRANCH RICKEY

2

Meet the Skeptics

FOR OVERSIGHT COMMITTEES, bringing new asset classes into a policy portfolio, or reducing overvalued asset classes, can be a blood sport. All the facts in the world may not be enough to prove the value of a decision that clearly bucks the trend. "Sell on strength and buy on weakness" is easier said than done. Certainty does not exist in any investment decision, and when markets are erratic, uncertainty is a powerful deterrent to rational actions. And committees find it hard to buck a trend.

In 1981 no high-yield, or junk, bond had ever been purchased by a pension fund. They were deemed imprudent, speculative, disreputable investments laden with bankruptcy risk. And yet if you took the time to read Edward Altman's seminal research on junk bonds and Z-scores (an Altman innovation that assesses the risk of bankruptcy by looking at different financial ratios),[1] you would have learned that they were investments that could pay off handsomely, even adjusting for probability of default; that they had strong risk-diversifying qualities; and that they contributed to the growth of emerging prosperous industries. Moreover, the evidence was that there could be higher risks in buying low-yielding, highly rated securities in industries like railroads that might end up downgraded and possibly in bankruptcy.

After bankruptcy, those bonds, now junk, were more attractive than when they were highly rated.

Having the World Bank Pension Finance Committee approve the addition of junk bonds to its fixed income assets in 1981 was a worthy battle. As with any hard sell, you can't assume the sale will occur in the heat of the battlefield. The sell has to be promoted slowly, almost one-on-one, giving decision makers a chance to express all their worries and ask all the questions they could possibly ask before formal committee meetings. It may require taking individual decision makers on fact-finding trips so they can "see and touch" what is behind investments that seem dangerous to them. It took us months to prepare the field for a final discussion of the benefit of junk bonds to the World Bank pension fund. We were proposing only to invest less than half of 1 percent of total assets in these junk bonds. Was it worth the time spent building the full committee's understanding of these instruments to the level where the comfort of the committee members would match the opportunity? We didn't know, and the only way to find out was to go through the process, start with small commitments, and grow them as we learned the best way to implement the strategy. As it turned out, the effort was supremely worthwhile. Adding those bonds, and several talented specialist managers in the field, has been one of the best, most enduring investment decisions we have brought to portfolios under our management. Since 1981, junk bonds have contributed substantially to our total funds' returns on both an absolute and risk-adjusted basis. The factors behind their long-term contribution to portfolio returns—regulatory constraints, market segmentation, behavioral patterns of different investors, and appropriate management styles—are explained further in Part III.

What instruments you choose to include in a policy, and in what manner, will be among the largest potential sources of value added to portfolios. Every month spent building the case for junk bonds in the World Bank pension portfolio was worth millions of added value over time. You cannot give up easily when you are introducing unknown but attractively priced assets or withdrawing from favorite but overpriced assets or managers. Removing Japan from our portfolios as Japan basked brightly in the sun of global competitiveness and slashing high tech from portfolios in the late nineties were equally arduous and equally valuable decisions.

Building the right policy portfolio to meet your investment objectives and tolerance for volatility and illiquidity can be daunting (see Figure 2.1). The policy portfolio is generally determined by using mean-variance analysis, a portfolio optimization process that seeks the most favorable trade-off between risk and return (further discussed in Part V). The inputs to the optimization are expected return, standard deviation of return, and correlations between asset classes. An optimizer program identifies combinations of asset classes that maximize expected return at each level of risk. These candidate portfolios, when plotted on a graph, form a curve called the efficient frontier, where the most efficient trade-offs between risk and return exist.

For the theoretical example in Figure 2.1, the prescient optimal portfolios for each 5-year period and the total 25 years complied with six constraints:

- No less than 10 percent in U.S. equities
- No less than 20 percent in U.S. and non-U.S. equities
- No less than 10 percent in U.S. Treasuries
- No more than 30 percent in private equity
- No more than 50 percent in illiquid assets
- Annual volatility tolerance of 12 percent

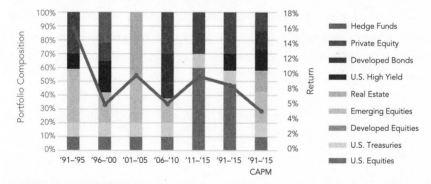

FIGURE 2.1   E pluribus unum.

These bars illustrate how daunting it is to assemble the widening array of investment choices into a global policy portfolio that will excel in the future. The first 6 bars show the optimal mix of 10 investments that a manager with perfect foresight would have chosen at the beginning of each half-decade. The radical differences mean that historical statistical analysis can fail you; returns, volatilities, and correlations are unstable. The jagged line shows that even with optimal portfolios, returns will diverge over time. For comparison, the rightmost bar represents an optimal portfolio generated by the capital asset pricing model without perfect foresight.

Figure 2.1 is a sobering reminder of how unstable historical statistics are, how difficult it is to arrive at truly optimal portfolios over time, and how important it is to add value to overcome optimal policy handicaps. It's a testament to the importance of generating risk-adjusted returns above the policy portfolio to make up for the shortcomings of before-the-fact optimal policy relative to after-the-fact optimal policy.

The policy portfolio should not remain unchanged forever. It should evolve with your and your competitors' expertise and with the appearance of new asset classes such as emerging markets, hedge funds, real assets, and commodities. New asset classes emerge as new assets are securitized. Hedge funds especially require expertise in finding the right ones. You won't profitably invest in them by buying a passive selection of the most representative index of hedge funds. The combination of changes in policy to incorporate new asset classes and our evolving expertise in the selection of active managers allowed us to achieve almost the returns of a perfectly prescient portfolio by allocating a significant amount to alpha-generating hedge funds and other active managers. (See Figure 2.2.)

The lesson here is that given the uncertainty of returns and correlations, you should deviate from your policy and your peers only to the extent that your deviations can add sufficient value. That value added will serve to make up for the uncertainty of optimal policy. Put another way: if you are confident you can add value, you should try; otherwise your calculated optimal policy choice might leave you wanting.

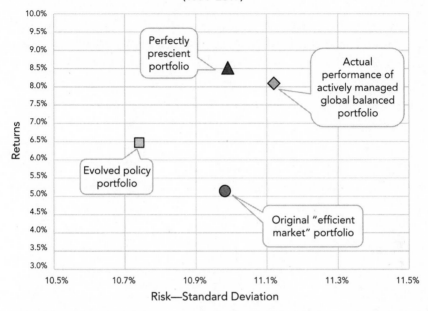

FIGURE 2.2   More than efficient.

Constant attention to changing opportunities and threats enabled us to verge on matching the performance of the portfolio that a theoretical prescient manager would have selected in 1991. The actively managed global balanced portfolio exceeded the returns of the original "efficient market" portfolio by 296 basis points per year. Of that, improvements in the policy itself (represented by the "evolved" portfolio) accounted for 133 basis points, and 163 basis points were gained through active management. This exercise includes only the years since 1991 because there are no reliable market data for all alternative assets before that time.

3
Investment Policy

Mission Objectives and Needs

THE INVESTMENT POLICY is the institution's fundamental document governing investments, focused on broad investment guidelines. It's separate from the more detailed guidelines used to limit the investment authority of individual investment managers. New fiduciaries joining an investment committee for the first time sometimes struggle to understand the reasoning that underlies the investment policy. A good place to begin this inquiry is to ask what the purpose of the policy is. The major purpose is to provide committee members with a logical framework for making decisions about managing investment assets. In a well-drafted policy, targets and guidelines are set forth in sufficient detail to be effective but not overly restrictive. Achieving this delicate balance requires a solid understanding of the purposes and pitfalls of investment policies.

Sometimes an investment policy exists within or alongside a much more comprehensive document that codifies all the organizational operations of the institution, including the roles, responsibilities, and procedures of the committee members, staff, and others. The investment policy itself is more limited in scope. It's intended to provide direction, discipline, and consis-

tency to the institution's investment decisions by establishing a policy portfolio—an asset allocation, defined by a set of benchmarks with target weights
and variation ranges, describing the asset mix most likely to meet the institution's return and risk objectives.

The policy portfolio serves several important functions. First, it's a guide-
post for measuring and controlling short-term deviations from the investment policy. It helps fiduciaries keep the overall portfolio from veering too
far off course, especially during times of market stress. Deviations from
the policy portfolio should be supported by a reasonable, well-articulated,
fact-based conviction of asset mispricing. There are times when assets are
not all fairly valued or when asset classes display an atypical relationship to
one another. Second, and often the most discussed function of the policy
portfolio, it serves as a benchmark against which performance of the actual
portfolio and its components are measured and evaluated.

The task of writing an investment policy gives an investment committee
a means of forming a consensus about the institution's needs and investment
goals. By requiring the group to codify its investment philosophy, biases, and
constraints, the document focuses committee discussions on specific aspects
of investment policy. The policy enables committee members to communicate investment goals and restrictions to present and future board members,
supporting staff, and external investment managers.

Like a constitution, an investment policy should be written broadly
and allow for ample flexibility or it won't survive long when circumstances
change. Even if the policy is flexible, committee members should expect that
it will need to be amended from time to time. It should be viewed not as holy
writ but as a living document, subject to routine review for relevance and
appropriateness. No matter how well a policy is thought out and written,
some of the considerations and data used to formulate it are necessarily time
dependent; they will eventually cause the policy to become obsolete.

The Essential Elements

Investment policies often begin with a general statement of the purpose of
the institution's investments—usually to fund future liabilities, as in pension

plans, or planned expenditures, as in endowments, foundations, and family pools—and proceed to describe the nature and timing of those future needs. The goal of funding program expenditures or liabilities, which after all is the primary purpose of managing assets, should be advanced by all the details of the policy.

In addition to the spending goals or liability structure, the institution's tax status, time horizon, and organizational type should be stated. They should lead logically to the return objectives and risk tolerance. After those are set forth, each of the asset classes—the building blocks of the policy portfolio—should be itemized with a target percentage allocation, allowable range for tactical shifts, and applicable benchmark.

State Your Investment Philosophy and Biases

The next step is to clearly articulate the institution's overall investment philosophy and biases. To state their philosophy, fiduciaries must truly know themselves and their risk tolerances. This is often not easy. If the group's philosophy is not clearly understood and agreed to by all, the committee members are likely to abandon their long-term policy during periods of underperformance. They won't have the philosophical anchor of knowing exactly why they took the positions. All policies are severely tested by market events from time to time.

Every effort should be made to ferret out unresolved issues, settle them, and state the policy. Special attention should be paid to the permitted allocations to alternative asset classes, such as private equity and hedge funds, since these are "frontier" areas for many institutions; the special characteristics of alternatives may be unfamiliar territory to some committee members. Likewise, the use of derivatives and leverage should be discussed. The allowable allocation to soundly developed "portable alpha" strategies, which often employ both hedge funds and derivatives, should be defined. (More on this in the portable alpha discussion in Chapter 12.) The emotional and rational characteristics of leverage and the use of controlled leverage in portfolio construction should be explicitly and maturely understood.

Setting Return and Risk Goals:
Blending Desirable with Plausible

The objectives set in various sections of the policy must be achievable under normal long-term market conditions that have historical precedent and are likely to recur. These goals must also be consistent with each other and the policy portfolio. A common pitfall in setting goals is expecting more return than markets can deliver. Some institutions, confronted with potential low-return environments, have a hard time adjusting their return expectations downward because of the implications for funding levels, required contributions, and spending. To avoid lowering their expectations, they may overestimate the return potential for certain asset classes. Another common pitfall I have observed is increasing the exposure to riskier assets rather than considering applying leverage to less risky assets in arriving at more efficient portfolios.

Ambitious return objectives sometimes lead to overreaching an institution's risk tolerance, or even ignoring certain risks altogether, such as peer risk. Underperforming their peers is often more psychologically painful for fiduciaries than underperforming market benchmarks. Ignoring what may be a real sensitivity to peer comparison in the policy-setting process can result in abandoning a reasonable investment policy at precisely the wrong time, after a period of disappointment and before the portfolio has had time to recuperate and resume its expected long-term return trajectory.

One solution is to acknowledge peer portfolios as an additional benchmark for the policy portfolio. The portfolio optimization process handles this by adding the dimension of peer risk as a constraint. With this change, the efficient frontier, a two-dimensional trade-off of risk and return (see Chapter 2), becomes an efficient surface with three dimensions: risk, return, and tracking error to peers.

Setting Ranges for Asset Classes:
Profiting from Disequilibrium

Ideally, the policy portfolio defines the long-term target allocations for asset classes under theoretical conditions in which asset classes are fairly valued. But at any moment, some prices may not perfectly reflect supply and demand—equilibrium, in economists' language. For those who acknowl-edge, as we do, that disequilibrium pricing does occur and can be exploited in financial markets, significant tactical shifts around the target portfolio should be expected and allowed by the investment policy, provided the manager or the committee has the analytical tools to make these shifts pro-ductively. One common mistake is setting the ranges for asset classes too narrowly around the target allocations. As a result, the investment policy must be revisited repeatedly to take advantage of opportunities that arise. Alternatively, even in the absence of a tactical asset allocation program, the portfolio may require frequent rebalancing, as assets drift away from target weights as their prices change. Overly narrow variation ranges, then, cause expensive turnover and prevent the institution's managers from profiting from tactical opportunities.

Another form of micromanagement is tightly specifying the asset classes in the policy portfolio, even down to the level of styles or other asset subdivi-sions. Listing an asset subclass and giving it a target and a range will not only constrain tactical shifts but also can open up a Pandora's box of definitional questions. For example, if a loosely defined and ever-changing equity style such as large value is specified and given a target allocation, defining large value can become a permanent nuisance issue. The fiduciaries should leave control of allocations at this level of detail to the investment staff and service providers.

For certain illiquid asset classes, particularly private equity, it's impractical to manage policy weights in the same way as for liquid asset classes because capital is frequently returned to investors and because it is often impossible to rebalance when gains are realized. Moreover, as these assets are revalued relatively infrequently, their proportional value in the portfolio can be influ-enced dramatically by shifts in other, more liquid asset classes. To solve this problem, the policy benchmark can be allowed to float so that it reflects the changing weight of these illiquid assets in the portfolio but keeps overall allocations in line with the long-term policy asset mix. In the case of private equity, the market equity benchmark weights could be adjusted to absorb the deviation from the long-term policy private equity allocation, "floating" the private equity weights.

Overcomplicating the policy portfolio should be avoided in general. The asset classes, their target weights, and allowed ranges form the outlines of a broad strategy and should themselves be broad. A policy portfolio is for setting major boundaries. It should not substitute for day-to-day oversight and monitoring.

Liquidity Needs: There Is a Reason for Liquidity Risk Premiums

Liquidity often gets insufficient analysis in investment policies, leading to too much or too little liquidity. A high demand for liquidity, to pay benefits or fund expenses, significantly alters how assets should be allocated. Some institutions, particularly endowments and foundations, invest heavily in illiquid asset classes, such as private equity and hedge funds (see Figure 9.1). Some pension funds, especially frozen ones (see Chapter 4), pay out a high percentage of their assets each month. In a serious market downturn, some of these institutions may find themselves strapped for liquidity and have to sell depressed assets to raise cash for operations. Other institutions may be staffed or have the management infrastructure to handle unexpected liquidity demands by leveraging their corpus and using futures to rebalance their asset mix after it has been brought severely out of balance.

The policy portfolio should reflect the liquidity needs of the institution by limiting allocations to illiquid asset classes as appropriate. To determine allocations that provide enough liquidity in various market environments, the portfolio can be stress-tested using a Monte Carlo simulation. With this technique, a computer generates thousands of return streams to model investment scenarios and their consequences in particular years. The simulation results will include the probability of running out of liquidity, a risk that can be reduced by adjusting the policy weights.

A Policy, Not a Panacea

Whether an investment policy works well or not depends in large part on the fiduciaries. As a policy is a tool for establishing a consensus, the policy portfolio's usefulness is affected by the behavior of the individual committee members, for better or worse. Some committees take too long to resolve policy decisions. Some too frequently amend their investment policy in response to short-term trends. Some committee members dominate policy discussions, while others don't fully understand the policy they have approved.

Such shortcomings (discussed more fully in Part VI) make the best case for having an investment policy. The harder it is to achieve consensus, the more important it is to have a document that helps create one. For any group of fiduciaries, the task of forging an investment policy is difficult, requiring a lot of discussion, clear thinking, and expertise. Yet since any investment policy helps an investment committee set goals and communicate its wishes, it's always worth the effort.

What Can We Expect?

Under generally benign capital market conditions—no world wars or other market-disruptive events such as capital controls—the typical return objective for a balanced long-term portfolio is about a 5 percent annual pretax real return net of all costs. As explained in Chapter 11, that produces a theoretical 4.3 percent annualized compound return at 12 percent annual volatility. This return objective allows the portfolio to maintain its purchasing power net of inflationary pressures and permits a 4.3 percent compound spending rate indefinitely. However, many endowments have to face higher than average inflationary pressures. As measured by the Higher Education Price Index (HEPI), college and university endowments needed to outpace the national inflation rate by about 0.8 percent per year for the 53 years through 2014. The consumer price index compounded at 4 percent for those 53 years and 2.4 percent since 2000. The HEPI index compounded at 4.8 percent for the 53 years and 3.2 percent since 2000.

Some policy portfolios may have slightly higher objectives than a 5 percent real return, some slightly lower, depending on risk tolerance, use of prudent leveraging, other sources of revenue, and management's perceived ability to outperform policy.

At present, the volatility of a 5 percent real return portfolio, if properly diversified, will range between 9 percent a year at the low end and 13 percent at the high end, depending on the asset classes and investment styles included. The more broadly diversified the portfolio, the lower the expected volatility over the long run. With a 9 to 13 percent volatility range, you can expect your 5 percent average annual real returns to range in any single year within –8 and +18 percent with 68 percent probability, between –21 and +31 percent (95 percent probability), or from –34 to +44 percent with 99 percent probability.

You have two levers at your disposal to increase expected returns: you can leverage beta (market risk), which will increase expected return and volatil-ity proportionately and leave your risk-adjusted return unchanged, or you can leverage alpha ("active" risk), which if done properly will increase your return more than proportionately to the increase in active and total risk. Market risk can be reduced only by adding less correlated asset classes. Active risks can be reduced only by adding less correlated, successful active-manager strategies while keeping the market risks at the same or lower levels.

Figure 3.1 includes a sampling of "optimal" ex ante (before the fact) policy portfolios ranging from two to six asset classes, as of 2017 (the NACUBO portfolio is as of June 2016). Which one best meets investor needs depends on the investor's skills in asset-class management and the relevance of com-peting peers. These optimal ex ante policies will not necessarily be those that are optimal 5 or 10 years from now looking back. In fact, one would bet big that they will not be!

Figure 3.1 lays out past portfolio returns for alternative asset mixes. The portfolios range from simple 60 percent equity, 40 percent fixed income through more globally diversified arrays, culminating in the E&F sample policy portfolio with increasing allocations to hedge funds and other illiquid alternatives. The figure shows that one can increase the potential returns without much increase in volatility by diversifying more broadly. Return and risk are not the only elements important in setting policy. Your own regulatory and competitive advantages as well as other special circumstances should affect the policy chosen. Among these special circumstances are taxes, liquidity needs, stability and quality of the governance structure, financial strengths of funding sources, and potential for additional revenue or capital expenditures.

Asset Class	60/40 Liquid	60/40 Global Liquid	E&F	E&F ex-Illiquid	NACUBO $100M–$500M	NACUBO Greater than $1 Billion
Equity	60%	60%	40%	52%	48%	32%
U.S.	60%	32%	20%	26%	27%	13%
Developed Non-U.S.		22%	14%	18%	25%	11%
Emerging Markets		6%	6%	8%	6%	8%
Alternatives	0%	0%	30%	18%	27%	43%
Private Equities			12%		7%	18%
Hedge Funds			18%	18%	19%	25%
Hedge Funds (Gross)			28%	28%	19%	25%
(Portable Alpha)			−10%	−10%		
Real Assets	0%	0%	10%	5%	7%	14%
Real Estate			5%		3%	7%
Commodities			2%	2%	4%	7%
TIPS			3%	3%		
Fixed Income	40%	40%	20%	25%	13%	7%
U.S. Fixed Income	40%		20%	25%	11%	6%
Investment Grade	40%	36%	18%	23%	10%	5%
High Yield		4%	2%	3%	1%	1%
Non-U.S. Fixed Income					2%	1%
Cash	0%	0%	0%	0%	5%	4%
Total	100%	100%	100%	100%	100%	100%
Real Net Return	5.1%	5.5%	6.2%	6.0%	5.9%	6.1%
Volatility	11.0%	11.4%	11.5%	11.4%	11.7%	12.6%
Real Compound Net Return	4.5%	4.9%	5.5%	5.4%	5.2%	5.3%

FIGURE 3.1 The impact of alternative policy portfolios on return and volatility.

As the three rows at the bottom demonstrate, the more diversified you are, the higher your likely compound rate of return. Replacing private equity and venture capital with hedge funds generally may lower volatility. Which policy is preferable depends on your competitive advantage in selecting asset classes and managers and on your liquidity needs. The sample endowment and foundation (E&F) policy portfolio is shown with and without ("ex-") illiquid private equities. A 12 percent allocation to private investment is included to show expected outcomes for a less seasoned, younger private equity portfolio. The NACUBO portfolios are the those of the National Association of College and University Business Officers, as reported by Commonfund Inc.

Some assets will give you near certainty of returns but generally very low returns, such as the 30-day U.S. Treasury bill. At a zero to 2 percent real return per year, you would exhaust your portfolio in a couple of decades if, as a not-for-profit tax-exempt institution, you have to spend 5 percent every year. The institution's half-life would be much shorter, not being able to recruit or retain expert employees or maintain its programs along the inexorable path to extinction.

Roger G. Ibbotson and Rex A. Sinquefield did a great service to our profession when they took on the mundane but extremely useful task of documenting the history of investment returns—initially U.S. stocks, U.S. bonds, and cash—since the early twentieth century.[1] At the World Bank pension fund, we started investing in non-U.S. stocks, real estate, high-yield bonds, emerging market equities, and hedge funds in the 1970s and early 1980s before there were reliable sources of long-term historical returns, standard deviations, and correlations for those asset classes. To build efficient portfolios, we had to extract information on those asset classes from a variety of sources. Our partner Antoine van Agtmael produced the first set of reliable emerging market equity returns while at the World Bank in 1984.[2] Gary Brinson published broader selections of global asset-class returns in 1986 and with Roger Ibbotson in 1993.[3]

Antoine coined the term "emerging markets" to put some shine on that segment's tarnished capital market history, once marred by misinformation and political instability. In the last 30 years, however, constructive macroeconomic policies and access to capital markets started creating a stunning reduction of world poverty, particularly in the emerging, less developed economies. There was a reason the statistics were not that deep or broadly chronicled: Many of these asset classes hadn't been around long, and others had stopped trading during the two world wars. Yes, under severely disruptive circumstances, such as wars, terrorist attacks, and government controls, even the highly liquid and reliable U.S. stock and bond markets can stop trading—and they have, although for just a few days. In Chapter 5 we cover when it is appropriate to adjust historical estimates to reflect special circumstances, such as expected fixed income returns in 2017.

Previous sample policy choices have been based on U.S. dollar–denominated portfolios designed to produce a sustainable long-term annual inflation-adjusted return of around 5 percent over 10 to 20 years with expected yearly volatility of 10 to 12 percent. At that level of volatility, actual compound real returns would be 4.3 to 4.5 percent, significantly less than 5 percent (see Chapter 11). Moreover, looking at today's more sedate yield and expected-return scenarios, some experts expect future real returns to average at best 4 percent per year with 12 percent volatility. If so, the effective compound return would be 3.3 percent—and a spending rate of 5 percent would deplete more than 20 percent of principal in 10 years.

These lower assumptions, used today among some foundations and endowments, are a more sustainable risk-return objective for reasonably well-diversified, not fully funded retirement plans and other long-term savings accounts. One may find portfolios likely to deliver 4 to 5-plus percent real returns over the long run with lower volatility, but quite likely by increasing liquidity risks—the chances of running out of needed cash—and by building on preferential access to the best, most restrictive managers of traditional and alternative asset classes, not generally available to the average institution.

A 4 to 5 percent compound real return may be necessary over the long run to meet the spending needs of many institutional portfolios as well as the retirement needs of fully funded open plans (those still accepting new beneficiaries) without creating the need to contribute extraordinary additional funds to avoid painful spending cuts.

4

Liability-Driven Investing

A Brave New World of Fiduciary Issues

ONCE DEFINED BENEFIT (DB) pension plans nearly reach fully funded ratios of expected assets to liabilities and are frozen and closed to new entrants, corporations may choose to hedge the volatility of future contributions. They can do this by adopting liability-driven investment (LDI) policies—adopting portfolios with much higher allocations to longer-duration fixed income assets (maturing in 20 or more years) that closely match the distributions of future benefit payments.

A frozen plan, with its relatively certain time horizon and fixed liabilities, often requires a lower-risk policy portfolio than an open-ended plan. The rationale for higher-risk asset classes, such as equities, depends largely upon the expectation that liabilities will grow indefinitely, and that the plan's long horizon will allow time to recuperate after the periodic negative shocks that equities can bring. In contrast, a frozen plan's ever-dwindling time horizon and shrinking asset base tend to reduce the plan sponsor's risk tolerance, and the act of limiting liabilities effectively turns them into a stream of more or less fixed payments that can be estimated. In many cases, the risk-return profile of the frozen plan calls for more exposure to fixed income and less to equity.

Full hedging of long-term pension liabilities is not really achievable because of normal benefit uncertainties, less-than-perfect hedging vehicles, and corporate mergers and acquisitions, which add uncertainty to future liabilities. Therefore it's sensible not to try to fully hedge your liabilities but instead to retain a portion of assets capable of generating higher returns (with higher volatility) to hedge the LDI risks. You'll need to continually increase or decrease the ratio of risky assets depending on funding levels and relative valuations.

Managing the Plan from the Liability Side

Liability-driven investing is a radical departure from conventional asset-maximizing strategies. It requires new portfolio structures, customized benchmarks, leverage, derivatives, and, above all, changes in investment thinking. It's a response to a fundamental change wrought in the world of pension plans by a new set of standards, contained in Financial Accounting Standards Board Statement 158, that govern the accounting treatment of a pension's *funded status*—defined as the difference between plan assets and the projected benefit obligation, or PBO. The standards require companies to report changes in their plans' funded status on their balance sheets. No longer are fluctuations in a plan's funded status to be smoothed out over several years or buried in footnotes.

Uncontrolled, visible volatility in corporate net income naturally gives heartburn to chief financial officers. The most exposed firms have pension plans that are large in relation to their business, often old-line manufacturers with a lot of retirees. As interest rates or asset valuations change, these companies could see swings in their pension contributions, financial position, bond ratings, and borrowing costs. For some firms, the risk could threaten their survival and therefore, in the event of bankruptcy, their ability to meet their pension and other liabilities. Some have chosen to enter a brave new world, adopting LDI plans managed with the goal of minimizing the volatility of their deficit or surplus rather than maximizing their assets.

Although the first firms to shift to LDI generally have been those whose financials are most at risk, all plan sponsors are potential candidates, especially those whose plans have a surplus. Punitive "surplus reversion" taxes severely limit a plan's ability to benefit from accumulating surpluses. Investing to increase a surplus generally offers a plan sponsor no significant benefits—only the dreaded risk of a future deficit requiring contributions. If a plan is open to new employees and benefits are still being accrued by active employees, market risks are arguably worth bearing to maximize assets to cover future liability growth. But if a plan is frozen, with benefits capped and new employees barred from admission, liabilities are much more certain and maximizing asset growth is commensurately less justifiable. LDI is an attractive option for such plans, as it increases the certainty of meeting the targeted payouts and lowers open-ended financial risks for the corporate sponsor.

LDI Portfolio Structures

Liability-driven investing is a form of hedging corporate funding risks. The overall portfolio is reconstructed to reduce the volatility of the funded status, particularly volatility due to interest rates. Equities, which produce most of the volatility of a conventional pension portfolio's assets, are replaced to a large extent by fixed income. The duration of the fixed income exposure is managed to offset fluctuations in the liabilities' present value, which varies inversely with prevailing interest rates.

Since it's difficult to build and manage a portfolio of conventional fixed income securities that accurately matches the long duration of the liability structure—often 15 years or more—interest rate swaps and other derivatives may be used instead of bonds. For example, a plan may need some leverage to boost its fixed income exposure to match the value of its liabilities. Even a fully funded plan may need leverage in its fixed income exposure to compensate for any assets that are allocated outside fixed income to produce asset growth.

In the rare case of a firm that knows its future pension liabilities with perfect certainty, fixed income can fully immunize the liabilities against interest rate fluctuations. Most plans, however, have numerous uncertainties about the value of their liabilities, such as those arising from the unknown longevity of the retiree population; continuing or conditional accruals of benefits by plan members; or potential benefit supplements. These firms are candidates for LDI that reserves a portion of the total portfolio for generating asset growth to address the uncertainties. This growth-producing segment may be an allocation to equities or alternatives, such as hedge funds.

A Different Mindset Required

Fiduciaries will find that adopting LDI necessitates a complete overhaul of their investment orientation. Benchmarking illustrates the shift in thinking that's required. The primary benchmark for an LDI strategy is a policy portfolio that best fits plan liabilities. The objective is to invest the asset pool so its value closely tracks the discounted value of the liabilities.

One of the hardest adjustments for fiduciaries is breaking the habit of trying to keep up with peer institutions. Since every plan's liability structure is unique, and a plan run under LDI is managed in a customized fashion to minimize deficit or surplus volatility, there are no applicable peers. Even if a sponsor identified a set of peers with a similar liability structure, which is unlikely, the degree of market risk taken as a complement to the hedging portfolio would vary for firms with differing financial characteristics. Market risk creates uncertainty about requirements for future contributions to the plan. An enterprise with a large pension liability relative to its assets and a cyclical business, for instance, is less likely to be able to bear that uncertainty than a cash-rich sponsor with a balance sheet much larger than its liabilities.

Regulatory and Legal Considerations

Fiduciaries bound by ERISA regulations have a duty of loyalty to the plan and an overriding duty to act in the best interests of the plan's participants. When these same fiduciaries are corporate officers who are seeking to use

LDI to reduce the firm's exposure to the plan's volatility, it may appear that they are in a conflict of interest. Despite the fiduciaries' dual roles, their actions in adopting LDI must be in the interest of beneficiaries.

Fortunately, in 2006 the U.S. Department of Labor rendered an advisory opinion on whether a fiduciary of a defined benefit plan may consider the liability obligations of the plan and the associated risks in devising an investment strategy. Although the opinion did not settle all issues, it wisely acknowledged that LDI offers a benefit to beneficiaries in "the reduced need for the plan to rely on the plan sponsor to meet its funding obligations." LDI's benefits to the plan sponsor as well can be regarded as incidental.

Lawyers advise fiduciaries to document their decisions regarding the adoption of LDI to show that they are acting on behalf of beneficiaries. Fiduciaries should ensure that they have records substantiating that their actions are expected to reduce the beneficiaries' reliance on the plan sponsor and its solvency.

Frozen but Not Dead

As fiduciaries will discover, freezing a pension plan has significant ramifications for the plan's oversight and management that go well beyond constructing the portfolio. Freezing a pension plan forces investment committee members to change their habits, posing new management challenges in the areas of investment policy, oversight practices, and staffing. The number of companies that have frozen or terminated their defined benefit plans has more than tripled since 2001. To date, most of the discussion about freezing pension plans has understandably centered on the effect the curtailment of benefits will have on employees, while the impact on fiduciaries charged with managing a frozen plan has received scant attention.

Governance may be more difficult, depending on how fiduciaries respond to the change in the plan's objectives. As the pension industry is reshaped by the freezing of many corporate plans, staffing an internal pension group may become problematic. New ways of supervising the assets, such as outsourcing, may become more appealing. Such issues may have been viewed as secondary by a firm's top management when it made the decision to freeze its plan, but they are primary for the fiduciaries.

These issues arise because freezing a pension plan does not kill it. In the typical case, a firm simply halts the accumulation of benefits for its current employee population. Although a frozen plan's liabilities no longer grow, the benefits remain to be paid. The assets must still be managed over many years, through often perilous market conditions. An otherwise well-constructed LDI portfolio might even encounter circumstances when the equities are doing great but fixed income is poor, making it hard to meet pension obligations. Hence, when a pension plan is frozen, it is effectively frozen alive. Furthermore, it will continue to live and breathe for decades, as long as any of its beneficiaries do.

Out of Sight, Out of Mind

Despite their legal obligation as fiduciaries, investment committee members may find that freezing a plan diminishes their ability to carry out their duties with the same level of care as before. Once a plan is frozen, the company may not demonstrate the same commitment to it, moving on to matters it considers more current. The committee members may not be as interested in devoting their time and energies to it, especially if the plan's investment complexity has been reduced. This situation may lead to inattention, which is likely to worsen as the plan's time horizon and assets shrink.

Knowing that a plan is being slowly liquidated may also have a negative effect on the internal pension staff. With many firms freezing their plans at the same time, potential staff members may view managing corporate pensions as a dying specialty, not only within their own firms but everywhere. Recruiting talented new staff members may become more difficult, as potential employees view a stint in the pension area as unattractive. An industry-wide deterioration in the expertise of internal pension staffs is to be expected.

If the quality of the internal pension staff declines, the risks to the firm of making investment mistakes will rise, and the firm will become more dependent on external talent for expert advice. But external staff may be harder to find, as experienced corporate pension officers become a rarity. At the same time, companies will find that the efficiency of managing the pension with an internal staff is declining in proportion to the asset base. Eventually, the plan assets will reach a size where internal management is clearly no longer cost-effective.

Outsourcing the Frozen Pension Plan

Investment committees as well as employees will be dealing with the consequences of freezing defined benefit pension plans for decades to come. Companies contemplating freezing their defined benefit plans should anticipate these effects, because managing a frozen plan will force them to adopt new policies and practices—and break some old habits. Perhaps the first and hardest habit to break will be the mental habit of thinking that DB plans in their current structure and the old ways of managing them will be around forever.

Staffing issues and cost pressures may drive many firms to outsource the entire function of managing their frozen pension plans. Firms that previously felt that an internal pension operation gave them control over their pension plans may choose to divest themselves of the burden. A trend toward outsourcing large corporate plans, like the current trend toward freezing them, is likely to take hold.

If outsourcing large plans becomes more common, competition for assets will intensify and the number of ways to outsource pension management should grow. Today the main option for corporations wishing to outsource their pension plans is the manager-of-managers firm, or outsourced chief investment officer (OCIO). Some OCIO firms, but not all, are willing to assume the role of named fiduciary and accept discretionary responsibility under ERISA. The OCIO model may provide co-fiduciary expertise. Alternatively, corporate defined benefit plans, once frozen, can be sold and their funding risks transferred to insurance companies, which will be pleased to manage them for an attractive implied return to the insurer.

One way for investment committees to lessen the appearance of conflict of interest is to engage an outside, independent fiduciary, such as an outsourcing firm. That creates an operational separation between the plan sponsor and the investment management of the plan. Furthermore, a qualified outsourcing firm is likely to be better suited than a plan sponsor to implement the critical but unfamiliar tasks involved in a dynamically managed LDI program. A host of activities, such as asset allocation, hedging, derivatives management, hiring and terminating managers, risk budgeting, preparing legal agreements, monitoring, and reporting can be integrated in a bundled approach by an outsourcing firm experienced with LDI issues.

Experience in trading and monitoring borrowings and derivatives is typically not available at the staff level. ERISA plans seeking outside assistance in dealing with swaps are required to use a qualified professional asset manager (QPAM). The QPAM should also be able to take on the burden of negotiating swap agreements, which demand specialized legal expertise.

A key service rendered by such firms is devising the LDI strategy, using actuarial information to propose an investment policy that will reduce surplus volatility to levels acceptable to the firm. Trigger levels can be established for downsizing or increasing the equity allocation and risk levels in general in several steps as successive surplus targets are approached. For example, the first reduction might take equities down from 60 to 30 percent, the next from 30 to 15 percent, and the last to 0 percent, if and when it becomes feasible and appropriate to seek full immunization. The timing of these shifts will depend on many variables, such as interest rates, the market environment, the liability structure, the size of the existing surplus or deficit, and the financial characteristics of the sponsor.

The extensive asset reallocations involved in LDI often entail portfolio restructurings, account terminations, and new manager agreements. The sweeping changes can significantly affect longstanding relationships and fee agreements with external managers, especially in cases where the manager has granted a low fee for running a large amount of assets. In general, manager costs for LDI may be lower than for a conventional asset-maximization strategy, as equity managers are replaced by fixed income managers. However, those cost savings may be offset by the increased (and profitable) use of portable alpha and alternative strategies, which come with high fees.

LDI Is Not Irreversible

Fiduciaries considering LDI can take comfort that although it's a major strategy change for any firm, it does not have to be permanent. Unforeseen circumstances could arise to make it advisable for a firm to revert to asset-driven investing. For example, a merger of two firms, one with an LDI plan and the other with a conventional plan, might result in a need for more asset growth in the combined plans. Perhaps some future change in the accounting treatment of pension deficits and surpluses will reduce the impact of volatility on financial statements. Maybe enlightened new government regulations giving firms reasons to bear the risks of running a pension plan—such as being able to apply a pension plan surplus to underfunded retiree health insurance plans, in ways not currently permitted—will someday encourage some firms to return to asset-maximizing strategies.

For the time being, though, LDI will continue to be the real-world choice for many fiduciaries. It's a risk-based approach to investing, with customized asset strategies managed to offset the volatility of liabilities, with unique policy benchmarks driven by interest rates, with leveraged fixed income swaps, and with no peer comparisons to provide safety or satisfaction. For investment committees used to conventional plans designed to beat market benchmarks, LDI is indeed a brave new world.

5

Moving from Theory to Practice

OUR ASSUMPTIONS FOR returns and risks are sure to be seriously tested by world events that can't be predicted with great accuracy, only broadly probabilistically. To find your truly optimal portfolio, you have to use not just historical statistics, but also a significant helping of judgment and wisdom based on your ability to identify asset classes and managers you trust to deliver acceptable returns for their expected volatility.

Figure 5.1 lays out estimates of expected returns and risks for major asset classes. These estimates modify historical statistics by taking into account some reversion to mean for asset classes that seem unsustainably overpriced. For example, government bonds exhibit negligible real yields compared with their more normal 2 to 3 percent real yields. In addition, conservative estimates of alpha (value added by the active management of the asset class) are added to returns. These estimates merely illustrate the impact of potential alphas. Investors should develop their own properly calculated estimates of returns, volatilities, correlations, and alphas, and update them (and include emerging asset classes) at least every three to five years.

Asset Class	Expected Real Return	Expected Alpha	Adjusted Real Returns	Expected Volatility
Equity				
U.S. Equity	6.8%	0.4%		16.8%
Non-U.S. Equity	6.9%	1.0%		17.1%
Emerging Markets Equity	8.3%	1.1%		21.5%
Alternatives				
Private Equity	8.5%	1.5%		23.6%
Directional Hedge Funds	4.2%	1.5%		9.8%
Market-Neutral Hedge Funds	1.4%	1.5%		7.9%
Real Assets				
Real Estate	2.8%	0.5%		10.8%
TIPS	1.5%	0.0%	0.2%	4.4%
Commodities	5.0%	0.0%		24.6%
Fixed Income				
U.S. Fixed Income	1.9%	0.3%	1.1%	5.9%
U.S. High Yield	3.9%	1.0%	2.8%	11.2%
Non-U.S. Fixed Income	1.7%	0.1%	(1.3%)	5.3%
Cash and FX				
U.S. Dollar	0.0%	0.0%		0.0%
Foreign Exchange	0.2%	0.0%		7.6%

FIGURE 5.1   Expected long-term returns and volatility.

The expected returns have been adjusted for inflation. Expected alphas are illustrative only. Source: "Endowment Management for Higher Education," Nicole Wellman Kraus, CFA, Hilda Ochoa-Brillembourg, CFA, and Jay A. Yoder, AGB Press, 2017.

In building portfolios from estimates, you should know what relevant peers are doing, to make sure you deviate from them only for well-thought-out reasons: to meet specific portfolio needs, to have access to unusual investment skills in certain assets over others, or to build or protect a robust, stable governance structure. Bear in mind that being too different from peers can be a death sentence for an institution responsible for delivering strong, trustworthy results if markets do not reward your choices. It takes years and hardy governance to build sustainable, valuable differences from peers in the nonmarketable asset classes. The Yale portfolio, including 30 percent in private equity and venture capital, 22 percent in hedge funds, and 8 percent in fixed income, took over 15 years to develop gradually as the team's confidence in alternative asset classes, management selection skills, and governance took hold.

Correcting for Unrealistic Return Expectations

Since the crash of 2008, bond markets have not reflected the prices at which they would clear without the copious liquidity that the Fed and the European Central Bank injected. Confronting the collapse of banking credit and the effect on the money multiplier, central banks increased money supply to maintain a sustainable growth rate and avoid a 1930s-style depression. Credit was curtailed when commercial banks, pressed for capital, adopted lending restrictions. The liquidity crisis thus forced a deleveraging of the world economy. Central banks intervened to restore the availability of credit in lending institutions through so-called quantitative easing, injecting new money into the economy by buying fixed income assets from the public and financial intermediaries. Both consumer and financial-intermediary debt levels were reduced, while increased government debt filled the gap to sustain employment and aggregate demand. And yet when and how these unsustainably low real yields will revert to normal is highly uncertain, judging by the experience of Japan, where 10-year bond rates have been very low since 1998.

The Fed has made it quite clear that it wants interest rates out of the basement, with an extended series of 25-basis-point increases in the Fed funds rate since December 2015. Figure 5.2 shows how challenging that effort is.

After years of disappointment, inflation has been moving toward a target of 2 percent (horizontal bar). Unemployment is now comfortably below the target near 5 percent (vertical bar), and we aren't facing new recessionary threats from other major world economies.

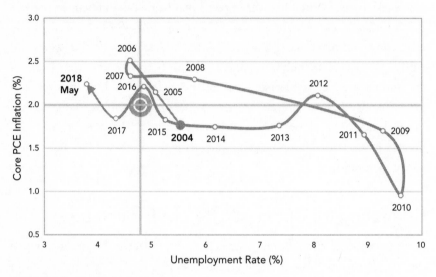

FIGURE 5.2   The Fed's dual target.

Source: U.S. Bureau of Labor Statistics, retrieved from FRED, Federal Reserve Bank of St. Louis.

In mid-2017 the valuation-adjusted returns for both bonds and equities were lower than historical averages in the United States. But considering that corporate earnings continued to surprise on the upside, equities appeared less overvalued than bonds, particularly if real interest rates remained at low levels. Therefore, at those levels one might not have lowered the expected return on equities for policy-design purposes. One might have tactically underweighted the more overvalued U.S. equities in favor of less overvalued ones (e.g., emerging and non-U.S. developed market equities).

Valuation-adjusted return and risk expectations change day by day with changes in earnings, inflation expectations, risk premiums, and interest rates. This turbulence should not necessarily affect your optimal long-term policy portfolio, particularly if that policy is reviewed only every three years or more. (Institutions that review policy yearly may choose to adjust their return expectations at the policy level and therefore change the policy.) But changing current conditions may affect *tactical tilts*—exposures to certain assets that differ from allocations in the long-term optimal policy portfolio and those of your peers. Figure 5.3 suggests possible tactical ranges around policy targets to allow for price volatility and tactical tilts relative to policy. The ranges should respond to the comfort level and skills of the team and service providers in taking tactical bets.

Category	Target	Range
Total Equity	40%	30%–50%
Total Alternatives	40%	30%–50%
Real Assets	5%	0–10%
Fixed Income	15%	10%–30%

FIGURE 5.3   Illustrative asset allocation target and ranges.

Source: "Endowment Management for Higher Education," Nicole Wellmann Kraus, CFA, Hilda Ochoa-Brillembourg, CFA, and Jay Yoder, CFA, AGB Press, 2017, page 36.

If you're changing the policy at a time when expected returns are not within "normal" ranges, the expected shorter-term, tactical returns, rather than the long-term estimates, should drive the speed and timing of the change. For example, many DB plans might be considering hedging a portion of their long-term liabilities by increasing long-duration fixed income holdings when real bond yields are near or below zero. If you do this, you should do it slowly, preferably in response to increasing yields rather than buying into declining yields. (See Figure 5.4 for the recent trend of Treasury yields and Figure 5.5 for the expected one-year returns on Treasuries of different durations.) Many small to midsize endowments that are shifting toward the larger-endowment model of fewer but longer-duration bonds may not need to reduce the speed if they are leaving the *total* portfolio duration—and therefore the interest rate risk—unchanged. But they should monitor the comparative attractiveness of the risky assets they are replacing with fixed income.

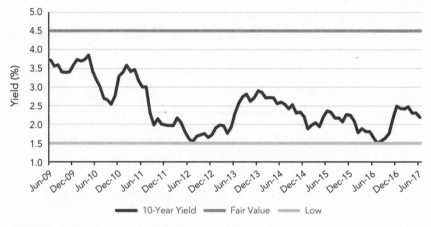

FIGURE 5.4   U.S. Treasury yields have revived from the bottom of the range. The top horizontal line is the long-term "fair value" yield.

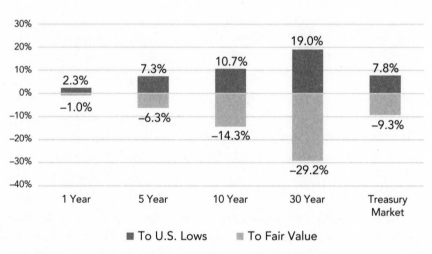

FIGURE 5.5   The range of expected one-year returns for U.S. Treasuries.

These were the likely annual returns as of June 2017 if the yields on Treasuries returned to either historical fair value or recent lows.

Assessing Alternative Scenarios and Ranges for Equity Returns

Benjamin Graham and David Dodd developed a useful table (Figure 5.6) to assess the response of equity prices to changes in interest and earnings growth rates.

Bond Yield	Expected 5-Year Annual Earnings Growth Rate								
	0%	5%	10%	15%	20%	25%	30%	35%	40%
1%	37.4	81.4	125.4	169.4	213.4	257.4	301.4	345.4	389.4
2%	18.7	40.7	62.7	84.7	106.7	128.7	150.7	172.7	194.7
3%	12.5	27.1	41.8	56.5	71.1	85.8	100.5	115.1	129.8
4%	9.4	20.4	31.4	42.4	53.4	64.4	75.4	86.4	97.4
5%	7.5	16.3	25.1	33.9	42.7	51.5	60.3	69.1	77.9
6%	6.2	13.6	20.9	28.2	35.6	42.9	50.2	57.6	64.9
7%	5.3	11.6	17.9	24.2	30.5	36.8	43.1	49.3	55.6
8%	4.7	10.2	15.7	21.2	26.7	32.2	37.7	43.2	48.7
9%	4.2	9.0	13.9	18.8	23.7	28.6	33.5	38.4	43.3
10%	3.7	8.1	12.5	16.9	21.3	25.7	30.1	34.5	38.9
11%	3.4	7.4	11.4	15.4	19.4	23.4	27.4	31.4	35.4
12%	3.1	6.8	10.5	14.1	17.8	21.5	25.1	28.8	32.5
13%	2.9	6.3	9.6	13.0	16.4	19.8	23.2	26.6	30.0
14%	2.7	5.8	9.0	12.1	15.2	18.4	21.5	24.7	27.8
15%	2.5	5.4	8.4	11.3	14.2	17.2	20.1	23.0	26.0
16%	2.3	5.1	7.8	10.6	13.3	16.1	18.8	21.6	24.3
17%	2.2	4.8	7.4	10.0	12.6	15.1	17.7	20.3	22.9
18%	2.1	4.5	7.0	9.4	11.9	14.3	16.7	19.2	21.6
19%	2.0	4.3	6.6	8.9	11.2	13.5	15.9	18.2	20.5
20%	1.9	4.1	6.3	8.5	10.7	12.9	15.1	17.3	19.5

FIGURE 5.6   Graham & Dodd's matrix of price-earnings ratios.
This table allows you to calculate the maximum P/E ratio you should pay to make both investments (bonds and equities) comparable at different bond yields and expected earnings growth rates. Embedded in the formula is that you discount equities' cash streams at the bond yield plus an equity risk premium.

Broad, Efficient Diversification

A well-diversified portfolio is likely to achieve higher compound rates of return over time than a less diversified one because it should reduce total portfolio volatility by adding additional, less correlated assets. However, you will inevitably encounter some period when diversification fails to lower volatility or increase risk-adjusted returns. There are periods when one or another asset class will do much better than a broader mix of assets. From 2010 to 2015, for example, a plain vanilla portfolio of public and private U.S. stocks and bonds would have greatly outperformed one including international assets and other alternatives.

The problem with any theory, and MPT is not an exception, is that in practice you will get different answers for what is the optimal portfolio *after the fact*. Measurements are extremely "beginning- and ending-period" sensitive. Of course, it's impossible to know for sure what investment environment we will be experiencing in the future. One can develop opinions about the future more or less substantiated by current developments, but these opinions are not facts, and they are frequently wrong. For example, the correlation between U.S. stocks and bonds has fluctuated from *positive* 0.6 to *negative* 0.6 over the past 20 years and has hovered around negative 0.4 since 2008 as the markets have pivoted between risk-off (recession) and risk-on (growth) postures. In risk-on situations, stock prices go up and bond prices stay flat or may marginally dip. When risk-off, stocks go down and bonds go up or stay flat. In periods when inflation is the greater risk, such as the seventies, the correlation between stocks and bonds tightens.

Maintaining target correlations among asset classes in a policy portfolio requires attention. Correlations among all asset classes have fluctuated quite dramatically over the past 25 years. Figure 5.7 depicts rolling five-year correlations among different asset classes. Of the four classes charted, only U.S. Treasuries have moved from positive to negative correlations with U.S. equities.

Dealing with Currency Risks

As desirable as it may be to diversify globally, currency risks have been a deterrent to some investors—often a more formidable deterrent than they need to be. We rightly emphasize global diversification as an efficient way to lower total portfolio risk. Yet international investments do encounter foreign currency risks that have to be addressed. As you increase investments outside

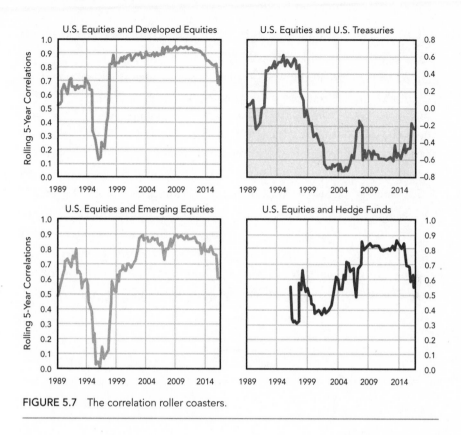

FIGURE 5.7   The correlation roller coasters.

your base currency (the currency in which you report results to your stake-holders), you incur currency translation and conversion risks. Translation risks are incurred at every reporting period when foreign currency asset results are translated to your base currency as they are marked to market. Conversion risks are incurred when the asset is sold and the proceeds are converted to the base currency. Therefore the optimal policy portfolio can be quite different depending on the investor's base currency.

Prices and interest rates will adjust to reflect changes in the exchange rates. Economists have developed the theory of purchasing power parity, which claims that, in equilibrium, traded goods will have the same price every-where. That is, the price of the good in one currency will be the same as the price in another currency times its exchange rate. Otherwise it pays a trader to move the good from one country to sell in another. The idea is that over the longer run all prices in the economy will adjust to a new exchange rate.

Unfortunately, currencies have a habit of behaving in surprising ways, as different governments use monetary, fiscal, and trade policies to increase employment and growth, attract capital, or increase exports by making their currencies or goods more attractive to investors or importers. Portfolio managers have to be attentive to the currency risk and its effects on total portfolio returns.

Let's look at the history of the three major currencies (euro, U.K. pound, and Japanese yen) against the U.S. dollar since the euro started on January 1, 1999. (See Figure 5.8.) By late 2017, both the euro and the yen had fallen about 3 percent vis-à-vis the dollar since the starting date. In contrast, the pound had strengthened by 27 percent. But over the whole of the period, all three currencies have had significant swings. For example, the euro weakened

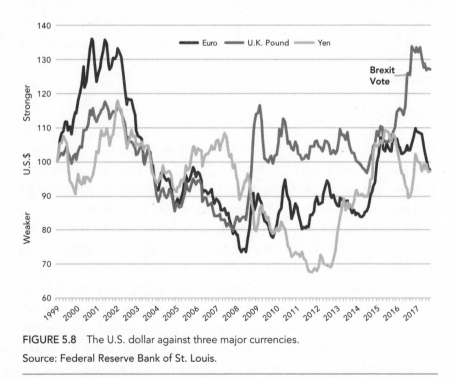

FIGURE 5.8   The U.S. dollar against three major currencies.
Source: Federal Reserve Bank of St. Louis.

by 30 percent within two years of its adoption, then appreciated 60 percent until hitting a peak in 2008. After the pro-Brexit vote, the pound and the euro dropped 7 to 15 percent in a few weeks.

The annualized monthly volatility of the exchange rates is 6 to 7 percent. The CBOE offers a product that trades this volatility—EUVIX (CBOE/CME FX Euro Volatility Index). This volatility is about half that of the U.S. equity market, which has averaged around 15 percent since 2010.

How Much Should Currency Risks Be Hedged?

The optimal level of currency risk hedging will depend on five factors:

- The impact of currency volatility on the portfolio's historical returns
- The correlation of the hedged and unhedged assets to the rest of your portfolio
- The size of foreign assets that you should ideally own
- Your tolerance for total volatility, particularly if there is no additional return for the volatility
- The expected hedging costs

Because of the diverse ways that currency movements affect asset prices, a depreciating currency and its effect on translation losses can be fully or partially offset by an exporting company's increased competitiveness, a growing earnings stream, and a higher stock price. On average, stock prices in exporting countries tend to compensate for currency movements. In economies that trade mostly within their own borders, prices are less sensitive to currency movements; therefore currency volatility has a larger impact on portfolio returns. Taking some uncorrelated currency risks serves to lower total portfolio risks.

When investing overseas, if non-U.S. dollar investments in developed country equity exceeded 30 percent of the total portfolio, I would hedge half the risk. This risk could be hedged at the portfolio level or by asking underlying managers to do it by giving them a hedged local currency benchmark for the portion of assets in need of hedging. Exposure to emerging market equities would be left unhedged for several reasons: The majority of those companies are exporters; the allocation would not be above 15 percent; and hedging costs have historically been higher than for developed markets. Foreign fixed income investments in excess of 10 percent would be hedged fully, because currencies and interest rates are highly correlated. More recently, as portfolios were diversified into a broader set of alternative U.S. dollar assets and allocations to nondollar bonds were negligible, there was less need to hedge the currency risks of nondollar marketable equity investments.

Foreign currency investments in real estate, private equity, and venture capital bring on specific currency risks associated with the time at which the investments are to be sold. You'll face regular translation losses or gains during the investment period, but when an exit is contemplated, short-term currency risks can be particularly high and require additional attention. If a sale is being contemplated over, say, a 12-month period, you may want to hedge the currency risk to preclude an outsize impact on your private equity or real estate returns when you are about to capture your final value.

The Price You Pay for an Asset Is the Greatest Risk

In my experience, the best predictor of expected return and risk may not be historical statistics, but how relatively overvalued or undervalued the asset is at present relative to its history. You may find that these overvaluations and undervaluations are a reasonable predictor of future returns for the one- to five-year horizon, but only if the assets are overvalued or undervalued by at least 1.5 to 2 standard deviations. If the valuation is inside that 1.5 range, you can use historical estimates of returns and volatilities. If the overvaluation or undervaluation is outside that range, you may consider decreasing or increasing your average return estimates roughly proportionally to the percentage by which assets are overvalued or undervalued, perhaps using a five-year horizon and assuming that the prices will revert to mean values.

You may use historical standard deviation estimates for marketable assets, but you might tweak correlations to a larger handicap for the diversifying asset if there's high demand for the asset in the market. Before doing that, you might want to check how sensitive the policy outcomes are to the change. Historical correlations can also be tweaked to handicap the diversifying asset in cases where the asset might have already lost some of its diversifying properties for other reasons. These exercises, driving toward an optimal policy, are useful in testing the reasonableness of your policy on its own and relative to peers' choices. They are particularly useful given how sensitive optimizer models are to small changes in assumptions. Sensibly deviating from peers' choices requires robust estimates and your informed assessment of your own superior skills.

The historically based optimal policy can be tested for reasonableness relative to the tweaked optimal policy, and allocations can be marginally increased or decreased. Changing demand for a diversifying asset can be established when peers' investment policy allocations to the asset are significantly increasing or decreasing. This can be checked by observing trends reported by media, custodial banks, and research institutions. As demand for a diversifying asset ebbs and flows, so does the correlation of that asset to the most liquid, widely held assets; the diversification benefits of the asset vary accordingly.

6

Changing the Policy

LONG-TERM POLICY PORTFOLIOS generally should be well diversified and optimized along historical estimates of returns, volatilities, and correlations, then course-corrected with a few qualitative tweaks to specific component assets. Estimates and weightings should be reviewed and updated with some frequency as new asset classes emerge or investor needs and circumstances change. You may check policy continually and effect a thorough review every three or four years. This review could trigger changes in the weights given to assets, increasing those with higher return expectations. The benefit of updating policy, incorporating new asset classes and management styles, can be seen in Figure 2.2 (in Chapter 2).

In the 25 years from 1991 through 2015, adjustments and improvements to investment policies likely increased our benchmark annual return by 150 basis points and reduced yearly volatility from 12 to 11 percent. *Actual* returns, including returns from active management, exceeded those enhanced policy benchmarks by an additional 2 percentage points, bringing results closer to the 8-plus percent compound annual returns that perfect foresight would have predicted for those 25 years. This incremental return over policy was achieved through tactical and structural tilts in favor of underpriced assets and emerging manager styles.

Some expertly managed institutions prefer to use shorter-term estimates of future returns in setting the policy. This approach changes the policy itself more often instead of leaving the long-term policy unchanged for three to five years or until conditions change while perhaps taking small tactical tilts above or below policy targets in response to market and competitive opportunities.

In theory, neither approach is better. In practice, yearly policy changes work best where the board or investment committee is actively responsive to changes in estimated returns based on facts, not opinions, and the staff or asset manager isn't inclined to take tactical positions too frequently. In these environments it's easy to change policy based on updated valuations.

In environments where policy discussions and changes require multiple quarterly meetings with complicated, unpredictable governance dynamics, it makes more sense to change the policy infrequently and allow the managers to make small changes to their tactical tilts in the asset mix relative to policy. In the absence of demonstrated managerial skill, the asset mix may be rebalanced to policy quarterly, or more frequently if prices have changed more than, say, 10 percent within the quarter. Tactical asset mix tilts generally have low evidence of consistent short-term value added. Managers with proven expertise in this area should change tilts *only when justified by extreme valuation disparities.*

In sum, the optimal frequency of policy reviews depends on the decision-making process at the top of the governance pyramid. If the board approval process is rational, fact-based, and easy, opt for reviewing and adjusting the policy frequently—say, yearly—based on robust, well-triangulated estimates of returns (not based on someone's pontification about valuations). If the board approval process is complicated by layers of formalities, contracts, and heterogeneous actors, opt for allowing moderate, risk-appropriate tactical tilts and leave the policy unchanged until a prudent in-depth review every three to five years. Exceptions, of course, need to be made when there are changes in the financial and other institutional needs, changes in liability structures caused by mergers or acquisitions, or new capital spending needs that could justify a different medium- or long-term policy.

Organizations need special discipline when decisions at the top are made by less experienced and more varied actors, including diverse knowledgeable but impulsive specialists. Even if they review policy relatively infrequently, they should avoid chasing trends, diversifying into new asset classes that have performed best over the last three or five years—unless the assets are in fact still undervalued. Instead, they should use the reviews to update assumptions and get all decision makers, particularly new ones, on board with the chosen policy. If a new asset class can be added only after plenty of evidence that it has the power to add value, and the evidence is strongest after a period of unsustainably high asset-class performance, then add the asset in small increments, ideally after it has come down in price. This is hard to do by committee. If decision makers want some action even at a terrible time in the market, dollar-cost averaging over 24 months—adding fixed dollar amounts to the asset class at regular intervals—serves the purpose of stretching the dollars when prices are lower and not chasing a runaway market. Speed bumps can reduce some accidents.

Relative Value Lost During Bubbles Can Be Recovered Quickly

The greatest mistakes we have seen in managing balanced portfolios have occurred under the banner of diversifying more broadly *after* the diversifying asset class has done unsustainably well. A few of our clients severely tested our relationship in the late eighties when we kept them out of the obscenely overvalued Japanese equity market while many other investors were moving to "diversify their risks" by *adding* Japan to their portfolios at the most overvalued possible time. Price appreciation had pushed Japanese stocks to account for more than 60 percent of the developed non-U.S. equity markets. (In 2017 they were a mere 23 percent.) Under the weight of excessive P/E multiples, low earnings, and high corporate debt, Japan's equity market collapsed in 1990 and has yet to recover to its previous high. Keeping Japan out of our portfolios—a tactical tilt that subtracted relative value for five years!—contributed significantly to our value added over time. The five-plus years of underperformance in international equities created by under-weighting Japan were made up in a mere 21 months (March 1989 through December 1990), and we continued adding value with this tactical policy through 2000. We then reweighted Japan to policy levels since it was no longer grossly overvalued and offered risk-diversifying low correlation with other equity markets.

Similarly, during the tech bubble of 1998 and 1999, we lost a few clients that chose, despite formidable arguments to the contrary, to adopt a fully indexed or, worse still, a growth strategy in U.S. equities.[1] With some ill-advised consultants on their side and trade media articles prompting them, they wanted to add many more tech stocks to the portfolios in which we had cut the exposure to tech. In their minds they were *decreasing* their risk of underperformance by moving into tech stocks at record prices. In our minds they were significantly *increasing* their risk by doing so. Simply put, *you do not diversify or reduce risks by buying overpriced assets!* Clients looking at past returns couldn't fully understand or trust that we were looking at expected future returns. They were blindly projecting the immediate past into the future. The tech bubble burst in mid-March 2000, and we recovered our underperformance in less than a year.

My suggestion is to make changes in the policy portfolio to increase future returns or reduce future risks *when assets are within one standard deviation of fair value*, which is 68 percent of the time. And use as many measures of fair value as you can find in estimating the normal range. Avoid exaggerated impressions of value that can be found among vocal portfolio managers more interested in making a name for themselves in the trade journals than acting prudently.

Beware of pulpit preachers in the investment or any other world. Anybody claiming extreme conviction about the value of an asset should be viewed with careful skepticism, unless the asset is overpriced or underpriced by more than two standard deviations relative to historical averages. If it is, the preacher might be right if too strident.

7
Selecting Appropriate Benchmarks

WITHIN A POLICY portfolio, performance benchmarks are an instrument both for targeting expected returns and for controlling the risks you are prepared to live with. They're also a measuring stick for how well you're doing relative to passively managed, low-cost, diversified market funds. Benchmarks should ideally encompass the breadth of global asset choices and the risks you're prepared to take in the pursuit of return objectives. Broad global diversification is generally preferable to narrow diversification.

A typical long-term portfolio should have reasonably achievable return objectives embedded in the policy benchmark. For endowments and foundations, assuming an annual spending rate of roughly 5 percent net of costs and inflation, the objectives should have more than a 50 percent probability of being achieved over 10 to 20 years. Spending rates for pension plans follow a different track: much lower for younger plans, much higher for mature plans.

As a performance measurement stick, the benchmark should be hard but not impossible to beat. Aspirational benchmarks aren't appropriate; they could be too hard, even impossible, to beat depending on market conditions—or too easy. For example, some investors use an absolute rate of real return of, say, 3 to 5 percent, depending on style, as a desirable return target for hedge funds, because it's difficult to find appropriate passively managed benchmarks for hedge funds. However, among hedge funds, that actually is an aspirational return; your hedge funds are unlikely to satisfy such a hurdle rate in the near to medium term, except by the luck of the draw. Well-managed, diversified hedge funds should exhibit low correlations with most other asset classes, and few if any investable assets can give you a steady 3 to 5 percent absolute return along with low correlation with other asset classes. You might need to wait 10 years or more for them to meet those objectives. That 3 to 5 percent benchmark won't reflect a powerful reason for including hedge funds anyway: the relatively low (but not zero) correlation and risk abatement power of a well-selected set of hedge funds. Warren Buffett was happy to report his winning a 10-year bet that an index fund would beat a package of hedge funds,[1] but he may have overlooked the major reason for holding well-diversified hedge funds in a balanced, tax-free institutional portfolio of stocks and bonds, which is to further diversify equity risks and deliver higher compound returns for the total portfolio over time.

Ideally, an asset-class benchmark should have the following qualities:

- Covers the broad tradable investment universe for the asset class
- Offers passive, low-cost, liquid, investable vehicles, including futures and options to help manage exposure to that benchmark
- Is difficult but not impossible to beat over a market cycle
- Is published by independent benchmark providers, not the asset manager
- Offers a wide set of active managers willing and able to manage to that benchmark

Better benchmarks are developed over time with additional liquidity and emerging assets. Investors should evaluate existing and new benchmarks regularly and introduce them in the policy portfolios with each review.

What Is an Asset Class?
Are Hedge Funds an Asset Class?

Asset classes organize and categorize investment decisions around investments with similar qualities aimed at delivering similar expected returns for
a given level of volatility and correlation with other asset classes. Investment
managers specialize in one asset class or another. An asset class should typically include all assets that are highly correlated with each other (at least 0.7
correlation coefficients) and are managed to a widely accepted market benchmark. Ideally, based on the list of benchmark qualities, an asset class should
have replicable, investable, and passively managed investment vehicles with
low management fees and daily liquidity against which you can measure
active strategies. Better still, they should have liquid derivative futures you
can efficiently trade for cost-efficient portfolio and liquidity management.

Most U.S. equities have a correlation* in excess of 0.7. That is, 49 percent
of their volatility is explained by the behavior of the broad equity market,
generally responding to similar external factors: economic growth, inflation,
market volatility, interest rates, and risk premium—how much investors
are willing to pay for volatility at any time. In contrast, government bonds
respond to inflationary expectations and attendant Fed policy, and less so to
economic and profit growth, except to the extent that growth increases inflationary pressures. Consequently the correlation between stocks and bonds
has varied widely between about −0.6 and +0.6 (see Figure 5.7 in Chapter 5).

There is no hard-and-fast rule about what constitutes an asset class. In
addition to the return and risk characteristics, how portfolio managers define
and compete within subsets of a larger asset class can also be a determinant of
an asset class. How a particular subset correlates or behaves relative to other
subsets can serve to define that subset as an asset class. *The purpose of defining asset classes is simply (1) to organize and facilitate investment decisions that
meet targeted expected returns and risk preferences and (2) to be able to assess the*

---

* Or more specifically, a coefficient of determination (the square of the correlation), which
measures the percentage of return explained by the market return. For example, a 0.5 correlation with the S&P 500 would mean that 25 percent ($0.5 \times 0.5 \times 100$) of the price
change of the asset is explained by the market.

relative performance of active managers within a similar asset class and market conditions. Another way of organizing and understanding asset classes is to look at them as return and risk "buckets."

Hedge funds may be considered an asset class distinct from equities and bonds. They don't behave like equities or bonds, although they hold equities and bonds (and many other instruments) long and short. The majority of hedge funds are relatively new derivative investment pools created from different types of financial instruments, precisely to serve as an effective risk diversifier to stock and bond assets without sacrificing expected average long-term returns. The more long-lived of these pools may not go back more than 20 or 30 years. They may achieve their return objectives because they are less constrained than a typical stock or bond manager, who will generally not sell short or leverage, and who will more typically try to beat a market benchmark in an asset class without deviating too much from peers' asset-class weights and the class's return and risk characteristics. Even hedge funds with disproportionate asset-class bets have a correlation of 0.7 or less with those asset classes. Those that have a correlation exceeding 0.8 could arguably be included in the asset class they are most correlated with, although they could add significant volatility to the asset-class returns in the form of active-management risk.

A diversified hedge fund bucket will ideally offer nominal returns and risks somewhere between stocks and bonds (say, a real return of 3 to 5 percent and volatility of perhaps 8 to 10 percent) and a relatively low correlation (less than 0.7) with both stock and bond buckets. Hedge fund managers transform the public equity and bond return-to-risk profile by use of multiple management tools including not only short sales and leverage, but also options, futures, and swap contracts. Some hedge funds also hold privately traded assets in so-called side pockets.

Some hedge funds will have higher and more volatile returns than stocks and bonds—and one should avoid those, certainly as risk diversifiers, unless they offer very low correlations, which are themselves rare and possibly dangerous. If you find two negatively correlated assets, chances are one of them will go bankrupt or otherwise cease to exist, and so will not be a good risk diversifier. When we first invested in hedge funds in 1981, we could find only two that had track records longer than five years. A handful in existence since earlier times had "disappeared" amid the market turmoil of the mid-seventies.

When accepting hedge funds as a separate asset class because of their different return and risk characteristics, you are not anointing them with a superior quality. They have to demonstrate they have the quality. Some investors include hedge funds as part of their equity and bond portfolios. We preferred to group them separately, because combining the assets made our overall risk management and return attribution process more difficult. It also made the process of transporting (leveraging or amplifying) alphas much harder to control. (More on this in Chapter 12.)

For illustrative purposes Figure 7.1 includes historical returns, volatility, and correlations from Hedge Fund Research, Inc. (HFRI). Our own experience with the class offered much better results than those averages.

There is a strong argument for keeping hedge funds as a separate asset class when hedge fund portfolios are used to reduce market or asset-class risk as much as we could. From inception of the asset class in our portfolios at the World Bank, we believed in searching for a well-diversified pool with positive alpha and low beta. To buy beta exposure through a hedge fund can result in paying up to a 2 percent base fee plus 20 percent incentive fee on returns above zero—an expensive alternative to paying less than 5 basis points for passive, indexed market-beta exposure and blending that exposure with reliable alpha sources.

Style	HFRI Historical		Correlations			
	Annual Returns	Annual Volatility	Equity Long/Short	Market Neutral	Macro	Merger Arb
Equity Directional	4%	8%	1.0			
Market Neutral	3%	3%	0.6	1.0		
Macro	5%	5%	0.4	0.4	1.0	
Merger Arb	4%	3%	0.8	0.5	0.4	1.0

FIGURE 7.1 Historical HFRI Index returns, volatility, and correlations among major hedge fund styles.

Source: Strategic and Hedge Fund Research, Inc.

One should also pay attention to hedge funds' beta effect on total risk and control the total risk of the portfolio to targeted levels. Figure 7.2 displays the beta exposure of our group of hedge funds over time relative to nine different factor risks, including equity, interest rate, and credit exposures.

10 Years Ended 2015

FIGURE 7.2   Betas and alpha of Strategic's hedge funds over time.

The bulk of our annual hedge fund return over time was attributed to alpha and a much smaller portion to market risk factors.

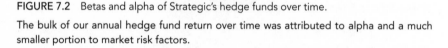

How Many Asset Classes: Somewhere Between Two and Eight?

In our experience in designing a policy portfolio, it's impractical to include more than eight asset classes and imprudent to include fewer than two, unless you're dealing with extraordinary circumstances. For example, if you have a very long horizon, are completely insensitive to annual volatility, and assume returns will revert to the mean, you could invest solely in equities. If you have no liquidity or spending needs, the assets could in principle all be private equities. Even then, however, some small amount of fixed income, say, 10 percent, is always advisable for rebalancing, seizing new investment opportunities, and dealing with unexpected changes to liquidity needs. Even in a 100 percent stock portfolio, there should be room to add international and emerging market stocks, private equity, and venture capital, assuming you are qualified or can find qualified service providers to select good managers in those segments; index funds can be used for international equities and even emerging markets but not for nonmarketable private investments. Obviously, an investor with a short horizon of less than about 10 years shouldn't invest in volatile assets.

More than 8 to 10 asset classes become cumbersome to manage. You are overspecifying the policy model and reducing management flexibility. Whatever the number of asset classes, each should be broadly diversified and inclusive of all tradable instruments with similar correlations to the others. The markets create appropriate benchmarks and indexes for each asset class that evolve with new securities and other market developments. Even within an asset class, diversification is a free lunch, yielding expected returns with less volatility.

How Small Can an Asset Class Be and Still Make a Difference?

Investors commonly balk at including asset classes amounting to less than 5 or 10 percent of total assets. Yale's Swensen has suggested 10 percent as a minimum.[2] But Yale now has three long-term asset classes in the policy portfolio that are much less than 10 percent.[3] (See Figure 7.3.)

The argument goes that at less than 10 percent exposure, the asset class makes no real difference to total returns, while small allocations complicate decision making and management. Worse still, small allocations distract attention from more important decisions. These are valid points, but we and others make exceptions. There are two reasons to include some asset classes at less than a 5 to 10 percent level.

First, they may be unique or *highly volatile*, yet exhibit *very low correlation* to the rest of the portfolios. Commodities fall in that category. Commodities are like salt to a meal. Some people may prefer to skip salt altogether; others add so much they make the meal unhealthy if not inedible. Yet just a pinch of salt may make a delicious difference to a meal. A pinch of commodities makes a noticeable difference to reducing the risks of a balanced portfolio without throwing the portfolio into a tailspin when commodities are crashing, as they do with relative frequency.

Portfolio	Yale Policy	Endowments Over $1 Billion (Average)
Domestic Equity	4.0%	13.0%
Foreign Equity	14.5%	19.0%
Fixed Income	8.5%	11.0%
Absolute Return (Hedge Funds)	21.5%	21.0%
Real Estate	13.0%	7.0%
Private Equity and Venture Capital	30.0%	22.0%
Natural Resources and Commodities	8.50%	7.0%
Total	100.0%	100.0%
Liquid Assets (less than 30 days)	27.0%	43.0%
Illiquid Assets (more than 90 days)	73.0%	57.0%

FIGURE 7.3.   Yale policy portfolio as of June 30, 2015.

Private equity includes 3 percent in distressed fixed income. Liquid assets are those that can be sold at publicly quoted prices without significant discounts even in liquidity-constrained markets. David Swensen has indicated recently that Yale maintains a liquidity target of 50 percent of the total portfolio. This may be accomplished by setting up hedge fund strategies in a separate account that can be liquidated at Yale's discretion. Source: NACUBO-Commonfund Study, 2015.

Second, small allocations can establish a beachhead into a new asset class that you want to monitor closely. They let you begin recognizing skilled managers and emerging styles within established firms without subjecting the portfolios to possible significant losses from inexperience with the asset class or style, or from simple bad luck in opting for the asset class at the wrong time. New asset classes and styles offer fewer if any experienced-manager choices, precisely because they're new. But because there's less competition, it's easier to add value. Inexperienced investors shouldn't bother with new asset classes or investment styles—they might not survive implementation errors. But for a seasoned investor, trading off the opportunity to add value in mispriced securities for some inexperience can make sense if you control the risks—inexperience and illiquidity—by limiting your exposure to be tolerable even if there is a near total loss.

We've used small exposures to asset classes when new assets appeared in the marketplace offering attractive return opportunities in relatively ineffi- cient markets, and where pioneering managers with adaptable expertise are learning to trade them. Examples were high-yield bonds, private equities, and hedge funds in 1981 and emerging equity markets in 1984. We made early, initial, modest (2 percent of total assets), and highly profitable investments in these and other securities, and we developed the skills to increase those investments with more confidence over time. Some of them increased to 5 to 10 percent, and sometimes 20 percent or more, of managed portfolios. Over the years, emerging and frontier markets, high-yield bonds, commodities, opportunistic capital, hedge funds, venture capital, private equity, futures, and others may have started with 2 percent allocations at the policy-portfolio level.

Human capital and personally owned assets—such as homes (e.g., Airbnb) and cars (Uber)—may be the new frontier for securitization of otherwise nontradable assets. An argument could be made to allocate a small percent- age of total assets into these emerging and hard-to-value securities, directly or through venture capital pools.

8

Rebalancing Versus Tactical Tilts

How Frequently and Why?

MOST OF OUR clients adopted monthly or quarterly rebalancing rules. That means we measure their performance monthly or quarterly against the fixed weights of the policy portfolio. In between rebalancings, the designated policy portfolio weights will "float" with the changing prices in the indexes. So will the actual portfolio, unless we want to effect some tactical trades.

In the latest edition of his book *Pioneering Portfolio Management*, David Swensen indicates that the Yale portfolio is rebalanced to the policy daily. We have to assume that what's rebalanced is only the marketable assets, which are less than 30 percent of the Yale portfolio (the nonmarketables would float), and that all daily rebalancing is done through futures or exchange-traded funds; otherwise it would trigger unnecessarily high transaction costs and potential loss of unrealized alpha from active managers. For proper risk management, assumptions have to be made about the prices and betas of the nonmarketables. Investors may price portfolios daily but rebalance monthly or quarterly, except in unusual circumstances. You may rebalance more frequently if markets experience a price dislocation of, say, more than 10 percent for nonfundamental reasons—caused, for example, by market reactions to political events that you conclude are triggering greed or fear. Greed and fear are prone to short-term mean reversion. You may also take carefully measured and controlled tactical exposures—tilts—relative to the policy.

Too frequent rebalancing in a well-selected portfolio of active managers incurs unnecessary transaction costs and destroys some of the value-added bets in their active portfolios. I like to think of a gardener metaphor to explain why too frequent rebalancing of active positions can kill a portfolio, the same way that an aggressive gardener can chop off the buds in wintertime so you get no spring blossoms. I lived through an aggressive gardener experience once and learned the lesson to be subtler in pruning our clients' portfolios. We have used fixed income and equity futures to implement quick rebalancing and tactical tilts when there is the need to do so.

Market Weights or Equal Weights?

The weights assigned to each asset class in policy portfolios and to the holdings within each asset class have generally followed combinations of three tracks.

1. **Capital asset pricing model (CAPM).** At the policy-portfolio level, the optimal theoretical track is to find the different asset weights that bring an optimal trade-off between expected returns and expected risks. This is the approach suggested by the CAPM: the theoretical price of risk is determined by the interplay of all world assets as they are arbitraged—bought and sold by all market participants to reflect relative value—and risk-adjusted returns are equalized by all market participants. Within this approach, each unit of volatility has a weighted average equilibrium price determined by all market participants. That price is the return per unit of undiversifiable risk of an optimally diversified, globally balanced portfolio. Expected returns vary constantly and recently hovered around 38 basis points per unit of volatility (standard deviation).[1] This portfolio con-

struction method generally ends up delivering policy portfolios inclined toward equal rather than market weighting of uncorrelated assets.

2. **Risk-parity model.** Another track is to try to equalize the risks among the two major asset classes, stocks and bonds, by extending the duration (the volatility and interest rate sensitivity) of bonds to the level of equity market volatility. These risk-equalized portfolios aim to deliver better return-to-risk characteristics, particularly during recessions, than portfolios in which volatilities are not equalized.[2] Risk-equalized portfolios attempt to equalize opportunity costs between each dollar put into each asset class. This process can be extended to asset classes other than stocks and bonds with more difficulty.

Academics and practitioners refer to this general risk-equalization process as the risk-parity approach. The most common use of risk parity is to implement the preference of many endowments and LDI investors to assign the U.S. bond asset class a duration of 20 years or more. This duration resembles the volatility of the U.S. equity asset class better than the six to eight years of the popular bond market indexes. Risk parity allows them to take full advantage of the diversifying power of bonds without placing more than 5 to 10 percent of their portfolios in this lower-return, lower-risk asset class. They can leverage the power of bonds to become more effective risk diversifiers in recessionary scenarios, while allowing additional investment weights to higher-return, higher-risk securities such as private equities and hedge funds.

This approach works reasonably well in many scenarios and is incidentally an application of fit theory. A longer-duration bond is not particularly attractive on a stand-alone basis but can be an attractive diversifying complement to a portfolio laden with equity risk. Caveat emptor: there will be times when bonds are greatly overvalued, and the factors that may trigger losses in bond portfolios are the same that may trigger losses in equity portfolios—an increase in inflationary expectations, for example, or an increase in interest rates from a less accommodative Fed policy. Therefore you have to be careful not to extend the duration of your bond portfolios at the wrong time, when correlations between equities and bonds are likely to increase, as could be the case currently. A critical yardstick in moving toward risk parity is to keep total portfolio duration constant when bonds' duration is overpriced and to make sure that the allocation to riskier assets is not placed in overvalued ones.

3. **Equal weights.** Equity weights can be equally divided among U.S., developed non-U.S., and emerging equities, all with similar volatilities and less-than-perfect correlation to each other. Equal weighting within the asset class is facilitated by introducing more active managers in place of passively managed market-weighted strategies. Active managers tend to equal-weight their positions within each industry group.

In the end, investors will choose policy portfolios that blend the three tracks to meet their comfort levels and their experience with less traditional asset classes. For most institutional portfolios, size is not a constraint given the current liquidity of major asset classes. Some state funds with around $200 billion in assets, however, might face significant size constraints in trying to equal-weight smaller, less liquid asset classes such as hedge funds, private equities, and commodities.

It might take a decade or more to build up a significant 10 to 20 percent exposure to certain alternative asset classes, particularly those in the private equity and venture capital markets; you want to diversify the inception year and liquidity risks of private investments over time. Diversification by vintage year is critical, as private equity and venture capital returns are sensitive to capital market pricing at time of entry and exit: their exit prices are generally driven by the cycles of innovation and the initial private offering (IPO) market. Assuming that it would take a 20 to 30 percent allocation to each of these classes to equal-weight them with stocks, it may take 15 years or more to appropriately diversify the allocations.

In the seventies and eighties, when international diversification was not as broadly accepted, dollar-denominated portfolios tended to be much more weighted toward U.S. equities, and those that were internationally diversified were likely guided by the relative weights suggested by the capitalization size of the international markets, then smaller than in the United States. Now policies of different types of institutions are diverging in interesting ways, as we see in the next chapter.

9

Policies Are Increasingly Diverging

INSTITUTIONAL POLICIES HAVE become increasingly divergent and peer comparisons much trickier. Differences among policy portfolios widen as investors seek to diversify more broadly: pension liabilities increase and mature, creating different hedging needs for the assets; new asset classes and styles emerge; and investors develop different management skills. The most striking divergence has occurred between endowments and mature, relatively fully funded, frozen corporate defined benefit plans. Many of those DB plans have moved to hedge their liabilities with increasing allocations to long-duration LDI strategies. According to Towers Watson, frozen DB plans are investing 50 percent of their assets in LDI–long-duration fixed income strategies to reduce corporate funding risks. Meanwhile, endowments *reduced* their fixed income allocations from 35 percent in 1993 to 15 percent in 2017 (those with more than $1 billion in assets have reduced their fixed income allocation to 7 percent) and moved heavily into alternative investments, including hedge funds, real estate, private equities, venture capital, energy, and commodities. As a percentage of equal-weighted endowments' portfolios, alternatives ballooned from 5 percent in 1993 to 28 percent in June 2017. Endowments with assets over $1 billion show alternatives allocations in excess of 57 percent for June 2017.

A majority of U.S. pension funds' portfolios still are largely U.S.-equity-centric, despite evidence that broader diversification would increase long-term risk-adjusted returns and despite significant efforts to diversify the same corporations' sales and operations overseas. Is this a case of cognitive dissonance among corporate decision makers or reluctance to face foreign exchange risks? By contrast, most large endowments are prone to weight non-U.S. equities more heavily (13 percent U.S. versus 19 percent non-U.S.).

Endowment and foundation portfolios tend to be more broadly diversified and equally weighted because they are more focused on reducing total portfolio volatility relative to their spending needs. Endowments, unlike corporate pension plans, fund a large proportion of the institutions' annual operating expenses. For all colleges, the average contribution of endowment flows to their spending budgets is 9.7 percent, while larger institutions on average count on endowments to contribute 16.5 percent.[1] The Harvard and Yale endowments contributed more than 30 percent of the universities' FY 2015 operating income, thus making them more sensitive to market volatility, while net tuition and room and board contributed only 10 percent.[2] Furthermore, colleges' endowment, tuition, and other revenues may be less diversified than corporate revenues.

Figure 9.1 drills down into these 15- to 24-year trends for corporate plans, endowments, and affiliated foundations.

Alternative-asset allocations have increased for all, but much more for endowments. This creates a need to better understand the factor risks embedded in alternatives—liquidity, inflation, recession, growth, size, momentum, value—which differ from the much better understood factor risks of marketable securities. Importantly, the distribution of risks tends to be more asymmetrical than in marketable portfolios. The asymmetry arises from the reality that nonmarketables don't necessarily revert to mean—*in extreme scenarios they are more likely to go bankrupt.*

Average Asset Allocations: Defined Benefit Plans,
Educational Endowments, and Affiliated Foundations

Type	Year	Equity Total	U.S.	Non-U.S.	Fixed Income	Alternative Strategies	Short-term Securities, Cash, Other
Defined Benefit Plans[1]							
Open	2016	47%			41%	6%	6%
Closed	2016	43%			41%	9%	7%
Frozen	2016	42%			46%	7%	5%
Educational Endowments and Affiliated Foundations[2]							
Over $1 billion	2017	32%	13%	19%	7%	57%	4%
	2002	45%	29%	16%	21%	32%	2%
All institutions,	2017	51%	30%	21%	15%	28%	6%
equal-weighted	2002	57%	47%	10%	27%	10%	6%
averages	1993	53%			35%	5%	7%

FIGURE 9.1. Birds of a different feather.

The most notable divergence from the old, plain vanilla 60 percent equity, 40 percent fixed income mix of the seventies and early eighties is the fivefold increase of nonmarketable alternatives in endowment portfolios from 1993 to 2017. For larger endowments, alternatives are now in excess of 57 percent. Fixed income duration has also diverged among open and LDI defined benefit plans. Alternatives include hedge funds, private equity, venture capital, commodities, and real estate. Fixed income includes U.S. and non-U.S. bonds. Sources: (1) https://www.towerswatson.com/en/Insights/Newsletters/Americas/Insider/2018/01/2016-assetallocations-in-fortune-1000-pension-plans (2) https://www.nacubo.org/-/media/Nacubo/Documents/EndowmentFiles/2017-NCSE-Public-Tables--Asset-Allocations.ashx?la=en&hash=63C84937673C6A0ECB083B98C6E3BD4B05D106E5.

The increased divergence in institutional policy portfolios is likely to create a more fragmented market for assets. *Diverging policies and low to negative interest rates help explain why some assets become significantly overpriced* as investors, driven by asset allocation and competitive pressures, become less sensitive to valuations.

The Lure of the New

As endowments have increased their allocation to illiquid diversifiers, they have increased their expected returns, but also the potential volatility of returns under extreme scenarios. Portfolio theory teaches that historical volatility of returns and historical correlations are much more stable than mean returns. Given their relative stability over time, quantitative portfolio analysis tends to leave returns, standard deviations, and correlations unchanged from their long-term historical estimates. In reality, as we have seen, all three measures can change substantially with changes in relative valuation levels, the internationalization and securitization of capital markets, and macroeconomic and liquidity conditions.

With bond yields below inflation rates by the end of 2017, expected real returns on U.S. bonds should arguably not be any higher than the 0.5 to 0.7 percent yields on TIPS (Treasury Inflation Protected Securities), instead of the 2 to 3 percent real returns in historical estimates, and could be zero or negative over 10 years. The volatility of bonds has come down significantly since 2010, from an average of 8 to 10 percent to an average of 4 to 8 percent, and should be higher if inflation picks up. We may expect the volatility of bonds to go up to 8 to 10 percent over the next 10 years on their path to mean reversion, and the correlation of bonds to equities to increase from negative to positive 0.2, 0.3, or more.

The most dramatic impact of changing correlations comes when external or internal events create market shocks and all risky assets fall or rise in price at the same time. *At crisis times, all risky asset correlations move to 1.* Correlations of newly securitized assets can appear to be low relative to established, more liquid asset classes. But as investors begin to invest in the new asset class and it becomes more popular among global investors, it will become increasingly correlated to traditional asset classes (see Figure 5.7). The set of expected returns, risks, and correlations you based your initial investment on will change maliciously. Expected returns will come down with rising prices. Volatilities might stay the same, but correlations will increase.

As a result of evolving correlations, diversification will still provide benefits, but they will be smaller than anticipated, and they may be negative if the diversifying asset has become overpriced. On the other hand, the liquidity of these assets will have increased; correlations and liquidity tend to move up together. All these variables go hand in hand toward higher capital market efficiency. Such has been the case with emerging market equities, which exhibited much higher, 10 to 12 percent, real expected returns when they first became available to foreign investors in the eighties. For a while, they were much better than a free lunch, in that they offered higher returns, somewhat higher volatility of returns, but really low correlations with other equities. As investors increased allocations to emerging market equities, returns and correlations increased and volatilities decreased. When flows reversed, prices fell, correlations decreased, and expected returns improved.

Today emerging market equities are no longer a homogeneous asset class. Some countries are net commodity exporters and others net importers. State ownership of publicly traded assets differs. Countries that are net savers or savings-strapped have different investment-return outlooks and fates. Some export-led economies have turned more toward domestic consumption. Some have become less sensitive to commodity cycles. Others, while still sensitive to commodity cycles, are priced to offer attractive, uncorrelated returns. And some governments have become freer of autocratic controls, offering better return-to-risk profiles and broader diversification opportunities to control industry and other factor risks. Differentiated in this way, emerging markets have lately again offered higher expected returns and lower correlations.

Skillfully adding new assets to your portfolio early can produce higher returns and lower volatility—until they become ubiquitous among institutional portfolios. As investors diversify more globally, the risk premiums of less traditional asset classes will come down, their prices will be bid up, and correlations will converge. Nothing as good as low correlation and high returns lasts forever. But correlations ebb and flow with new and newly orphaned assets (assets that investors have exited after performance disappointments), and opportunities to add less correlated assets at the right price appear with relative frequency. For example, decreasing growth, fears about the future macroeconomic outlook, and diminishing trade have reduced emerging market equity prices, but they have also reduced those stocks' correlations with the developed equity markets and each other, thus reinforcing their diversification attributes.

And then there is Japan . . . never say never! The only market that continues to exhibit a relatively low correlation to most other equity markets is Japan (0.5 since 2000). While Japanese equities aren't particularly profitable, their correlations are so low relative to other corporate equities that they are a welcome risk diversifier, a great stabilizer in any equity portfolio despite their lower expected returns. Of course, prices matter. Japanese stocks definitely were not a good risk diversifier in the late eighties when they had become 60-plus percent of the non-U.S. equity market index at exorbitant 60-plus P/E multiples.

So What Do You Do About Unstable Volatilities and Correlations?

First, as mentioned before, you can tweak them both a bit to "punish" or handicap the asset that previously appeared to be a great risk diversifier. There is no scientific way of handicapping an asset that doesn't have a long statistical history. Pay attention to the relative overvaluation of the asset and whether it is a "crowded trade" (too many investors investing in the asset) and avoid or slow down allocations to that asset.

Second, when you stress-test portfolios, you may assume that the less liquid asset classes should lose more value than the more liquid ones. However, that doesn't always happen. *Because less liquid assets aren't fully marked to market, investors in crisis will sell the liquid asset they can sell at the smaller discount.* In the liquidity crisis of 2007–2008, higher-quality senior bank debt lost more value than lower-quality high-yield bonds. There was a market for senior bank debt, but bid-ask spreads were so large for high-yield bonds that potential sellers abstained from selling.

The point of stress-testing portfolios is to make sure the portfolio and beneficiary can survive an extreme scenario. If the investor wouldn't survive, you have to take steps to ensure that the portfolio and the client can live another day. Reduce the risks to a level the investor could tolerate if badly damaged, and rebalance in pursuit of reversion-to-mean prices. Some of the best returns and added value can be achieved after a crisis if you have stabilizing liquid alternatives to rebalance the portfolio and buy good assets at bargain prices.

10
Responsible Investing

One More Source of Divergence

AN ADDED ELEMENT of divergence in policy portfolios comes from the increasing trend among endowments and foundations to add multiple social responsibility and quality-of-governance criteria to their investment policies and manager choices. Regulations inhibit corporate pension funds from incorporating such constraints; ERISA and Labor Department rules require them to manage the assets for the exclusive benefit of the retirees.

The term "responsible investing" (RI) has come into currency in recent years, propelled in part by the growing embrace of the United Nations Principles for Responsible Investment (UNPRI, to which our company became a signatory in 2014). For those of us who have devoted decades to investment management, the very term is a bit problematic: as one of our clients observed, if the new mode is investing responsibly, what is it that we'd been doing all these years? This short chapter will clarify the various approaches to RI and the practical implications and concerns we have learned from long experience with these approaches.

Sometimes also referred to as "sustainable investing," RI generally incorporates nontraditional, nonfinancial metrics into investment analysis. RI seeks to complement conventional financial analysis with a broader assessment of an underlying business and its long-term viability. From my perspective, the relevance of environmental, social, and governance considerations in valuing a business is self-evident. Even a casual survey of recent corporate scandals suggests that the ability to assess corporate culture and behavior in a broad sense can be critical in discriminating between future winning investments and losers.

Mission-Related Investing

While we may believe that the integration of responsible investing practices is beneficial for all investors, many institutions wish to further align their portfolios with their missions. In the current parlance this has come to be known as mission-related investing (MRI), which can be thought of as a subset of RI. Increasingly popular among U.S. foundations, endowments, and healthcare systems, MRI seeks to avoid incongruities between an institution's core values and its portfolio. Several distinct approaches to MRI have emerged.

Socially Responsible Investing (SRI)

The idea of excluding certain securities or categories of investments from portfolios for ethical reasons has existed probably as long as people have deployed their assets into capital markets. SRI prohibits investments in the securities of publicly traded companies whose products are antithetical to an investor's mission and values. SRI has been a common approach of investing for many decades, and we have implemented SRI criteria in specific client portfolios since 1989. Common negative screens include tobacco, weapons, and coal companies, but in practice SRI can be applied anywhere to any investment. SRI is the earliest and most straightforward approach to applying ethical guidelines to investing.

Environmental, Social, and Governance Investing

Environmental, social, and governance (ESG) investing favors the securities of firms with environmental, social, or governance attributes that resonate with specific investors. It therefore focuses not on excluding investments that are inconsistent with an institution's values, but rather on emphasizing investments that are mission-aligned. Specific examples include businesses that can contribute to solving the challenge of climate change and those that embrace workplace and board diversity.

Impact Investing

Impact investing is an approach focusing investments on areas of social and environmental concern, typically in a private equity structure and often in the early stages of a business's growth. Examples include venture capital investments in alternative energy companies. Impact investing typically seeks to earn a competitive investment return while also materially advancing other mission-related objectives—a "double" bottom line.

Does Responsible Investing Help or Hurt Investment Performance?

Certainly the inclusion of broader information in making investment decisions is likely to improve decision making. At the same time, as with all investment analysis, only superior skill will lead to outperformance. A flawed assessment of business sustainability can cause just as much damage as a flawed assessment of margins. When executed well, RI has the potential to enhance performance, and a burgeoning academic literature is beginning to shine a light on promising avenues of analysis. As an empirical issue, the realized performance of actual strategies in this space is still open to question.

In the special case of socially responsible investment strategies, the performance implications are less clear. In theory the exclusion of potential investments can only harm the portfolio, while in practice the particular exclusions may or may not be related to future returns. One subtlety of SRI approaches is that they sometimes aim to deprive undesirable businesses of funding sources, driving up their cost of capital and thereby impairing the businesses. Because the security issuer's cost of capital is the investor's return on capital, the success of this approach could directly lead to underperformance relative to other investors who do fund the targeted businesses.

In my experience, the mission of each institution is as unique as a fingerprint, requiring customized investment solutions. For both RI and MRI mandates, we have seen little convergence toward shared objectives, even among institutions that might appear to have significant commonality. For example, the definition of what constitutes "zero carbon footprint" can differ widely from client to client even though most of these investors hold similar environmental concerns.

Because of the need for customization, the advent of pooled solutions for RI and mission-related investment mandates awaits a broader consensus on terms and objectives than exists at the moment. When considering the implications for portfolio performance, the adoption of MRI objectives may preclude the use of desirable active managers who don't offer customized versions of their process. While some institutions have sufficient scale to obtain customized, separately managed accounts with many managers, the dominance of commingled vehicles in some market segments generally means that at least some active strategies must be ruled out. Some institutions have concluded that the loss of expected alpha from excluded active managers more than offsets the potential benefit of implementing an MRI strategy.

All these approaches and their definitions have evolved over time and continue to evolve in definition and application. We support the concept of eliminating mismatches between a client's ethical concerns and investment objectives. However, we also recognize that reconciling the two goals requires trade-offs, and we make the fiduciary implications of those trade-offs clear to our clients when proposing appropriate solutions.

11

The Uses
of Volatility

THE INVESTMENT WORLD today hears much nonsense about volatility. Many less experienced investors, some of whom may even sit on investment committees, have come to believe that the interim ups and downs of a security's price are of legitimate interest mainly to traders and hardly at all of interest to long-term investors. Their supporting text is Warren Buffett's 1997 declaration that "Charlie [Munger] and I would much rather earn a lumpy 15 percent over time than a smooth 12 percent." But the pertinent follow-up question is, Would you rather earn a smooth 12 percent or a lumpy 12 percent? The lumpier, bumpier ride is costly.

Here's why. As an example, a globally diversified $100 portfolio delivering an annual average real return of a more typical 5 percent, with an average annual volatility of 12 percent, will compound at 4.3 percent (not 5 percent) and lead to a total value of $154 after 10 years ($237 after 20 years). If that same portfolio, with the same annual return, experiences a volatility of 20 percent, it will reach only $137 after 10 years ($188 after 20 years)—almost 11 percent less wealth in 10 years and 21 percent less in 20 years, despite the same 5 percent real average yearly return.

Volatility can't be ignored, because it is a frictional cost that will undermine your ability to create wealth over time. Not understanding compound interest and how to temper yearly volatility can be your greatest source of loss of principal. Unstable principal is a particular problem for endowments and pension funds that have to make monthly, quarterly, or annual payments to beneficiaries.

Volatility is the price you have to pay to accumulate returns above inflation over time. Volatility is not your friend, unless you are an active trader who can successfully surf through the waves of volatility, buying low and selling high. Volatility reduces compound rates of return over time. Most portfolio managers should aim to build long-term portfolios that can withstand annual volatility in good stead. Figure 11.1 illustrates that, at any average annual rate of return, the higher the volatility, the lower the compounded return and the lower your terminal wealth.

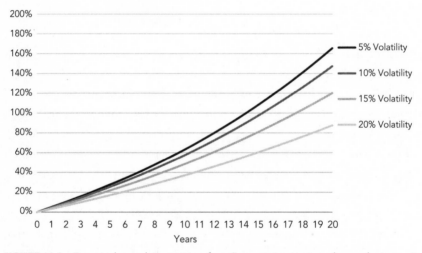

FIGURE 11.1   Expected cumulative returns from 5 percent average real annual returns at various volatilities.

There are shortcut formulas for calculating estimates of the impact of volatility on compound rates of return, using average return and standard deviations.[1] Figure 11.2 describes the nasty impact of volatility on wealth accumulation over time as well as the cumulative drag (ending-wealth shortfall) created by volatility over 10- and 20-year periods.

Arithmetic Mean Returns	Volatility				
	5%	10%	12%	15%	20%
	Compound Returns				
4%	3.88%	3.52%	3.31%	2.93%	2.13%
5%	4.88%	4.53%	4.32%	3.94%	3.15%
6%	5.88%	5.53%	5.33%	4.95%	4.16%
	Accumulation of $1 in 10 Years				
4%	$1.47	$1.42	$1.39	$1.34	$1.24
5%	$1.63	$1.57	$1.54	$1.48	$1.37
6%	$1.80	$1.74	$1.70	$1.64	$1.52
	Accumulation of $1 in 20 Years				
4%	$2.17	$2.02	$1.94	$1.80	$1.53
5%	$2.65	$2.47	$2.37	$2.20	$1.88
6%	$3.24	$3.02	$2.90	$2.69	$2.30

Standard Deviation	Cumulative Downside Return* Horizon (Years)				
	1	5	10	15	20
0	4.4%	24.1%	54.1%	91.2%	137.3%
−1	−7.4%	−5.1%	5.4%	20.1%	38.8%
−2	−17.9%	−27.4%	−27.9%	−24.5%	−18.9%
−3	−27.2%	−44.5%	−50.7%	−52.6%	−52.6%

*5% Mean Return/12% Volatility

FIGURE 11.2 The long-term impact of volatility on compound real returns and terminal wealth.

Over time, higher volatility erodes compound returns and therefore how much an invested dollar grows. The bottom table shows worst cases: how much growth is lost by money held for various periods—unmonitored and unchanged—at various levels of volatility.

Figure 11.3 adds visual insight to the impact of volatility on investment returns. It depicts the annual arithmetic returns you have to generate at various volatility levels to match a 5 percent compound geometric return.

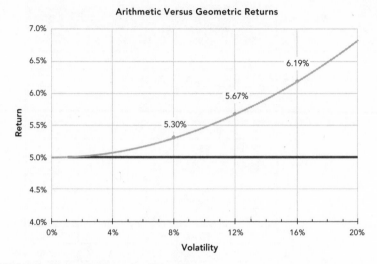

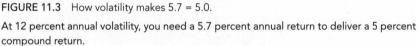

FIGURE 11.3   How volatility makes 5.7 = 5.0.

At 12 percent annual volatility, you need a 5.7 percent annual return to deliver a 5 percent compound return.

Alternatively, Figure 11.4 shows the performance drag of higher volatility. At 12 percent volatility, your 5 percent annual average return drops to a 4.3 percent compound return.

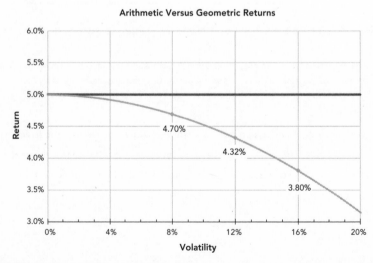

FIGURE 11.4   How volatility makes 5.0 = 4.3.

Finally, Figure 11.5 depicts worst-case scenarios. Over 20 years a typical institutional investor would expect wealth to more than double but stands a small chance of losing half the initial wealth if volatility swings by three standard deviations around the average 12 percent.

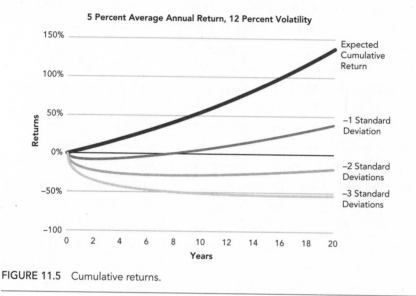

FIGURE 11.5   Cumulative returns.

Volatility as an Offensive and Defensive Tool

The portfolio manager's challenge is to bring down volatility without sacrificing long-term returns. But even better, use volatility to your advantage. After a market crash, many investors are so concerned with surviving volatility and protecting assets from unexpected losses that they miss the opportunities that appear then. No one likes a crash, and no one knows when one is coming; it could be this or any other year. A 20 to 30 percent 1-year loss occurs about every 10 to 20 years in the U.S. equity market and every 15 to 20 years in a balanced portfolio. And of course deeper drops are possible.

The most human and least profitable response is to panic and run for cover—building cash *after* the loss has occurred—or to increase allocation to the asset that suffers the least. The second most frequent response is to retreat into inaction and a ruminating state. There are reasons for both responses. At crisis time no one can give you assurances that things might not get worse, when you may have already lost a third or more of your wealth and can ill afford to lose any more. It's more probable that you'll regain the wealth and more if you buy at cheaper prices, but it's also possible you could lose another 20 or 30 percent before you recover the losses. Reinvesting into assets that have just produced significant losses appears as inviting as a game of Russian roulette. We know. We've been there a few times in our careers. But as Buffett has rightly said, "A simple rule dictates my buying: Be fearful when others are greedy, and be greedy when others are fearful."[2]

Managing portfolios to be able to pounce on the markets when prices collapse is a critical component of your liquidity management policy, though many endowment managers have underestimated it as a defensive tool. Seeking excessive illiquidity in pursuit of more stable and higher long-term returns is unwise. The venerated Yale model has yet to be proved successfully implemented by many less experienced endowments, which have stretched their tolerance to levels of illiquidity they couldn't handle well under extreme scenarios. It stretched even Yale's tolerance for illiquidity and peace of mind in 2008, but Yale's robust governance and warranted trust in its team's management skills held the day. Yale had arranged sources of funding to handle such extreme circumstances, including access to commercial paper financing initiated in the early nineties to fund working capital needs. This access made a huge difference by giving it unique flexibility to rebalance exposure to risky (and by then cheaper) assets. When others were selling illiquid investments, Yale was buying. Few other institutions have established access to short-term financing when there is little or no liquidity. Yale has since put in place mechanisms that allow it access to 50 percent liquidity if needed.

By contrast, other investment pools, including many defined benefit plans, have exaggerated levels of liquidity in their portfolios and could diversify more broadly into less liquid alternative assets with longer horizons and higher expected returns. Volatility is not always your enemy, but you need liquidity and discipline to turn it into an ally.

The Trade-Off Between Volatility and Illiquidity

The right trade-off between volatility and illiquidity stands on three pillars:

- The ability to identify superior providers of illiquid assets. Indexing is not an option.
- The ability to position your policy portfolio to take advantage of average expected returns and volatility of returns, with sufficient liquidity to allow rebalancing to policy under extreme market conditions.
- For portfolios with large allocations to illiquid assets, particularly private equities (35 percent or more), a better understanding of the factor risks embedded in the illiquid assets, many of which are ex ante (before the fact) blind pools with no obvious, measurable, well-diversified exposure to the broader equity markets. Much trust has to be placed in their managers' ability to respond to high stress with the right strategy.

Outsourced service providers including OCIOs (outsourced chief investment officers) such as Strategic, or the investing institution's internal staff, need to control total portfolio volatility and need sufficient liquidity to meet operational needs as well as to rebalance on a timely basis. For service providers, the appropriate level of liquidity may be roughly 50 percent of assets under current market conditions and assuming the appropriate ability to manage margin and futures. Given the recent explosion of OCIOs, among which only a handful have verifiable, audited track records for more than 10 years (since the last liquidity crash), it's unlikely many have the necessary expertise to handle high levels of illiquidity under stressful market circumstances.

Liquidity needs have to be reassessed continually in light of market developments, margin requirements, and investor circumstances. Portfolios with excellent internal management, strong, stable, disciplined governance, and a lot of client goodwill in their favor have more leeway. Their liquidity needs might be managed in extreme scenarios with about 30 to 40 percent of the total portfolio (but not much less), depending on spending and borrowing flexibility and the amount of puttable debt on the balance sheet. They could risk creating a panic among their debt holders, who might put back the debt to them at a time of restricted liquidity or turn off potential donors apprehensive about adding capital to a sinking ship. In practice, endowment debt holders didn't panic during the 2008 liquidity crisis, although some donors, whose philanthropic resources had also been hammered, curtailed their donations when universities and colleges needed them most. *It turns out that markets, private net worth, and donations may have a relatively high correlation.* The most critical factor—frequently overestimated because it can change unexpectedly—is the reservoir of goodwill and the sturdiness of governance structure that the institution's investors can count on in times of crisis (more on this in Part VI).

Yale's outstanding performance is a tribute to its competent staff, but just as importantly it's a tribute to a solid governance structure and the overseers' ability to withstand extreme scenarios and maintain discipline. Skilled staff and good governance structures feed off each other, a virtuous case of codependency. But we have seen other seemingly strong governance structures crumble under duress, with superb management destroyed by unexpected events and governance disrupters.

Risk diversifiers that reduce the volatility of the total portfolio and still give you an attractive equitylike return are hard to find. Savvy investors seeking to stabilize the annual budgetary impact of volatile endowment returns have focused on the qualities of illiquid alternative assets. Trading off annual volatility for illiquidity can seem unambiguously attractive for a long-term investor with limited liquidity needs. You give up some liquidity, for which you don't have much need, and reduce your total portfolio's annual volatility. A perfect trade-off, up to a point. Holding an asset to maturity and avoiding the quarterly mark-to-market pricing is a sure way to reduce volatility and increase long-term compound returns, *but* you have to make sure the asset will deliver the expected compound return in the end, and that you aren't giving up so much liquidity that you can't meet operational and portfolio rebalancing needs under extreme scenarios.

This trade-off did not elicit much discussion among endowment managers before 2007. Endowments that had diversified into illiquid or less liquid assets were doing much better than those focusing on traditional stock and bond liquid assets. Investment pools holding mostly stocks and bonds, however, were carrying a much larger proportion of equity market volatility than just that implied by their allocation to equities. A 60-40 equity–fixed income portfolio in fact carried *90 percent* of equity market volatility despite a 60 percent allocation to equities, simply because equity market risk was so much higher than fixed income risks. Over their long history, equities have exhibited an annual standard deviation of about 17 percent, compared with 6 to 8 percent for bonds.

Illiquid assets tend to and should yield higher rates of returns to compensate for being illiquid, and their short-term volatility is muffled because they are not marked to market until they are actually sold, ideally at close to peak prices. The theoretical benefits of diversifying public equity market risks by including hedge funds, private equities, and long-duration fixed income are significant. A 60-40 plain vanilla U.S. equity–U.S. fixed income policy leaves equity contributing 90 percent of the total portfolio risk. The same 60-40 mix with bond duration at 20 years reduces the equity contribution to risk to about 75 percent while leaving the contribution to return relatively unchanged. Portfolios that include 50 percent in hedge funds reduce the equity contribution to risk substantially; they leave expected returns at the same or higher levels, assuming the hedge fund portfolio is well diversified and has a low correlation to equities.

The so-called endowment model, which allocates more assets to alternative investments, began to be adopted by most university and college endowment managers in the nineties and became their norm by 2017 when alternatives comprised 53 to 57 percent of their assets. (See Figure 9.1 in Chapter 9.) Illiquid assets provide an illiquidity premium, justified not only by their longer holding period, but also by private firms' opportunity to better manage the underlying companies. Private companies can manage operations with longer investment horizons, without the constraints of managing for quarterly earnings that meet or exceed analysts' expectations. Their managers can more constructively focus on the long run. Furthermore, given their relatively smaller size, they can make meaningful investment and operating decisions that foster innovation and sustainable growth. And in the absence of daily marking to market, the influence of leverage on volatility is hidden.

Liquidity was perceived to be overrated anyway, particularly in equities. Once their prices had collapsed, there was no benefit to selling them. Government bonds were liquid, but their historical average after-inflation returns of 2 to 3 percent could not compete with 7 to 10 percent from less liquid assets. If there was no question that illiquid assets were better than liquid assets and the need for liquidity was overstated, why hold less than 70 or 80 percent of illiquid assets? Why hold more liquidity than needed to meet your operational cash needs? So went the talk.

For good reasons, liquidity should not be less than 50 percent of total assets, and in many cases it should be even higher. We sounded a prescient word of caution in early 2007 at one of our annual conferences, in Washington, D.C., by pointing out that many investors wouldn't be able to rebalance their portfolios into collapsed security prices with such extreme levels of illiquidity. This concern was so far removed from attendees' minds that they couldn't even understand the question posed to them in an interactive survey: "How much liquidity do you think you need in your portfolio if equities fall by 50 percent and you would like to rebalance your portfolio?" After we tried, we received the following answers:

Less than 5 percent	11%
Between 6 and 10 percent	5%
Between 11 and 20 percent	37%
Between 21 and 50 percent	32%
Over 50 percent	11%
Don't know	5%

A second, related issue was raised at that session and another in San Francisco: "I think those institutional investors who have more than 50 percent of their assets in illiquid instruments could have a problem rebalancing portfolios in extreme cases." The responses:

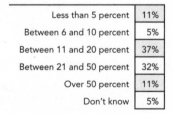

	D.C.	San Francisco	Combined
Strongly Agree	41%	56%	49%
Agree	41%	17%	29%
Neutral	6%	11%	9%
Disagree	6%	17%	11%
Strongly Disagree	6%	0%	3%

A third statement focused on accounting for liquidity risk: "I believe the most important risk associated with leverage and liquidity is that:"

	D.C.	San Francisco	Combined
Investors underutilize the leverage options available to them	22%	24%	23%
Investors overutilize the leverage options available to them	4%	0%	2%
Investors under-account for their potential liquidity requirements (as in a major market disruption)	66%	71%	68%
Investors have not put in place prime brokerage accounts	4%	0%	2%
Other	4%	5%	5%

Many endowments are still ignoring the risks. With up to 57 percent in illiquid assets in 2015, few appear to have open margin accounts or experience in managing financial futures. Portfolios should be kept at about 50 percent broadly diversified liquid assets, because bad events can exceed three standard deviations and one wouldn't want clients to go through the stresses that so many endowments faced for a few years. Few clients' governance structures and reservoirs of goodwill match the required ability to tough out extreme adversity.

Some large, sophisticated endowments perhaps could handle extreme illiquidity, because they could use bond holdings equal to 5 to 8 percent of their portfolios as margin against which to buy close to 100 percent of the total portfolio in equity or bond futures. With futures, they could easily rebalance the portfolio or meet spending needs without liquidating assets at bargain prices. This exercise would amount to leveraging the 5 to 8 percent liquid component by as much as 20 times, depending on the targeted rebalancing and spending needs. The obstacle is that the internal teams of most endowments and foundations might not have the leveraging arrangements, nor likely the support of their boards or the backbone to do that in a crisis. Many of the endowments that reduce bond holdings to such levels may also have issued puttable debt, with its possible unpleasant repercussions.

Large, sophisticated university endowments with great governance structures and confidence in their internal investment management have valuable options in a liquidity crisis. They can delay disbursements, dig into their endowments to meet operational needs—albeit at the worst possible time—or find multiple ways to borrow against hard assets. Other institutions' governance and decision-making process can sink into a sort of bankruptcy-of-process mode, abandoning long-term policy at the worst time. A shift of policy after big losses prevents the institutions from recouping the losses when markets revert to mean.

Risky Rebalancing with Nonmarketables

In the liquidity crisis of 2008, some endowments with large allocations to illiquid assets simply moved the measuring stick: rather than trying to rebalance to policy into cheaper assets, they changed the policy to specify more illiquid assets so it would match what was left of their holdings. That risky strategy worked because private equity and venture capital recovered more than nicely over the next several years. A very loose monetary policy, low to negative interest rates, and technological breakthroughs made the environment for private investments quite hospitable. That may not always be so. What's more, the allocations to nonmarketables in 2008 were much lower than today's 50 percent or so.

In some environments, an already high allocation to nonmarketable assets cannot be increased further without creating extreme operational stress on institutions. Maneuvering with 60 to 80 percent of illiquid assets at a moment of increasing interest rates and collapsing venture capital and private equity multiples would be a high-wire act few could handle regardless of how robust their governance structure and how skilled their staff. When a large portion of your assets are illiquid, the makeup and style attributes of your nonmarketables need to be considered, as their ability to react to changing market conditions will be critical to portfolio health.

Investments in private equity and venture capital, and to a lesser extent real estate, are made through partnerships that take a few years to call in their capital. Their 2-plus percent fees are paid on undisbursed commitments—

amounts the investors have promised but not yet paid in—which are called in when attractive assets are ready to be purchased. Because it usually takes three to five years to disburse committed amounts, and some partnerships begin distributing gains before the disbursement period is complete, investors may properly commit much larger amounts than are specified in their policy portfolios. An endowment or foundation that wants to maintain, say, a 20 percent allocation to private equities might have to commit 25 to 30 percent of total assets to maintain the 20 percent allocation over time, depending on total asset returns and private equity distributions. Defined benefit plans have much lower exposure to private equities, so the need to overcommit is also much lower unless they intend to build up their exposure. DB plans exhibit allocations to private equities of 3 to 5 percent. They may overshoot commitments by 1 or 2 percent or commit at the policy level and let the disbursements lag without a significant impact on their risk or liquidity profile.

These undisbursed commitments are functionally akin to leverage. In a way, endowments and foundations are "borrowing" shelf space in the partnership and paying an interest rate for the borrowed shelf space equal to the fee on the undisbursed commitments. A 2 percent fee on undisbursed commitments can make the effective flat-fee component of private equity partnerships rise to 8 percent on disbursed amounts over a few years, assuming a 10 percent, 20 percent, 30 percent, and 40 percent four-year call schedule on commitments. Other than the impact on fees, these overcommitments are generally not a problem—*except* when the market crashes and you are short of liquidity to rebalance, to fund operational needs, or to meet sudden calls on committed assets. In 2008, overcommitments to private equities, venture capital, and in some cases hedge funds in which shelf space was limited and desirable led to uncomfortable situations. Quietly, universities and foundations dissuaded their private equity general partners from making calls. Managers acquiesced because they themselves were in shock, assets were hard to price or trade with no market for them, and they understood how scandalous and counterproductive it would have been to penalize loyal clients with forfeiture of assets under the circumstances. Few if any mean words were likely exchanged in these moments of codependency.

Managing Government Bonds, ETFs, and Futures In-House to Enhance Liquidity

Soon after we entered the asset management business in the mid-seventies, it became clear that to compete effectively in complex global capital markets, it made sense to outsource the management of assets to specialized external active managers. The only rationale to manage assets in-house would have been to build a bureaucracy and promote our careers inside the World Bank by eliminating external management fees at the expense of increased returns and management flexibility, a penny-wise and pound-foolish strategy. We focused instead on developing the competitive advantage awarded to investors who can move easily into new assets and investment styles and pick among the best and brightest around the world, and we worked at building a small, competent, cohesive team of modelers and market strategists for different types of assets. We wanted to be able to manage assets not just efficiently but also effectively. We wanted to add value net of all fees. We were less interested in managing a large number of people, who would be hard to find and retain, and who would be next to impossible to fit or fire in response to changing investment needs. Flexibility in investment choices and hiring and firing decisions is paramount when competing in global markets.

When many of our more successful peers were bringing assets in-house to focus on picking stocks and bonds, reducing management costs, and furthering their corporate careers, we were hiring small external managers and incubating some new ones with competitive advantages and fees appropriate to their added value. We nurtured over 20 new strategies and emerging managers, many of whom, like Ray Dalio's group at Bridgewater, have risen to outstanding success. We weren't fully aware of it at the time, but in a way, as innovators in our field, we were creating a new business model, one that has been labeled "investment outsourcing," or more commonly, if not elegantly, "OCIO." Manufacturing firms such as Dell that adopted an outsourcing production approach were called platform companies. A platform company is hidden among most of the tech service providers that are improving our distribution networks. Uber and Airbnb are examples.

Although most client assets have been managed by external specialist managers, government bond portfolios were managed in-house for many years to control total portfolio duration and liquidity risks. Other investments managed in-house included exchange-traded funds (ETFs), swaps, and futures, amounting to 10 to 20 percent of total portfolio assets. This was done at no extra charge to clients, to make sure it was possible to rebalance portfolios and manage portfolio risks dynamically and cost-efficiently.

12

Transporting
Alphas (or Betas)

INVESTMENT RETURNS HAVE two sources. One, the return that comes from the premium that investors are willing to pay for each unit of undiversifiable market risk multiplied by the riskiness (beta) of the specific asset. Two, the value that an active manager can get from buying low and selling high and the ability to reduce the *management risks* taken through portfolio construction. The evolution of portfolio theory, analytical tools, and the great variety of investment vehicles allows an investor to separate market returns (betas) from active-management returns (alphas).

Separating Alphas and Betas

Today it's possible to separate and build (very cheaply) purely beta-based globally balanced portfolios and (more expensively) alpha-based portfolios and to combine them to suit the level of market and active risks the investor is prepared to take. The separation between market (beta) and active (alpha) risk is important, not only to properly allocate risk in the portfolio construc-

tion process, but to allocate management costs efficiently and proportionately to the expected value added.

Market risk can be purchased at very low cost by buying index futures,
while active alpha can cost up to or more than 2 percent plus 20 percent of
profits. You should place great effort in making sure you are not paying high
management fees for exposure to market returns you can buy at trivial fees.

To construct portfolios that have a targeted exposure to high-fee alpha,
you can recombine pure alpha portfolios with pure beta (low fee) exposures.
This process has been called "portable alpha." To explain: portable alpha is
the process by which you superimpose a "pure alpha" portfolio over a "pure
beta" exposure (equity or fixed income) to arrive at a policy portfolio that
meets the targeted level of market and active risks as efficiently as possible
from a cost and execution perspective.

Futures in stocks and bonds are well suited to implement portable alpha
strategies. The internally managed pool of assets allows tight controls over the
duration exposure (interest rate sensitivity) of portfolios, as well as dynamic
and cost-effective control of liquidity and asset-class risks.

In the initial approaches to combining betas and alphas explicitly and
efficiently, in the early nineties, we and others asked the alpha (hedge fund)
manager to buy a market future (equity or bond) and deliver the firm's alpha
plus a market return in equities, fixed income, commodities, or other classes.
Not many hedge fund managers were willing to do this for clients then or
now. With the emergence of different, uncorrelated hedge fund strategies,
we were able to wrap a diversified group of uncorrelated hedge funds with
an index-future exposure (equity or fixed income) to produce a combined
market plus alpha return in excess of the long-only asset-class manager's and
control the liquidity underlying the beta exposure. Figure 12.1 illustrates the
management structure within which one can manage and transport alpha
and beta exposures.

We chose the highlighted structure, which allowed us to best control alpha
and beta exposures and access liquidity. With appropriate staff support and
futures management capability, we would select a diversified group of hedge
funds capable of delivering positive alpha and overlay them with beta-market
exposures that met our policy and risk management objectives. This process

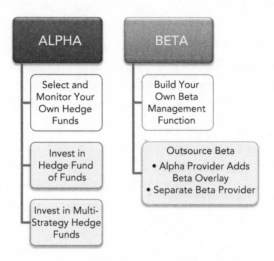

FIGURE 12.1   Major options for structuring a portable alpha program.

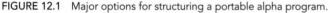

allowed us to deliver a targeted combination of beta and active-manager risk to complement other active equity and fixed income managers.

The amount of portable alpha in a total policy portfolio has been as low as zero and as high as 20 percent. Portable alpha limits are bound by the liquidity needs, attractive long-only management strategies, hedge fund opportunities, and tolerance for active and passive management volatility. A 10 to 20 percent exposure to portable alpha strategies, properly executed, can add significant risk-adjusted value to a total portfolio relative to the exclusive use of long-only alternatives.

Factor-Driven Policy Portfolios

The returns achieved by any asset depend not just on which opportunities and risks the asset captures as part of its asset class, but also on what the macroeconomic factors driving those returns are—inflation, recession, growth, contraction, leverage, liquidity, volatility. Academic research offers a factor-based policy construction process that attempts to disentangle such factors to arrive at unique drivers of returns. For example, equities might be better than bonds in hedging inflation risks, but not as good as real estate or commodities. Factor analysis sheds light on the expected returns of asset classes under different macroeconomic scenarios, but pure factor exposures are difficult to implement when portfolio managers are still focused on markets and asset classes rather than on individual factor opportunities. Asset-class allocations should come from well-measured factor bets, but pure factor bets are not yet a real alternative to asset classes in building policy portfolios.

For investors emphasizing factor-based policies, some managers—Bridgewater, AQR, and others—do offer portfolios based on balanced factor bets. Sometimes they work, sometimes they don't, but they can show a relatively low correlation with some policy portfolios and can serve to lower total portfolio risks while maintaining long-term return targets. However, factor managers, as well as all other factor users, have to translate factor exposures into investable instruments like stocks, bonds, and commodities.

PART III

Structuring the Asset Class

$$\alpha$$

A spirit of innovation is generally the result of a selfish temper
and confined views. People will not look forward to posterity,
who never look backward to their ancestors.

—EDMUND BURKE, *REFLECTIONS ON
THE REVOLUTION IN FRANCE*, 1790

13

New Maps of Value

CONSIDER YOURSELF LUCKY if you're an innovator and Edmund Burke is not one of your investment committee members. A few years ago we were attending an investment committee meeting for a large foundation client. The room was warm and plates were piled neatly around the buffet consoles. Food was waiting, papers spread out on the table. Attendees, about eight of them, had been hard at work for a few hours. Noon was approaching. Not an ideal time to dive into a complicated portfolio-restructuring proposal.

The stakes were high. For starters, we planned to change their more traditional passive-active management structure by initially investing 10 percent of their U.S. equity portfolio in equity futures layered over a well-diversified group of hedge funds. The hedge fund combination on its own was likely to deliver 6 to 8 percent annual real returns with no more than 6 to 7 percent volatility (hedge funds were doing better then than now!). Layered over index futures, we expected this change would add about 60 basis points of annual returns to the foundation's total portfolio with no significant increase in risk, a welcome improvement over keeping their traditional active managers. We expected to increase this allocation as their confidence in the proposed structure increased.

We believed our proposal would bring them closer to achieving their long-term investment objectives. If it were turned down because of its perceived complexity, we would have to find more traditional and less reliable ways to improve their returns. The stakes were really high. We very much wanted the proposal to succeed.

We thought the proposed construct would offer higher and more stable risk-adjusted returns than a good set of active equity managers. Although hedge funds command higher fees, the total cost to the foundation per unit of expected value added would be the same or less. Active managers collect fees for the full set of assets, the majority of which are actually tracking an index; seldom more than 10 percent of their total assets is really actively managed. Although hedge fund fees appear higher, they may in fact be lower relative to the broader scope of assets actively managed and the expected value added—assuming both kinds of managers meet return and risk expectations.

A couple of committee members were apprehensive. "That would be leveraging 10 percent of the portfolio," one said. "We do not like to add leverage."

"Yes, adding futures is a form of leverage," one of us answered, "but we wouldn't increase the volatility of the portfolio beyond the volatility of your active equity manager. We'd control the volatility of the alpha generated by the hedge funds and the volatility of the futures overlay with the same tools your active equity managers use to control their own volatility."

The next question followed without any sign that we were making headway. "Why don't we just ask one of our existing hedge fund managers to lay the equity futures over their holdings?" asked another committee member.

"Would you only use low-risk hedge funds to control the risks?" asked a third.

We answered, "It would be better, more transparent, and less risky as a line item in the portfolio to overlay the future over a diversified portfolio of hedge funds, rather than just one hedge fund. If you ask one of your current managers to layer futures, that fund's return would be more volatile than if you layered the future over a diversified group of funds. That would add line-item risk, which can spook you. Also, if we layered the future over a well-diversified set of hedge funds, we'd have better control over the size of the equity market exposure. The effect on the total portfolio would be the same, but the risks would be better displayed on your performance reports and you'd get more direct control over the size of the futures." On the issue of just picking low-risk hedge funds, we explained that it would be better to diversify the hedge funds broadly to achieve the highest alpha we could, not just including relatively low-risk, low-return funds.

The discussion was developing hairy twists and turns. It was undoubtedly leaving some of the committee members bored and disengaged—a deadly trap when you need lively counterbalancing points of view to reach a difficult consensus. Plowing ahead, we stuck patiently with the line of inquiry. Additional benefits included better management of the exposures to any of the hedge fund managers and more liquidity available for rebalancing purposes at times of stress. Detours along the windy road of the arguments! More efficient portfolio constructs than they were used to required a deeper understanding of the sources and stability of returns under different asset-class structures. Oh! If we could only stop for lunch . . .

You may guess that at long last we did get approval for the proposal. And it did generate 60-plus basis points of additional portfolio returns over their planning horizon. But the arguments about complex versus less complex structures will keep cropping up from time to time, particularly when there is a new committee member.

The outcome was worth the struggle that's familiar when innovations in portfolio construction appear to create more complex portfolios, such as through the use of futures. Why the struggle? The risks perceived in quantum leaps may be too great to seem profitable. A perfectly Burkean argument: small mistakes are easier to correct than big ones. We need sequential steps to climb a ladder. We knew that. Adding an overlay of futures over hedge funds in only 10 percent of the U.S. equity portfolio was a marginal improvement to the foundation's dependence on traditional long-only active managers. We were creating a ladder.

As Burke would attest, revolutions are costly and their outcomes highly uncertain. Humans fear revolutionary changes unless they are desperate. As Burke's view of historical progress explains, the most useful and sustainable innovations evolve over time and are not the products of abrupt change. Investment committees operate as a social network. As imaginative and creative as an idea may be, it needs to be anchored on existing thought structures and comfortable frameworks. *Incremental innovation is easier to implement than disruptive innovation within existing governance structures—except when people (and committees) get really frustrated.* Then they are ready to start a revolution, and legacy ideas get guillotined!

Managing Each Asset Class

The arguments in that committee meeting, nerve-racking as they were, quite properly zeroed in not just on the broad concept of futures overlaid on hedge funds, but also on the components of each. The management structure and allocation for each asset class can be designed in almost infinite shapes. You can hire generalist managers, indexed or active, or you can identify pockets of the asset class that deserve specialized expertise because they are more complex and inefficient, because they respond to different macroeconomic events and opportunities, and because they offer the potential for higher value added.

Hedge funds are an almost unique array of idiosyncratic investment approaches grouped under the same heading. Investors group them because it's hard to handle an unlimited collection of haywire actors without assembling them as cast members in a risk-diversifying strategy play (even though some of them may not be good risk diversifiers and should be avoided, and all, like long-only active managers, can suffer periods of producing negative alpha). Hedge funds can be quite different from one another, thus truly offering diversification, but each fund tends to have stable behavioral patterns. This is a quality they share with managers of other asset classes, and it makes analysis of their unusual strategies more feasible and their results more predictable.

Using hedge funds complemented with futures overlays is an improvement you can bring to structuring an asset class, but there are many others. In managing each asset class, there are several decisions to make:

- Whether to use *passive- or active*-management strategies and how much to allocate to each style. In other words, how much will you deviate from the market benchmark weights, how often, and why?

- How you plan to manage within asset-class allocations. We refer to these as *structuring* decisions.
- Whether to tilt the asset-class management structure to take advantage of diversified opportunities. We call these *asset-class tactical tilts.*

Active-management styles vary according to asset class. Figure 13.1 offers a schematic view of each asset class's characteristics, differentiated by market segment, management style, and strategy.

Market Segment	Management Style	Approach
U.S. Equities		
Large Cap	Passive	Top Down
Mid Cap	Value: Price Sensitive	Bottom Up
Small Cap	Growth/Momentum	Quantitative-Risk Controlled
	Quality: High and Stable Returns and Low Leverage	Concentrated
	Growth at Reasonable Price (GARP)	
	Rotational/Opportunistic	
Non-U.S. Equities		
Developed	Passive, Value	Top Down
Emerging, Frontier Markets	Growth/Momentum/GARP	Bottom Up
Regional/Local	Rotational	Quantitative
Fixed Income		
U.S. Governments, Corporate	Passive	Top Down
High Yield, Bank Loans	Active Duration	Bottom Up (Security Selection)
U.S. Mortgage, Asset Backed	Active Credit	
Non-U.S., Emerging	Arbitrage	
Hedge Funds		
Equities	Market Neutral	Quantitative/Risk Controlled
Bonds	Directional, Macro	Security Selection

FIGURE 13.1   Structuring asset classes: a simplified map of choices.

(continued on next page)

Market Segment	Management Style	Approach
Hedge Funds (*continued*)		
International	Arbitrage	Value
Commodities	Diversified, Distressed	Momentum
Futures	CTA	Quant Trading
Private Equity/Venture Capital		
Public to Private	Operational Leverage	Industry Specialized
Earlier Stage, Pre-IPO	Financial Leverage	Diversified
Later Stage	Operational Engagement	
New Economy, Old Economy		
U.S., International		
Real Estate		
Office, Commercial, Hotel	Income Producing	Low Leverage
Residential, Specialty	Active Property Redevelopmental	High Leverage
Non-U.S.	Active, Operational Involvement	Development Risk
Commodities		
Oil and Gas	Momentum	Operations
Minerals and Other	Value	Asset Managers

FIGURE 13.1 · Structuring asset classes: a simplified map of choices (*continued*).

Equities Styles

Equity managers can be price sensitive, seeking investments that trade below fair value based on balance-sheet or discounted cash flow estimates (price to book or to earnings) or momentum (increasing revenue, earnings, or price). They may focus on small versus large capitalization or on different regions of the world. Most price-sensitive styles work over time in the hands of experienced, disciplined managers. Momentum styles work until they do not: when momentum shifts, losses can be larger than prior gains. Over time, therefore, some managers use a combination of value and momentum. When the two contradict each other, managers stay close to benchmark— match the index. If value and momentum agree, managers take an active bet. Managers can also use quantitative methods, the specialty of analysts known as quants, or fundamental analytics, controlling risks by controlling the probability of loss. Both types have a role in a diversified portfolio, but quantitative approaches should generally be favored for liquid, efficient markets. Fundamental, nonquantitative security selection works better in the more inefficient segments, where bid-ask, buy-sell spreads are larger.

Fixed Income Styles

In the fixed income sectors, styles generally combine duration (the price sensitivity of bonds to changes in interest rates) with sector bets. Duration bets tend to have low "information ratios"—the value added of the bets is small relative to the volatility of the value added. Duration bets are binary—up or down—and not diversified across many factors. Unlike red or black at the roulette table, for which you can try many times, with duration you only get a couple of useful bets a year, with relatively low payouts. In addition to duration bets, you can judge disparities in credit risk, which allows more diversified bets, or look for yield curve disparities between governments and high-grade corporate bonds. Opportunities can be found in asset-backed mortgages and many more types of fixed income securities in the structured credit sector, consisting of pools of securities divided into tranches segmented by credit risk. In assessing the attractiveness of different fixed income strategies, it's important to understand how a strategy responds when people react to changes in interest rates—for example, mortgage prepayments rise when interest rates go down—and in credit risks—defaults increase when rates rise, when the economy or specific industries contract, and when corporate leverage is high.

Alternatives Styles

In the alternative asset classes, you can find many more and more complex differences. Many styles will work *unless* you adopt them after a long successful run and the style is overcrowded and overpriced. That's an often-repeated mistake even among experienced investors: they cave into market trends or client demands. Diversifying expected alpha among styles and managers is a way to increase total alpha over time.

Criteria for Diversifying: Indexes, ETFs, and Smart Betas

Investment theory prescribes broadly diversified asset-class structures because diversification reduces asset-class and total portfolio volatility. Modern portfolio theory rightly prescribes holding the broad market portfolio to diversify risks efficiently. The most efficient way to hold a broadly diversified market exposure is through a passively managed fund. Passive management can be achieved cheaply though indexed vehicles such as ETFs and, for larger portfolios, commingled or separate accounts or futures. But watch for management fees and other costs, and for performance drift from market indexes at times of stress. The primary advantage of a separate account for an indexed portfolio is that it may allow you to use your own portfolio (instead of the ETF) as margin if you need liquidity for rebalancing or other purposes. The liquidity of commingled accounts is not controlled by the asset owner but by the manager. A large sponsor may be able to put in place separate margin agreements with a broker-dealer to access margin debt from commingled accounts, but they require time-consuming administrative contracts that may not be available to or prudent for smaller institutions. Many but not all commingled vehicles offer daily liquidity and extremely low costs. At present, the costs of investing in indexed vehicles, including custody and administrative expenses, can be less than 2 basis points per year on assets for the most liquid U.S. equity and high-quality fixed income markets.

At any time we may have held 10 to 20 percent of total liquid assets in ETFs, swaps, and futures for asset mix and risk control purposes. The global market in ETFs has exploded, going from $500 billion in assets in 2008 to $4 trillion in assets in early 2017.[1] The total costs of the more liquid ETFs are extremely low and falling. Less liquid ones are more expensive and may trail their benchmarks. Futures are a cheap means of holding liquid equities and fixed income, but futures require more complex administrative arrangements, including opening margin accounts with broker-dealers. They are useful in managing day-by-day rebalancing and policy portfolio control needs without upsetting your active manager lineup. But managing futures requires experience, appropriate staffing, the analytical tools to measure and control asset allocation and manager risk, and registration as a commodity pool operator, with its regulatory and reporting requirements.

Despite investment theory, until 2006, when we tilted portfolios toward undervalued, large-capitalization, high-quality growth stocks, we often preferred to weight equity assets more equally within an asset class rather than by their market capitalization.

Doing so amplified the benefits of diversification and, even more important, forced the value-added effect of rebalancing portfolios to the fixed weights. In the past decade, new quasi-market indexes have been offered under the label of "smart beta" portfolios, designed to take better advantage than the pure market portfolio of many fundamental value and size factors. The smart beta approaches are backed by a plethora of statistical research. Most worthy of note is an article by Robert Arnott, Jason Hsu, and others showing that the most formidable explanatory variable behind all smart beta approaches is that they force periodic rebalancing of the portfolio.[2] The rebalancing effect appears so powerful that even portfolios constructed from the *worst*-ranked stocks by many factors outperform capitalization-weighted indexes *because those poorly selected portfolios are rebalanced regularly*. They sell high and buy low, adding value more frequently than would have been expected from the poor fundamental quality of the holdings. In contrast, market-weighted indexes are rebalanced less frequently.* As we saw in Figure I.3 in the Introduction, simple rebalancing to equal weights can add 180 basis points to the return of a market-weighted U.S. equity index.

The weight of any stock in the S&P 500 index goes up and down with the price of the stock. Market-weighted indexes "trend" with prices. In trending markets, when prices keep rising, it becomes harder to beat a capitalization-weighted index. The index will instantaneously move with the rising price of the asset (no trading required), while fixed-weight methods will waste time and money rebalancing. In contrast, during trendless or volatile markets, fixed-weight methods will outperform capitalization-price-weighted methods. In falling markets, indexes will generally trail active managers because the active manager will hold some cash for trading purposes, and cash will hold its value while risky securities are losing theirs.

---

* An index committee meets once a year or more often to add or subtract holdings in the portfolios or change country weights in response to an analysis of appropriateness. Planned changes to the index are announced before they are implemented to allow index users to adjust their portfolios according to their needs. Surprises are unwelcome.

Standard practice today among some institutional investors using multiple external managers is to assign a fixed weight to each manager's style within an asset class and rebalance among the managers quarterly or yearly or when there are cash flows in or out of the portfolios. Let's call these "style buckets." Depending on the size of the assets, you may want to use more than one manager style for each of the style buckets, to diversify manager risk.

It's wise to concentrate active-manager risk budgets in sectors that are less efficient. Generally speaking, one can manage large-capitalization stocks and government bonds passively while actively managing small-capitalization stocks, emerging and frontier markets, high-yield bonds, hedge funds, real estate, private equities, and venture capital. Importantly, though, if we found evidence of mispriced securities falling through cracks in the style buckets, we wouldn't shy away from opportunistic managers who do not stick to a particular style.

In short, in structuring portfolios one may not necessarily use fixed or market weights; instead the weights may respond to perceived pricing inefficiencies that exceed one standard deviation from historical fair value. Active or passive management can be used depending on expected value added. Part V describes other methods for allocating risks between passive- and active-management styles and by asset class, paying close attention to expected value added by asset class and management style, volatilities, and the correlation between asset classes and manager styles.

The Art of the Tilt

All asset classes offer opportunities to tilt the policy's allocation to an asset class in the direction of securities that appear to be offering a higher return per unit of risk. *Tactical tilts* respond to value-added opportunities over a 12- to 36-month period. *Structural tilts* respond to pricing inefficiencies that may last longer than your policy portfolio review horizon (say, more than 36 months). Structural tilts may be incorporated into the weights of the policy portfolio. Most of the time these apparent deviations from fair value are relatively small, say within one standard deviation from the historical average ratio of price to fair value. Price disparities that fall within one standard deviation of historic averages may be exploitable by external active trader-managers, and you trust they will be exploiting them.

For institutional investors seeking to add value over and above the underlying managers' security selection and trading skills by emphasizing some
styles over others, additional style tilts are warranted, in my experience, only
when price disparities are exceeding 1.5 standard deviations from historic
means. To identify those tactical tilt opportunities, track the valuations
regularly. Like a bird searching for its prey, we have tracked all investment
styles, more than 50 of them, around world capital markets. Investors should
review their value dispersions from historic averages at least quarterly, searching for 10 or more opportunities for tilts, 2 to 3 in each asset class. The tilts
should be small (10 to 20 basis points of total portfolio risk) because these
opportunities appear infrequently and can take as long as three years to pay
off. Therefore you have to make sure they are well diversified across asset
classes and investment styles to avoid timing and random risks.

Examples of these portfolio tilts within and across asset classes have
appeared and may continue to appear over time between the styles and market segments shown in Figure 13.2. New styles and market segments are
likely to offer additional opportunities in the future.

U.S. Equities	Hedge Funds
Small vs. Large	Market Neutral vs. Directional
Value vs. Growth	Diversified vs. Specialized
Non-U.S. Equities	**Real Estate**
Japan vs. Developed Ex-Japan	REITS vs. Closed-End Funds
Emerging vs. Developed	REITS vs. Open-End Funds
Small Emerging vs. Emerging	Closed-End vs. Open-End Funds
Latin America vs. Asian Emerging	Regional vs. Property Types
Frontier vs. Emerging	
U.S. Fixed Income	**Private Equity and Venture Capital**
U.S. vs. Non-U.S. Bonds	Later Stage vs. Earlier Stage
High Yield vs. Government	Private Equity vs. Venture Capital
High Yield vs. Corporates	Diversified vs. Focused Styles
High Yield vs. Stocks	U.S. vs. Non-U.S.
Mortgages/Asset Backed vs. High Grade	

FIGURE 13.2 Sample opportunities for tactical tilts.

The subtle art of "texturing" a portfolio through a series of specialized strategies and subtle interventions—when necessary and for relatively short periods, generally 18 months or less—is a tool to manage investment risks. It may successfully replace the blunt, expensive instrument of terminating strategies and managers. It's a risk management art akin to an expert gardener's touch in pruning and feeding a tree. The ability to prune managers' exposures without reducing their accountability can increase your ability to manage complex portfolios with more precision, and it allows you to cast a wide net along a diversified set of active bets. At any time a global, multi-manager portfolio may have 15 or 20 small, well-diversified "top-down" bets, from each of which you may expect 20 to 30 basis points of value added or 10 to 20 basis points of risk reduction to the total portfolio. Such broad diversification in tactical bets, *over and above all of the active managers' active positions*, makes the potential for value added over time less susceptible to unexpected market turns.

In support of this philosophy of more rather than fewer value-added bets, Richard C. Grinold devised a most insightful formula[3] confirming that the certainty of value-added active bets will increase with the skill developed in each bet *and* the number and diversifiable nature of the bets you have in your portfolios. That's why individual asset-class bets (overweighting one asset class over another) have a relatively low payoff in any short period, while 15 or 20 value-added bets have a much larger expected payout. That these bets are multiple and small sometimes seems counterintuitive to certain clients, who would like to see more conviction and more heroic bets—that work out, of course! Years of experience have taught us that Grinold's formula is a strong deterrent to high-noon confrontations with the market that may take years and a lot of patience to pay off.

We did engage in high-conviction types of "career bets"[4] in the past—shunning Japan exposure in the late eighties and high tech in the late nineties—and suffered the consequences of loss of clients and increased active-manager risk, although we more than earned back significant returns by sticking to our discipline. Since 1999, we have learned to be much more nuanced in our risk taking and more aggressive in finding more uncorrelated opportunities, and clients greatly benefited from less volatile absolute and relative returns—a more comfortable and profitable boat ride ending in higher compound value added and terminal wealth.

Structural Tilts Within Asset Classes

In addition to 1- to 3-year tactical tilts in each asset class, there may be opportunities to tilt asset classes within portfolios for 3 to 10 years—structural tilts. These wonderful finds are identified by expected returns relative to expected risks and the correlation of the opportunity to the rest of the portfolios. These structural, long-term opportunities were most numerous from 1981 through 1998. Declining inflation, interest rates, and trade barriers, along with increased opportunities in emerging countries, opened new markets and newly securitized assets.

During the eighties and nineties, the world saw one of the most aggressive rounds of monetization or securitization of theretofore illiquid assets, as well as the creation of all types of financial instruments. Financial futures entered the U.S. capital markets in 1982. Options, swaps, CDs, mortgage-backed securities, and dozens of associated derivatives, hedge funds, and all sorts of new assets and investment opportunities blossomed as inflation was brought under control, international trade quickened, and economic growth and institutional savings exploded. Wealth flowed widely, including to very poor sectors of the world, from the early eighties through the liquidity and commodity crisis of 2008. More recently, credit and regulatory restrictions on banking and the increased participation of central banks in capital markets have slowed innovation in investing and hedging instruments and increased the use of passive, low-cost, liquid investment vehicles such as ETFs. But opportunities for well-chosen structural tilts may increase as interest rates and market volatility rise.

14

Where the Structural Tilts Are

WHEN MARKETS HAVE engaged in new rounds of securitization, we have found generous opportunities to exploit market inefficiencies created by these new securities. These opportunities tend to last three to five years, until they become more widely exploited and their price per unit of risk tends to equalize with more seasoned securities. (See Figure 14.1.) New securities are less liquid, and to some extent their cheaper prices reflect that risk. But their prices and correlations with the rest of the markets start out low, reducing other risks. If you can assess the probability of their widespread adoption by the investment community over time, and the expected return assuming liquidity will improve, you can usually extract significant excess annualized returns from them with the same or less risk.

We seldom would initially invest more than 1 or 2 percent of total assets in these opportunities. But as our experience with them grew, say over 6 to 12 months, we'd increase that exposure, always conscious of not creating more than 10 to 20 basis points of total portfolio risk in each active tilt. In some cases these small risk exposures can generate up to 30 percent annual excess returns, contributing 30 to 60 basis points to total returns.

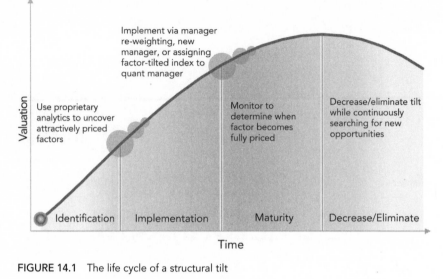

FIGURE 14.1   The life cycle of a structural tilt

A contrasting example of tactical asset-class tilting appeared a couple of years ago when one foreign market offered a limited window to invest in otherwise restricted securities. The restricted securities were trading at lower prices than the unrestricted ones. We bought all the limited amounts made available. Because the vehicle through which they were made available wasn't perfectly liquid, we had to hedge the underlying risk as the restricted securities ballooned to unsustainable price levels. We shorted correlated futures until we could liquidate the less liquid securities.

Unlike past securitization cycles, most securitized assets since 2009 have been financed by the venture capital community through their interests in new technologies. Investments in these large illiquid securitizations are more constrained than before—you acquire them only through venture capital partnership structures. The purchase multiples are high, and their prospects are hard to assess. In 2017, Tesla, the electric car maker, surpassed the valuation of General Motors ($50 billion-plus) with a minute fraction of GM's sales volume and no profits. Investors have to assign a present value to the prospect that Tesla will dominate transportation technology over the long term. We have found it hard if not impossible to create reliable value added through these types of investments. Perhaps the only prudent way to enter those risky, hard-to-assess new markets is through small allocations to quality VC partnerships.

High-Yield Investor Segmentation

We've found long-lasting opportunities for structural tilts in the U.S. high-yield markets through specialist, unconstrained active managers. At appropriate yield spreads, the high-yield markets continue to offer opportunities for active investors because of the many factors constraining investors' participation. The markets are segmented by regulatory constraints or by the idiosyncratic behavior of investors that could trade them but don't:

- Insurance companies are required by law to hold certain reserves in highly rated instruments regardless of how attractively priced the high-yield market may be.
- Mutual funds investing in high-yield bonds sell the virtues of the funds on the basis of yield rather than total return. They tend to favor riskier, higher-yielding securities over undervalued, less liquid ones. Mutual funds value liquidity to meet redemptions. They suffer untimely liquidations by retail investors when prices begin to fall as a result of threatened or actual defaults or investor interest in other assets. Strategies focused on total return, not just yield, outside the mutual fund constraints, provide better returns in the right manager's hands.
- Pension plans, endowments, and foundations that normally focus on total returns have generally been advised by their staff or external consultants that any fixed income in their portfolio should serve only to protect them against deflationary environments or to meet their liquidity needs. So they're advised to avoid the high-yield portions of the fixed income markets, which may be less liquid or less countercyclical. Were they to focus on the opportunities to add alpha and calculate the expected return, risks, and correlations—how well high-yield bonds may *fit* in their total portfolios—these institutions would find significant value added from exposure to these markets, compared with high-grade corporates or most other asset classes, as long as they don't enter the class when yield spreads are abnormally low.

Small Versus Large Stocks

Less liquid, more volatile, relatively underresearched small-capitalization stocks, which force managers to rebalance more frequently, offer opportunities for structural tilts in the equity markets. We took advantage of those tilts for many years until 2007, when large-capitalization, higher-growth, high-quality U.S. stocks became undervalued. Our subsequent multiyear tilt in favor of large-cap growth stocks increased returns and reduced the volatility of returns while we kept it. This opportunity caused us to tilt away from small-value stocks for longer than we could have anticipated in 2006.

Emerging Markets

Markets develop long-lasting aversions to certain types of securities that eventually offer opportunities for structural tilts. Opportunities arise when their expected return per unit of risk and correlations with the rest of the market begin to offer that appetizing free lunch, in this case a blend of higher return *and* low correlation. In 2015 and early 2016, prices of emerging market equities were beginning to signal significant aversion by global investors. These equities were once again offering higher-than-average returns and likely lower future correlations. As explained in Chapter 9, emerging markets were no longer the homogeneous group they had become in the years leading into the 2007–2008 liquidity crisis.

Nonmarketables

Tactical tilts in less marketable and nonmarketable asset classes are seldom available. Timing in and out of these investments is severely constrained by the delays between commitment, disbursements, and distributions, as well as the lack of control by investors over disbursements and distributions. Hedge funds are more liquid than private equity, but some managers may constrain entries and exits at inconvenient or preset times. Investors may slow down commitments at times of significant overvaluation of underlying assets, but at the risk of losing attractive shelf space among preferred providers. The best way to handle the timing of these investments is to maintain a relatively constant investment stream and diversify the funding and manager risks over time, while managing liquidity needs around the rest of the portfolio and focusing on partners with access to better-priced and more promising non-marketable opportunities.

The nonmarketable asset classes do lend themselves to longer-term, structural tilts. These tilts should respond to each class's expected returns and risks, related to both asset class and manager, or to the strategic interests of the investor (fit theory at work). Some investors have a strategic interest in certain technologies or industries as feeders into their own corporate acquisition target. Others may have interests in promoting causes through "impact investing": doing well by doing good. Many more investors might prefer more diversified, steadier sources of return.

Two relatively distinct approaches to investing in nontradable equities are those of managers who specialize in private equity and venture capital. They attempt to identify investments outside the more competitive public equity segment that can benefit either from operational and marketing efficiencies or higher leverage (private equity) or from investments in emerging technologies, products, and services (venture capital). These nonmarketable equities do tend to generate higher returns and higher risks, including liquidity, than public equities. In the venture capital segment, innovation and its attendant risks and capital requirements make diversification more critical and at the same time more difficult to achieve. Venture investment carries more asymmetrical risk (more risk than potential) than private equity, in that when funds encounter difficulties it is harder to find sufficient refinancing to rescue them from failure.

Private Equity

One may favor seasoned midmarket, small to midsize private equity players because they may play in less competitive segments that borrow less and focus on supporting operational improvements in the target firms. The larger private equity players (funds of at least $10 billion in 2017) usually bid competitively for public companies, pay higher multiples, and expect they will add value mostly from selling underperforming assets and from using financial, rather than operational, leverage. Some large activist managers do improve operational efficiencies.

These more leveraged, higher-multiple strategies, while indispensable to large pools of capital, may be riskier than strategies banking on lower valuations, operational rather than financial leverage, and sustainable competitiveness and growth, and to a lesser extent on step-ups in their original P/E ratios ("multiple expansions") at exit. A few of the larger funds have done a good job timing entry and exits and managing leverage, but this is a riskier strategy, as it may be more dependent on financial engineering than operational acumen.

The small to midmarket strategies may be less dependent on the IPO market at exit, as they have more potential strategic buyers. Corporate strategic buyers tend to pay higher multiples for the right-fit target company that complements their portfolio. The fortunes of small to midsize private investments are therefore less dependent on market cycles and exit timing. Larger private equity firms are beginning to invest in pools of small and midsize private assets to take advantage, if they can, of the higher expected returns. That trend could reduce and possibly eliminate the comparative advantage of smaller private equity buyers.

Investors in private equities favor companies that are already seasoned, with observable profits and growth trends, but that need new capital either to replace an original investor or to expand their operations and market share. These investments are generally offered in the form of limited partnerships, with a general managing partner responsible for selecting and allocating partnership capital among nonpublic companies until a final and ideally profitable exit 10 to 15 or more years after the initial investment. Exceptionally, private equity partnerships can begin distributing profits within three to five years of initial investment. In our experience, the more successful private equity investors have brought superior strategic planning skills, operational synergies in human resource management, and access to additional capital providers or clients. Investors aiming to enter private equity on a large scale may prefer larger funds that can handle significant allocations and may be more reflective of the private equity "market."

Venture Capital

A risk-averse investor may maintain a higher allocation to private equities than to venture capital (VC) partnerships over time, because seasoned private equity's return-to-risk ratios are likely to be more predictable and sustainably higher. Other institutional investors may maintain a higher allocation to venture capital because they have preferential access to certain funds or they accept higher volatility in their nonmarketable portfolios. A large portion of VC funds fail to meet return expectations.

The U.S. capital market is the birthplace of venture capital financing. Particularly since the internet and biotech revolutions, many of the most profitable breakthrough technologies have been financed by venture capital investment, not by the R&D budgets of publicly traded companies. It's hard to maintain disruptive innovation as a publicly traded firm; size and market share make it difficult to "move the needle," and rare breakthroughs are seldom worth the career risks for executives. Increasing demands for growth and profits create a conflict between entrepreneurial risk taking and sustainable earnings growth from legacy products and services. Even entrepreneurial public companies generally see themselves growing through acquisitions rather than internal innovation once they become large enough to attract substantial institutional-investor followings.

There's significant room to invest in venture capital start-ups. But the risks are large. Most early investors in start-ups end up being diluted or forced to risk additional funds at higher multiples, as the companies require additional rounds of capital injections to maintain competitiveness and growth and manage other sources of asymmetrical risks. Many end up with poor returns or complete loss of principal, as many innovations fail in the marketplace.

Given the inherent risks in venture investments, diversification is critical. Successful venture investing has to rely on a few big wins to cover many losing ventures. The industry tends to reward past success by attracting promising technologies to the more successful partnerships. Unfortunately, as the partnerships grow, their returns tend to come down. Given the hurdles to overcome in successful venture investing, we concentrated our VC allocation in the few partnerships that balanced the tension well between size of assets under management and access to the most promising ventures.

Private Investment Styles

Among private equity and venture capital managers, several approaches depend on the stage of development. *Early-stage investing*, generally the riskiest, is usually left to the entrepreneur's friends and family, who most believe in the promise of success. Most public companies were venture start-ups at some point. Neither banks nor institutional investors tend to invest in start-ups. The risks are too high and arguably unjustifiable when you are a fiduciary for other people's assets. *The greatest distinctions between private equity investment and venture capital rest on the stage of development, the visibility of profits from the sale of the product, and access to credit.* Although private equity investors hope to get profits from operational improvements, they also expect P/E multiples to expand. Some VC investments in the technology field experienced record exits and valuations two to five years from inception in the late nineties and again in the past few years. Private equity, however, has earlier access to bank and bond market lending, and it may have a quicker exit into the public markets or strategic corporate buyers.

Hedge Fund Styles

Before discussing potential structural tilts in hedge funds, it may be useful to describe the swarm of different hedge fund styles. The field offers many opportunities for unconventional management since a fund's benchmark is not tied to any market index. Hedge funds' implied benchmarks for performance-fee calculation are *zero*, or in a few cases the broker-dealer lending rate, even though many of them have significant equity or other market exposure. Oversimplifying a bit, we can find hedge funds grouped in 10 styles, all exhibiting quite different characteristics from one another. Within each style we can find them specializing in one or another region of the world. The styles are these:

Market Neutral

Market-neutral funds tend to have the lowest correlation with marketable segments. A typical market-neutral portfolio will exhibit relatively low beta (zero to 0.3). The portfolios are designed to be long and short the asset class in roughly equal proportions. The long portions of the portfolio comprise securities that the managers deem relatively cheap and likely to outperform the markets. The short positions are put in place by borrowing stocks whose prices you expect will come down over time, selling the borrowed stock at the current higher price and buying back the stock at the lower price later to return it to the investor that lent you the stock, capturing the difference between the higher price at which you sold the stock initially and the lower price at which you bought it back later on. It's complex to explain in writing but has become quite simple to execute in most developed market environments.

Market-neutral funds offer the broadest opportunities for style diversification within their own segment because they have low correlation with one another and can significantly reduce equity market risk. These funds tend to have the most quantitatively controlled risk profiles, carefully controlling for style, size, capitalization, industry, and other factors, leaving only exposure to the relative mispricing between securities held long and short. If well managed, reliable returns and risks should be about half those of equities, but their lower correlations to equities make them efficient risk diversifiers.

Equity Long-Short and Directional

These two styles hold equities both long and short, like the market-neutral funds, but their long positions are typically larger than the shorts. Their expected returns and risks, and their betas to the equity markets, will also be higher. Long-short funds commonly show betas between 0.5 and 0.7. If they're good at managing risks, their expected returns and risks will be lower than those of equities but higher than those of market-neutral managers.

Risk and Merger Arbitrage

These hedge funds will also be relatively directional, moving with the total market, with higher betas to the market than the market-neutral funds. They are most directional at times of great market turbulence, when liquidity is threatened. Unlike typical directional managers, the merger arbitrage managers buy the stocks of companies targeted to be acquired and short the stock of the acquirer. The managers' expectation is that the acquirer will end up over-paying for the target acquisition and the acquirer's stock will lose some value during or after the process. The managers will use several risk management instruments, such as shorting the acquirer's stock and put and call options, to manage changing risk patterns during the tender process, carefully assessing the probability that the deal will go through at a particular price.

Merger arbitrage strategies tend to do poorly during significant market downturns. Their relative attractiveness tends to be cyclically dependent on the frequency of mergers and acquisitions, and the appetite for acquisitions and acquisition financing dies down during market turbulence. They will not likely temper your losses in a severe market downturn. You may prefer to invest in merger arbitrage through diversified hedge fund managers rather than strict merger specialists; what you lose in specialization, you may make up in the ability to diversify the cycle risks and avoid paying high fees for a strategy that's not always profitable. Fee savings by accessing the merger arbi-trage strategies through diversified managers can be quite large, and you are assured the requisite shelf space when cycles turn in favor of merger arbitrage.

The merger arbitrage strategy is riskiest in overvalued equity markets. In a sudden market fall, merger arbitrageurs tend to suffer worse losses than most other hedge fund managers or the market. With sudden loss of value, merger financing or merger appetite may vanish. Over a market cycle, the expected returns and risks from good specialized merger arbitrage managers may closely match those of equity managers in similar sectors, with higher downside volatility in serious market declines.

Distressed

Distressed security investment is another cyclical strategy that does best after a significant market correction, when capital is scarce and expected returns for abandoned segments of the market are high. It focuses on assets with little liquidity. There may not be great benefit in maintaining a permanent high-fee presence in segments that come alive every few years. One may participate in distressed markets through diversified hedge fund managers. You can also participate in the distressed market indirectly through changing exposure to the high-yield market, in which the fees are lower than in the closed-end distressed funds; you may have tighter control of your exposure, increasing exposure when high-yield spreads are large and decreasing it when the spreads are narrow; and you may be able to achieve better diversification and liquidity. The level of credit risk exposure can't be easily controlled over time if you choose to invest in distressed securities through closed-end partnerships. Some investors may still see some benefit in investing in superior specialized distressed managers if they have no exposure to managers of marketable high-yield bonds.

Fixed Income Arbitrage

This is a relatively low-return, low-risk strategy, with significant leverage attached. There are many forms of fixed income arbitrage, but most exploit positive yield spreads. A few fixed income arbitrageurs will be "long volatility," focusing on shorting overvalued, narrow spreads and other option- and swap-based strategies. If spreads widen, they'll do well. Others are "short volatility" and will underperform when volatility increases and spreads widen. They are hoping to short the lower-yielding bond and buy the higher-yielding security.

The short-volatility strategies are sometimes referred to as carry trades. They work well for long periods until the trend in yield reverses, occasioning significant losses. Long-volatility strategies are fairly scarce but bring attractive diversification to hedge funds and total portfolios, because if successfully implemented, they do relatively well when other strategies aren't working. Long-volatility strategies have fared poorly over the recent years of heavy central bank intervention, declining interest rates and spreads, and lower volatility, but they rebound as interest rates edge up and spreads widen.

Macro Managers

Macro managers place bets based on the relative valuations of broad categories of global assets, mostly using the futures markets. As the name indicates, their strategies respond to macroeconomic or political events. Macro managers come in quantitative and qualitative flavors or combinations of both. They focus on global stocks, bonds, currencies, and commodities, and some diversify risks by adding merger arbitrage and distressed securities. Their returns can be good but episodic because they are less diversified across individual securities. One may hold a few of them in diversified hedge fund portfolios, favoring those that exhibit low correlations with the other hedge fund managers and with broad markets. If the returns are episodic, their assets should at least diversify the risks of other assets.

Diversified

True to the name, diversified hedge fund managers include skilled portfolio managers who can cover more than one asset class. In the better-diversified hedge funds, you will find capital structure arbitrageurs, macro, merger arbitrage, distressed, directional, market-neutral, and opportunistic private equity and fixed income strategies. The allocation to each strategy will depend on the opportunities offered, with a senior portfolio manager, the "face" of the firm, making decisions on how much to allocate to each, based on broad discussions with portfolio managers and on quantitative or qualitative methodologies. These diversified managers offer relatively high return per unit of risk and strong performance over time. A few of the better ones aren't accepting new investors, and those of us who found them early in their careers benefit from maintaining significant shelf-space access to their funds. They tend to have larger pools of assets accumulated over many years of attractive performance. In a few instances these managers have returned part of their assets to clients when their set of investment opportunities is reduced.

Activist

This is the label assigned to a group of investors aiming to change or replace management practices in corporate America. The style first appeared in the mid-eighties with what were called at the time leveraged buyouts, largely financed by high-yield bond issues concentrated in the hands of Drexel Burnham. Some of the players in the LBO market were greenmailers—investors threatening an LBO for the purpose of being paid to go away at market prices higher than pre-threat. But the majority were change agents who took the U.S. market by surprise and shook up management complacency. Highly leveraged and very large takeovers occurred between 1984 and 1990, when Drexel's innovator and lead market maker, Michael Milken, was declared guilty of illegal stock parking, bringing down one of the most successful firms in Wall Street at the time, to the delight of some competitors. After the Drexel collapse, high-yield bond financing for hostile takeovers practically disappeared and eventually was replaced by bank debt, which financed less hostile takeovers and mergers. "White knights" and PIPES (private investments in public equity) began raising funds, as well as new LBO–private equity funds that generally engaged in nonhostile leveraged or management buyouts of private and public firms. Recently a large asset manager announced a new fund to invest in a select group of long-term marketable equity holdings—maybe a new kind of PIPE? Media comments saw it as a way to counteract the competitive erosion in the firm's management fees.

Aggressive and sometimes hostile investors have made a comeback. Activist investors enter the shareholder proxy process expressing their intent to improve the management of targeted company assets, usually but not always first contacting the management of companies they consider ripe for restructuring. These funds run relatively concentrated and not highly leveraged portfolios (the leverage is placed on the target firm), holding 10 to 20 stocks at most, with few accounting for more than 10 percent of their total assets. The more successful activist funds have constructive plans to enhance the firms they target, by selling less productive or uncompetitive assets while improving the operation of assets where management can bring a competitive advantage.

Some activist funds are just interested in selling off the more liquid or valuable assets, in some cases destroying a valuable enterprise. Activists have been blamed for shortening the investment horizons of corporate management, excessive focus on quarterly earnings, and declining innovation and risk taking among publicly traded firms. Activist funds offer a risk profile similar to that of equities with additional, significant company-specific risks. Activist managers span a large range of investment horizons. Some will attempt a proxy fight for board control and be happy to be bought out of their position at a premium. Others won't be satisfied until they substantially control a firm's operations over extended periods until exit.

Short Sellers

These funds invest mostly in securities held short, hoping to benefit from a decrease in their price. The interest earned on the cash they receive at the time of sale covers some of the interest they pay for borrowing the stock. Short sellers are the least visible and most controversial group of hedge funds. While they do hedge some of the risks taken by other hedge fund managers, which generally hold net-long positions, it's much harder to achieve consistent performance over time as a short seller, particularly when stock markets are generating positive returns, as they normally do. Rising equity markets are a strong headwind to overcome by identifying profitable short positions. Because short sellers' results are negatively correlated with the equity market, they could reduce total portfolio volatility. But their general lack of success has left a scarcity of short sellers from which to choose outstanding managers.

CTAs

Commodity trading advisors (CTAs) are not strictly hedge funds, although they trade futures and options and may use hedging instruments in managing their returns. Many CTAs have also become macro managers, wielding both their expertise in trading financial futures—most effective in dealing with commodity futures—and their unique insights into macroeconomic developments, particularly to identify trend reversals. CTAs have had mixed success over the years, and investors seem to have veered toward macro managers as CTA substitutes.

Hedge Fund Structural Tilts

Structural tilts in hedge fund portfolios should depend on the role that hedge funds play in your strategy. A tilt toward market-neutral managers may reflect a use of hedged strategies as beta risk diversifiers and alpha engines. Diversification and lower correlation with equities and bonds are easier to find among market-neutral managers. You may favor directional strategies if you're convinced they will enhance the performance of the underlying asset class as diversifiers of the active risk within that asset class, rather than total portfolio risks. You might favor diversified multistrategy managers over cyclical specialty managers because you want to reduce fees (see Figure 14.2) and better manage shelf-space needs or because you detect superior skills.

Assets Under Management		Returns		Fees*		
Type	Size	Year 1	Year 2	Year 1	Year 2	Total
$ U.S. Millions		% Per Annum		$ U.S. Millions		
Merger Arbitrage	$50	30.0%	−20.0%	$4.20	$1.20	$5.40
Distressed	$50	−5.0%	15.0%	$1.00	$2.00	$3.00
Separate Managers	$100	12.5%	−5.0%	$5.20	$3.20	**$8.40**
50/50 Diversified Manager	$100	12.5%	−5.0%	$4.60	$2.20	**$6.80**

*2% base+ 20% incentive; $100 million account.

$1.6 Million Savings

FIGURE 14.2   Simplified schematic fee example for specialized versus diversified cyclical managers.

Assuming that no incentive fee is charged until prior losses are recovered and that the base fee is charged on average annual assets, the diversified hedge fund manager's total fee is $1.6 million—20 percent—lower than the combined fee charged by two specialized managers (merger arbitrage and distressed).

Hedge funds' diverse styles can serve multiple needs for multiple portfolios and asset classes, or none for investors who dislike their fees and relative illiquidity or are uncomfortable with complex strategies that don't always work as hoped.

Real Estate

Let's start with an anecdote illustrating the difficulties in timing strategies that are less liquid, even if you combine them with more liquid vehicles, and the risks you take when you try to match different skills with the same benchmark. In 2007 we transferred about 5 percent of total assets from open-end real estate funds to the rest of the portfolio assets, reducing real estate exposure from 10 to 5 percent. This well-timed structural reduction of real estate assets increased our total portfolio return by 60 basis points per year for the next two years and 34 basis points per year until 2011, when we began reinvesting in open-end funds. Despite this significant contribution to total portfolio returns, we had trouble maintaining appropriate diversification within the real estate segment. As intended, by liquidating the more marketable portion of real estate—open-end funds and REITs—we increased total returns but left the real estate segment with only closed-end funds, which exhibited different characteristics from the open-end funds: closed-end funds are less well diversified and have more leverage. Over the long run they tend to outperform open-end funds, but there can be significant performance differences between the two types, particularly during times of high stress in real estate.

We knew that, and we did all we could ahead of time to address the higher risk in closed-end funds: We slowed our reinvestment; we favored funds with the least leverage and diversified into less overvalued segments; we avoided higher-risk funds such as those specializing in hotels. However, while our total portfolios benefited substantially from redeploying real estate assets into other asset classes that performed much better for years, our line-item real estate performance suffered when compared with the broader real estate benchmarks, which contained a significant amount of open-end funds. This was one more lesson about the hidden costs of illiquidity—in this case illiquid closed-end real estate funds.

The closed-end funds we held did well in the six years ended in 2016 and continued to outperform other closed-end funds after that. None were liquidated at a loss. They survived the wrenchingly restricted credit cycle. But their higher-than-average leverage and less diversified portfolios decimated years of above-average returns in the real estate segment during the drastic real estate correction of 2008–2010. It would take another two to three years to overcome the drag on the asset-class performance relative to a benchmark that included a significant allocation to open-end funds, despite the positive impact on total portfolio returns. This kind of risk is sometimes referred to as "line-item, benchmark risk." It's the risk of appearing to be underperforming in a particular asset class or investment style as a result of controlling risks of underperformance or absolute losses in the broader portfolio.

For reference only, we added an additional pro forma closed-end benchmark to our performance charts and communicated frequently with our clients to emphasize the effect of the restructuring of real estate assets on their total portfolios and on the real estate segment. But these explanations take airtime and may seem defensive, particularly to newcomers to the governance process. Committee members may want to assess the value added by a change in policy relative to the old policy benchmark, not just at the total portfolio level, but also at the segment level. Since there was no way to resolve the dual policy change to all parties' satisfaction, the benchmark was left containing all types of real estate funds when we only had closed-end funds in the mix. This is a case where strong governance, unity of vision, and a high level of trust are critical for appropriate performance measurement.

Real Estate Investment Vehicles

Broadly speaking, the real estate asset class consists of investments relating to real property, generally focused on land, rentable buildings, and other improvements. Real estate investors earn a return both from the income generated through leases, net of expenses, and from the potential for appreciation in the value of the property. Real estate investments can be publicly traded or privately structured and can be implemented across the capital stack from senior debt to mezzanine to preferred equity to equity. Investments are further structured to offer a wide variety of risk-return profiles. In addition to its basic return characteristics, at fair value real estate provides a hedge against unanticipated inflation; rent escalations and expense pass-throughs are typically structured into leases.

Real estate investment opportunities may be accessed through multiple vehicles, including illiquid limited partnerships (closed-end funds), evergreen structures (open-end funds), separate accounts, direct investments, and publicly traded real estate investment trusts (REITs). However, since REITs have been included in stock market indexes, their prices behave more like stocks than other real estate. Key characteristics of the major investment vehicles are these:

■ Open-end funds
  • Liquidity dependent on cash flows
  • Strategies tending to be "core" (see below)
  • Diversified by geography and property type

- Relatively low leverage (on average, 20 percent of total assets)
- Closed-end funds
  - Finite fund life
  - Wide variety of strategies
  - Typically more leveraged than open-end funds
  - Higher fees
- Separate accounts
  - Customized strategies fitting specific needs of investors
  - High level of investor control: investor can buy or sell depending on needs
  - Higher specific-property risk
- REITs
  - Liquid
  - Pricing determined by public markets (potentially more volatile)
  - Daily market-based valuation

Strategies

Investments in real estate funds typically focus on one of these three strategies:

- **Core.** The core strategy provides exposures to properties enjoying a dominant position in their respective markets and emphasizing the generation of a steady income stream.
- **Value-add.** The value-add strategy focuses on so-called lease-up, renovation, and repositioning opportunities to generate superior returns from both income and capital appreciation. Real estate managers have multiple avenues for enhancing property value through operational improvements, rehabilitation, or redevelopment.
- **Opportunistic.** The opportunistic strategy seeks to capitalize on market inefficiencies and asset mispricing with a greater emphasis on capital appreciation.

Additional common characteristics of each strategy are listed in Figure 14.3.

	Core	Value-Add	Opportunistic
Focus	Property	Property	Property and Equity
Markets	Primary	Primary, Secondary	Primary, Secondary, Tertiary
Leasing Risk	Limited	Modest	High
Leverage	Low	Modest	High
Return Driven by	Income	Income and Appreciation	Appreciation
Risks	Stabilized Properties	Repositioning Rehab	Development, Entitlement, and Zoning

FIGURE 14.3   How the strategies differ.

The illiquidity and lack of transparency in the real estate market, in addition to the unique nature of individual properties, offer the potential to exploit pricing inefficiencies.

Property Sectors

Four main property sectors generally dominate institutional portfolios, and numerous secondary sectors appear in larger, more diverse portfolios. The main property sectors are office, industrial, retail, and multifamily. Secondary property sectors include hotels, self-storage, senior housing, student housing, affordable housing, single-family rental, medical office, net lease, and land.

The investment returns of all the property sectors are somewhat correlated because of the shared impact of economic cycles on rents and of interest rates on the yields from real estate investments. But different sectors react more quickly or slowly to cycles, generally based on the duration of their leases. For example, hotel values are most sensitive to economic outlook based on their lease terms of a single night, versus an office building that may have a rent roll with contractual cash flows locked in for 10 years or more with inflation-sensitive escalation clauses.

Portfolio Construction

When building a real estate portfolio, consider risk and return objectives, overall diversification including any legacy investments in a portfolio, the desired control over individual investments, client tax status, liquidity needs, leverage levels of individual assets and the overall portfolio, and fees. For example, if an investor has a low risk tolerance and places a high priority on liquidity, you might overweight core open-end real estate funds, with their lower leverage and higher liquidity than closed-end funds.

While REIT investing has a distinct liquidity advantage over direct or fund investing, the correlation to public equities is high over time, reducing the diversification benefit of real estate investing. According to the National Association of Real Estate Investment Trusts (NAREIT), in late 2001 the REIT-stock correlation increased to around 70 percent, likely as a result of the inclusion of REITs in the S&P 500 and other broad stock indexes. During the 2008 global financial crisis, it rose to over 80 percent.

During 2016, REITs were carved out of the broader financial sector of the S&P 500. It remains to be seen whether this breakout will reduce the correlation of publicly traded REITs and the broader equities market. Such reduction in correlation would occur when investors show cyclical appetite changes for REITs over financial stocks or the S&P 500 index itself.

One should actively monitor property type and geographic allocation and seek to exploit inefficiencies in both the real estate and capital markets. Regional diversification is just as critical as sector diversification to diversify the risk of certain areas highly dependent on one or two industries. At the core of expected success is an ability to identify and gain access to superior investment opportunities. Sourcing new partnerships comes through multiple channels, including proprietary databases, your reputation as an institutional investor, and industry conferences. We've been an active investor in real estate since World Bank days, expanding our proprietary network of relationships. We've banked on this competitive advantage developed over many years.

Construct portfolios of partnership funds that you believe have the potential to improve total portfolio efficiency. This starts through diversification across a number of factors including strategy, property type, geography, and vintage year, and it continues with careful monitoring and midcourse corrections, or tilts. Aim to enhance the portfolio with diversified value-add and opportunistic strategies from generalists or region-sector specialists with the potential to generate alpha.

Over time, certain structural tilts in real estate may underscore its role as an asset with return and risk characteristics in between equities and fixed income. Real estate yields tend to track fixed income yields more than equity yields, but real estate prices tend to mimic equities and their positive response to economic growth and inflationary protection. The real estate portfolios have been structured to favor cash-generating assets in primary markets over holding land or funding development projects. For years, we maintained a structural tilt away from retail properties, expecting continued harm from e-commerce. As with other nonmarketable investments, we favored the U.S. markets and have asked the few non-U.S. managers to hedge risky currency exposures on our behalf. These structural tilts would be adjusted or reversed if significant price anomalies turn least-favored assets into attractively priced opportunities.

Blending and Hedging Manager Styles

While managers are selected based on demonstrated ability to manage well within a style or sector of the market, there are occasions to "blend" two managers into a portfolio, rather than terminate one of them because you find the asset class less attractively priced or because the manager is overexposed to a sector not quite in tune with the rest of your portfolio.

These occasions are infrequent and do not last long, but they may be significant if they result in not terminating a good manager. A few years back, for example, we found high-yield bond spreads versus governments too narrow relative to history, suggesting a risk that both government yields and spreads might increase and prices slump. Instead of reducing the allocation to our active high-yield managers—a relatively simple and more common action—we hired another manager who worked with credit default swaps; if spreads widened, we hoped he would protect some of the capital losses in the high-yield portfolios. We didn't reduce the allocation to high yield because we expected value added from active management of the sector. We didn't want to short the high-yield index, because it was expensive: When shorting any security, you have to pay the yield on the security to the long holder, from whom you are borrowing the security to implement the short position, and high-yield bonds' high yields create a high carry cost on the short. The credit default strategy appeared to offer a better risk-return trade-off. As it turned out, the hedge didn't work as well as we had anticipated. But the alpha added by the high-yield manager during the period offset most of the cost of the hedge.

We have also sometimes hedged managers' exposures to currency or sectors that appeared temporarily overvalued. In other instances, we have changed the manager benchmark to restrict or favor certain assets. For example, during the Japanese market bubble of the late eighties, we reduced and eventually eliminated Japan from the non-U.S. equity managers' benchmark so they wouldn't feel compelled to hold significant amounts of Japanese stocks.

In controlling exposure to certain risks without having to terminate a good manager or jeopardizing the manager's accountability, which tool is used depends on the hedging costs, the vehicles available to hedge, and the time during which you expect to keep the hedge in place. One should also weigh the difficulty of putting the hedge in place against tilting away from the manager.

PART IV

Selecting and Terminating Managers

$$\alpha$$

Markets make managers.

—INVESTMENT PROVERB

15

Asking the
Right Questions

YOU'VE HEARD THE saying "There are three kinds of lies: lies, damned lies, and statistics." It is so true. We demonstrated in Part II how unstable statistical measures of risk and return are and yet how unavoidable they are as a starting point in estimating probabilities in an uncertain world. Financial history is rife with stories about seemingly bulletproof statistics leading investors astray. I have a favorite of my own, involving not just statistics and cash, but also a bottle of Burgundy's most esteemed wine, Romanée-Conti. It started in the early eighties with a meeting at the World Bank with a superb outside manager whose team of financial product developers was one of the most innovative at the time. To respect the manager's identity, I'll call him Peter.

Peter's team had come up with a "yield-based" equity strategy that promised exceptional returns relative to the S&P 500 index. Yield-based strategies, focusing on stocks with high and sustainable dividends, do work well in certain periods, including the recent five years. The statistical analysis was superb, proving the superior qualities of the research team and strategy. Peter brought it to us because he knew we wouldn't mind providing seed assets to incubate new strategies. We had done so with a few of his team's novel strategies before.

But not this time. Yield-based equity portfolios seemed overpriced relative to other stock groups. We suspected the trend behind them had reached the point where statistical significance would be highest but returns going forward would disappoint, as may be the case today with some aggressively marketed smart beta ETFs. But Peter's certainty was as strong as our reluctance.

We found a fun way to resolve the impasse. We wagered a bottle of the best wine, to be chosen by the winner, on whether yield-based would beat the S&P over the next few years. Five years after the date of the wager and over a full market cycle, we concluded it was time to call the winner. The yield strategy had not done well. Peter accepted defeat. I selected a bottle of 1978 Romanée-Conti, retailing then for a very expensive $300.

Peter delivered the bottle personally, the way you might deliver a puppy about to be reluctantly given up for adoption. We invited him to join us in drinking it. He declined. To get maximum leverage from the single bottle, we put together a four-couple dinner, to which each of the couples would bring a similarly valuable bottle of wine, or two. The dinner included two bottles of '78 Romanée-Conti plus examples of Richebourg, La Tâche, Chateau d'Yquem, exquisite champagne, and aged port. The eight of us each drank the equivalent of a full bottle of wine.* One of us ended up with a severe sinus attack the day following, leading to sinus surgery.

The experience flagged several lessons. All winnings are temporary. Enjoy them, because joy cannot be stored. But always keep your focus on the risks that follow winnings; even the best come with some kind of aftermath. Any strategy or management style works if you buy it at the right price, and the best strategies may fail miserably if you invest in them at their peak. Relative valuation is many times more valuable than any historical statistical analysis. As Jeremy Grantham, founder of the GMO investment group, has said,

---

* We should have kept the Romanée-Conti instead of drinking it. In 2015 Sotheby's offered the '78 Romanée-Conti at auction with a price range of $14,000 to $20,000 per bottle. Serena Sutcliffe of Sotheby's described it with unbridled exuberance: "It has incredible taste, rich, young and untamed . . . this wine should be censored."

"Ninety percent of what passes for brilliance or incompetence in investing is the ebb and flow of investment style." These lessons apply not just to asset selection, but to every aspect of our business, not least the vexed area of hiring and dismissing managers.

Manager selection and termination are often handled in the manner of beauty pageants. A manager is swiftly selected or terminated by committee consensus based on one preponderant quality or another (including personal charm), without sufficient time or facts to make a better-informed, more nuanced decision. The typical behavioral flaw is identified by Daniel Kahneman as "small sample bias": hiring decisions are mostly based on recent superior performance, although there is strong evidence that top-quartile performance may not be repeatable (see Figure I.4 in the Introduction). Managers who have been underperforming aren't even included in the mix, though some have other outstanding qualities, including highly undervalued, attractively priced portfolios that are most likely to outperform over the next few years. Performance chasing is a poor practice, plagued with conflicts and personality and behavioral chemistry traps, even accidental factors such as the time of day of the meeting. Meetings after meals tend to find committee members, like juries and judges, more forgiving of outliers, while mid-afternoon or late-morning meetings tend to be mortal for the idiosyncratic manager. Intelligent, likable managers tend to win and grumpier characters tend to do poorly: "The chemistry is not right."

Some of our best managers have been poor presenters or lacked charm. They may not even be able to explain well the crux of their strategic advantage to a lay crowd, particularly in 15 minutes. Personality and communication brilliance should not be the determining qualities in a manager. It usually takes many meetings with and research on a manager to evaluate all the quantitative and qualitative factors that support a selection. The factors are:

- **Culture.** Does the candidate have a record of ethical, superior human-capital management and client-centric service, whether or not warm and fuzzy?
- **Outlook.** How do we assess the quality and valuation of the portfolio *looking forward*? (Price is the greatest risk.)

- **Process.** How do we assess the uniqueness, competitiveness, and repeatability of the manager's process given competitive pressures in the past and expected conditions in the future?

Other key questions to ask and verify:

- How widely spread have their winning bets been: one-off or many wins? Some firms have a single stock that explains superior returns over many years, a feat unlikely to be repeatable.
- How broadly are the excess returns distributed over individual years? Some outstanding years can cover many years of lackluster performance.
- What is the average value added, and what is the volatility—the information coefficient (IC) or information ratio (IR)?
- How strong is the research and innovation process?
- How talented, cohesive, and experienced is the management team?
- Is the size of the organization appropriate for the style? You want alpha growers, not asset growers.
- Can you identify the manager's clear competitive advantage and the competitive disadvantage? What are the scenarios in which the manager will do poorly? Are you expecting such circumstances, or alternatively, is that risk well diversified?
- How robust is the risk management methodology? It should rely on multiple risk controls.
- How strong are their internal controls (operational due diligence)?
- What's the quality of the manager's strategic thinking and reports? Exceptional strategic thinking might extend the manager's input into the larger portfolio.

Few nonprofit investment committees, typically composed of supportive volunteers and meeting infrequently, are equipped, or have time during the presentations, to cover these questions and understand the answers well. Quite often the determining factors are just the chemistry between the candidate and the more vocal committee members established at best over 45 to 90 minutes of presentation time, the firm's past performance, or consultants' commitment to the firm (which may have brought them clients). Since the internal staff or committee members may not be sufficiently qualified or trustworthy to make the decisions, a consultant may have the final say. There are excellent consultants, and some poor or conflicted ones.

The faults in this process have been good for us. They are the reason so many institutions are outsourcing full or partial management of global, complex, multiple-manager portfolios. This is a trend that we anticipated would become best practice 30 years ago when we adopted our business model, that of a dedicated, client-centric, ethical, unconflicted, expert investment outsourcer (OCIO). It has only become well-accepted best practice in the last decade.

We suspect the reason we may have outperformed averages in the management selection and termination process is that we have avoided adding a manager style at the top or terminating a manager at a bottom. We continually interviewed managers in every style, asset class, and region of the world, whether we needed them or not at the time, adding managers gradually over time as the need arose. Figure 16.1 in Chapter 16 illustrates the value added in hiring and firing managers in all marketable asset classes, relative to market averages. Industry averages exhibit significant difficulties beating market averages.

We tended to add managers when we were adding to the style or needed to diversify the manager risk. We would look at the correlation of the manager relative to other managers we had in the asset class and at the correlation of the manager's value added (alpha) to that of other managers' alphas. We searched for new styles, new asset classes, or orphaned asset classes that seemed undervalued and perhaps underrepresented in our clients' portfolios. In any year we would be adding or terminating 5 to 10 percent of the managers in our clients' portfolios—seldom for poor past performance. Reasons for terminating or reducing exposure to a manager, other than future performance expectations, included reducing the allocation to the asset class or style, finding a better manager, or determining that the firm had become too large, dysfunctional, or complacent.

That's definitely not to say we didn't care about performance. Performance is a critical variable in the manager selection process, but performance has to be understood in the context in which it has been delivered and relative to forward-looking expectations. You need to review all the statistical measures used to diagnose past, audited performance to make sure the results are statistically sturdy. For me, observing the monthly returns of the manager over a number of years, compared with the style-appropriate benchmark and the market, is one of the most revealing analytical tools. The manager may be asked to provide compelling explanations for significant deviations. Even more important, of course, is the valuation of the portfolio looking forward. Are the holdings trading at fair or less-than-fair prices? Are they grossly overvalued or undervalued? Is the manager's value added a diversifier to sources of value added by your other managers in the asset class?

One should hire managers that fulfill all the criteria, even if the absolute or relative results of a portfolio haven't been good at certain times, provided that the securities are attractively priced, the manager has demonstrated ability to deliver value added within its style, and the value added has low correlation with other managers' value added. Otherwise you can add a low-cost, equivalent indexed vehicle or future to fill the need.

16

When to Retain a Seriously Underperforming Manager

MANY YEARS AGO we had a manager of high-grade fixed income securities from which we expected 50 basis points of yearly value added after fees. The management firm unfortunately held some mortgage-backed securities that underperformed severely during an extreme reversal in prepayment schedules: as interest rates dropped, mortgage holders refinanced their mortgages at the lower rates so the mortgages were paid ahead of maturity, not allowing us to capture the full cycle of lower interest rates and the price appreciation they brought along. All of a sudden the duration of the bonds shrank to nothing. The manager underperformed that quarter by over 300 basis points, an extreme departure from its expected small but steady value added. This single-quarter underperformance ruined more than five years of outperformance. A natural response could have been to fire the manager on the spot for such a miscalculation of prepayment risks.

Worse still, we knew that it could take five years or more for the firm to pull itself out of the hole it had dug. Every quarter, we would have to remind investment committee members why we were retaining a manager that had underperformed for five years. But we also knew the firm wouldn't make the same mistake twice and expected it to reliably deliver 50 basis points of value added to the portfolio it was managing. With the backing of the investment committee, we kept the manager. As we expected, it delivered 50 basis points of alpha per year, but for many years we would find ourselves reminding the investment committee why we had kept the firm.

With the benefit of hindsight, we might have been better off terminating the manager and hiring a new one with similar style and similar abilities but no legacy baggage to defend. A lot of political capital and time was spent with our decision, despite its wisdom. At the time, we didn't have an appropriate alternative, and we wanted to do what was "right" despite the provocative line-item handicap in our total portfolio reports—a manager that appears to be underperforming for a long time. Well, this time doing what's right paid off. The manager dug out of the hole in four painfully long years. We were counting on the goodwill of that committee. We were counting on a robust governance process, including trust in our arguments and judgments, which is not always there.

You terminate a manager when a deep look into the portfolio and the manager's methodology for identifying value does not meet your expectations looking forward. The questions listed in the previous chapter have to be asked regularly to validate a continuing management relationship, regardless of performance. Academic research has demonstrated how ill-advised the process is by which individuals and institutions hire and fire managers: most do not add value through management selection.[1] By contrast, the governance process we put in place for selecting and terminating managers has been a central pillar of our value added. (See Figure 16.1.)

Despite its importance, few institutions have learned how to implement the process of identifying superior active managers constructively. Yet the process can and needs to be improved upon through appropriate analysis in experienced hands. If experienced hands are not available, you're better off indexing the more marketable, more efficient asset classes.

Net Value Added by Hired Portfolio Managers Minus Fired Managers

FIGURE 16.1. The difference the right managers make.

Strategic's process has added significant value (alpha) through portfolio-manager selection. Three years after replacing managers with new managers, the average institution gave up a cumulative 1.4 percent during the period of the study. Strategic added 3.5 percent over the 10 years ended December 31, 2016. (Sources: Strategic Investment Group; industry average analysis from Goyal, Amit, and Sunil Wahal, including all marketable equity and fixed income managers, "The Selection and Termination of Investment Management Firms by Plan Sponsors," *Journal of Finance*, 63, 4 (2008), pp. 1805–1847.)

Risks of Retaining an Underperforming Manager

In addition to the political risk of having to explain at every meeting why you are retaining an underperforming manager (when some would prefer to punish the manager for underperforming), there is the risk that the manager's holdings won't recover in time to prove their worth. Sometimes underperformance can lead managers to terminate themselves before they recover past losses—times when you are more patient than the manager! Managers who have accumulated large wealth tend to be less resilient in the face of large losses and may be more inclined to quit the business. We have seen a handful of managers, particularly among the well-paid hedge fund group, close shop not long after they experienced bad performance (or regulatory probing).

Consequently, you may find yourself, as I have, in deep discussion with several managers after serious underperformance to make sure they will remain steadfast at the helm of their firms and the portfolio. *Good managers will rebound from serious losses if they have the commitment and discipline to continue managing the portfolios.* An excellent manager will have demonstrated such commitment over time. In most cases, serious performance reverses are not permanent losses or impairments to the assets, just artifacts of abnormal market volatility that can be adroitly managed as you move forward.

Some investors fire a manager after a specific performance shortfall, no questions asked, invoking so-called limit-loss rules, which vary depending on asset class and style. As with any rule, experience tells you it might be wiser to use informed judgment based on thorough, factual, contextual analysis, including a meaningful discussion with the manager, assuming you have the knowledge to do so and are addressing an ethical professional. If the portfolios have been permanently impaired because of fraud or insolvency of individual investments, there may be no comeback. Managers in that situation usually will return assets to clients or end up behind bars. These disastrous temporary or permanent losses afflict mostly but not solely hedge fund managers, who are also generally those with sufficient wealth to declare "Life is too short" and quit managing assets before recovering your losses.

In my experience, it has generally paid off to stay with an able management firm after a loss rather than changing the manager, even when the individual manager decided to retire after a while under the "Life is too short" clause. The performance after the loss has generally been more attractive than the performance of an alternative manager.

The probability of significant loss for any manager is the reason you diversify manager risk, particularly when putting together portfolios of hedge funds. It's important to make sure that even the highly unlikely case of a total loss in a hedge fund won't inflict more than, say, a "tolerable" 1 percent or so loss in a total portfolio, though some investors may be willing to tolerate a higher total loss. This kind of loss can be made up over time in the normal course of adding value to a portfolio through a diversified set of management styles and assets.

Manager Turnover

High manager turnover in institutional investors' portfolios is a serious symptom of poor governance. A well-selected, diversified management structure should require little turnover. Certain consultants are motivated to churn managers because they get paid for searches or feel they impress their clients if they act quickly to terminate an underperforming manager, but investors should know better. Managers shouldn't be hired at peak performance or terminated at bottoms.

Low correlation does not mean negative correlation. There are few if any negatively correlated assets. Low correlation just means one asset class or style will not mimic another asset class or style; it does not mean that they will perform in opposite directions. Owners of a diversified portfolio of active managers and assets should expect some managers and assets to underperform while others are outperforming. You should feel guardedly happy when your portfolios are firing on all cylinders, but we know the synchronicity should not be permanent in a well-diversified portfolio. Wholesale hiring and firing are seldom if ever wise. Gradual portfolio tweaks and dexterous pruning are generally the best course.

PART V

Measuring and Managing Risks

$$\alpha$$

I am sufficiently proud of my knowing something
to be modest about my not knowing all.

—VLADIMIR NABOKOV, *LOLITA*

17

The Boundaries of Risk

SOME YEARS AGO, we were advising a prospective endowment client on potential changes to its portfolio that could improve the return and risk profile. As with many midsize and smaller endowments that aim to do as well as the larger endowments by increasing their investments into less liquid, higher-returning assets, this one had increased its exposure to alternative, illiquid investments to about 60 percent of assets. In the world of investing, the most compelling trade-off is swapping market price volatility for the book-value stability of private equity holdings. That's why many endowments have moved aggressively to divest their marketable equity and bond holdings in favor of nonmarketable alternatives. This trade-off is particularly attractive if a long-term horizon grants you the freedom to engage in that trade at little apparent cost. Better still, illiquid alternatives can bring a greater reward if you can capture an illiquidity premium, by paying less for an illiquid asset than for a liquid one. But there can be a catch.

We stress-tested the endowment's portfolio to three standard deviation levels and established that when market prices dropped to low and intrinsically attractive levels, the endowment probably wouldn't be able to rebalance the portfolio to meet their policy allocations. Furthermore, they didn't have futures-trading capabilities that would allow them to buy or sell futures in the rebalancing process. To make matters worse, they had committed to larger additional investments than they could afford in a crisis. If they had to honor those commitments in tough times, they might not meet their payroll.

This was a wake-up call. We began to feel alarmed that in the quest to do as well as some of the Ivy League schools, less well-equipped endowments were ignoring a new set of risks that were potentially larger than the short-term market volatility they were trying to avoid. I began to be more vocal about the illiquidity risks we were observing from our multiple vantage points as advisors, portfolio managers, members of investment committees, and speakers.

What I generally encountered was a reluctance of decision makers to discuss the facts. I heard comments such as, "If we would have a problem, imagine the problems that others would have!" A sympathetic, cliquish laugh would ripple around the table, and nothing would be done about the risk, which was clearly manageable at the time. Some of the reckless comments were coming from broadly admired, brilliant minds. "Well, when it happens, we'll worry about it," said the head of a prestigious firm with a chuckle. "My operating philosophy is not to worry about trouble until it happens." Again one could hear complacent snickers.

These distinguished minds were profoundly wrong and even irresponsible. Although the probability of a liquidity crisis was small, perhaps 5 percent or less in any year, the impact of such an event would be costly to those institutions. In fact, as time passed, illiquidity has deeply hurt the returns, self-confidence, and governance quality of a few of them. They could do the math; they just didn't want to do the math, or they felt wimpy focusing on those low-probability risks that others were paying no attention to. Was it because they felt lucky? Was it hubris?

Dead-end discussions like these might have taken place in many of the large banks as they were adding to their unsustainably high levels of leverage, off-balance-sheet financings, and underwritings that led to the financial crisis of 2008. Hubris among decision makers is probably one of the costliest liabilities an institution carries. It's an implacable enemy to overcome. Facts and grace might not be enough. Spending time with some decision makers away from formal meetings is a way to start moving complacent followers to realize the risks of voter indifference on boards. But few people want to spend time discussing and protecting against low-probability casualties.

Accurately identifying and managing risk exposures is essential to efforts to add value over policy benchmarks while limiting unintended shocks to the portfolio returns. This section presents a framework for distinguishing between market and active risk exposures.

Damage Versus Loss

Taking risks is the unavoidable consequence of investing. Luckily, investment risks can be managed reasonably well. The critical component of managing risks is a clear understanding of a client's tolerance for volatility *and* loss at any time and over time. *Volatility is recoverable; loss can be permanent.* Some loss of principal is embedded in historical measures of volatility and should be expected and managed properly. Each asset class exhibits measurable volatility over its history and generally displays a "normal" or "lognormal" distribution that can reasonably capture up to 99 percent of probabilities. But sometimes event distributions are abnormal, as during major wars or unexpectedly large bankruptcies that bring large financial intermediaries to insolvency—so-called systemic risks. Then historical measures become less relevant. A most thorough understanding of the wayward nature of risk and the discontinuities of market prices, which create deep risk pockets, can be found in Benoit Mandelbrot's work.[1]

Normal volatility is measured in standard deviations around an expected mean (average) return. For example, U.S. equities show a historical average annual real return of roughly 7 percent with an average volatility of about 17 percent. This means that equities have about a 68 percent probability of delivering annual average returns within one standard deviation above or below the mean. In other words, in two out of three years their returns will be between –10 percent and +24 percent. The probability that returns will stay within *two* standard deviations (–27 percent to +41 percent) is 95 percent (9.5 out of 10 years), and the probability that they'll stay within three standard deviations (–44 percent to +58 percent) is 99 percent. You can never reach 100 percent certainty because the probability distribution of returns has "fat tails," meaning it never reaches zero or 100 percent. Past history does not necessarily explain every possible future event. To be realistic, an investor investing all her or his assets in a broadly diversified basket of U.S. equities has to be prepared to experience a price decline of 50 percent or more in any one (terrible) year, which could be followed by another bad year.

The longer the investment horizon, the more likely the investor will experience that 7 percent average real return for equities over time; but also the longer the horizon, the more likely the investor will also eventually experience that terrible year—or a sensationally good year. Furthermore, the range of possible outcomes increases with time (see Figure 11.5 in Chapter 11). Successful investors make sure they can survive extreme losses (or gains) without losing their cool and selling out at the bottom or increasing the position at the top. Managing risks requires a good deal of understanding of your tolerance for volatility as well as permanent loss, and also requires the ability to measure the volatility of all investable assets by looking at their historical behavior and applying sensible adjustments looking forward.

Acting on greed and fear, under the pressure of extreme loss or gain, is the most underestimated risk an investor faces. More than market volatility—the standard definition of risk—investor behavior when faced with the reality of loss (or gain) is the most damaging of all risks: volatility can fix its own damage over time, as prices revert to their mean values, but selling at a bottom or buying at a top portends a permanent loss. We're genetically programmed to react to collapsing prices with excessive fear and, although less so, to react to gains with excessive enthusiasm. Under the adrenaline rush of the moment, we tend to think that extreme losses or gains will be a new normal. *Diminished wealth increases our fear of additional loss. Increased wealth makes us more willing to take risks. Both encourage irrational choices.*

In Part II, we included adjustments that may be needed when assets are priced unsustainably low or high after a period of excessive losses or gains. For example, bond yields have been unsustainably low over the past 10 years, with inflation-adjusted yields negative in the United States, Japan, Germany, and Switzerland. A sensible adjustment to expected bond returns and volatility would assume that in 2 to 10 years bond yields will return to average levels—say, 2 to 3 percent real yields on long-term bonds. For that to happen, current bond prices will have to decline. If you don't make that modest assumption, you will most likely overestimate the expected *return* on bonds based on memories of the unique circumstances of the last 30 years of globalization, lower inflation, lower risk premiums, and, since 2008, massive central bank intervention, which brought bond yields to unimaginably low levels and bond prices to breathtaking highs. An adjustment to expected bond returns could also force you to adjust U.S. equity returns, assuming higher discount rates for earnings and possibly lower earnings multiples.

Stress Tests

Stress-testing portfolios assuming extreme scenarios goes a long way in evoking the effect of possible outcomes on your behavior and financial equilibrium. Testing for "breaking points" is also important. Those tests include the maximum tolerance for loss, allowing for access to additional sources of financing and portfolio rebalancing. Unfortunately, not all decision makers take these tests with the level of maturity and diligence required. Not infrequently a decision maker responds with some cynicism that all we are trying to do is to *justify* rather than *assess* investor tolerance for possible losses. Far from it. Assessing tolerance for infrequent events is paramount in the exercise of your fiduciary duty.

When stress-testing your portfolios, you have to estimate returns under extreme positive and negative scenarios (one, two, and three-plus standard deviations), and you have to calculate each asset class and total portfolio performance absolutely and relative to policy and peers. This exercise will help you assess the level of objective and subjective comfort of the institution's governance pyramid with your investment stance and evaluate whether the finances of the enterprise can withstand the worst case. This exercise should be done yearly or more often when the financial circumstances of the sponsor are no longer what they might have been.

Stress-Testing Illiquidity

In addition to stress-testing institutional and emotional tolerance for extreme volatility, test portfolios for extreme illiquidity—conditions in which normal trading flows and the functioning of markets are interrupted by the collapse of large service providers, such as Lehman Brothers and others in 2008. When markets malfunction, price spreads between sellers and buyers become so large that transactions slow down or stop, creating credit anxiety for many and even insolvency for a few intermediaries with asset-backed contracts. Stress-testing the liquidity needs of your portfolios to confirm that your operational and rebalancing needs could be met within, say, 30 days or less in such circumstances is essential in risk management.

Counterparty Risks: Monitor Price and CD Spreads

No liquidity analysis is complete without a daily assessment of counterparty risks. Your liquidity tests are only as accurate as the health of counterparties; an insolvent counterparty is the ultimate illiquidity. A simple daily tracking of counterparty stock prices and CD spreads relative to Treasuries can serve as an early alert to deteriorating counterparty conditions, signaling potential liquidity problems and increasing counterparty risks. Continuing deterioration in these two variables can cause us to ask probing questions of the counterparties and the funds using them, and it may cause us to stop trading with such counterparties to reduce portfolio liquidity and other risks. These measures served us well in the case of two large counterparty risks: Bear Stearns and Lehman Brothers in 2007 and 2008.

Assessing Risks in Each Asset Class

Diversification goes a long way in reducing asset-class and total portfolio risks. Particularly for less-than-expert investors, buying the market portfolio is a good way to start (assuming it is not overvalued), as that is the portfolio available for purchase by all investors through index funds and ETFs. The market portfolio contains all tradable securities in the benchmark marketplace, weighted in proportion to the size of the asset as a percentage of the total market. Market-weighted portfolios are generally the least costly and most efficient way to invest and trade, because they are the most widely held and traded.

Portfolio managers have developed different if not necessarily more efficient processes by which to determine the weight of each security in the index—the so-called smart beta funds, whose apparent value added comes mostly from the portfolio-construction process that rebalances the securities more frequently. In addition, portfolios may be reviewed and if necessary rebalanced monthly or quarterly to ensure that the assets are allocated among types of securities and strategies that are attractively valued and skewed against strategies or securities that are significantly overpriced (i.e., by 1.5 or more standard deviations above fair value).

The sources of risk are quite different for each asset class, so each asset class has its own underlying risk descriptors. For example, for equities: size of company, growth, valuation, beta, leverage, currency, industry. For fixed income: yield, maturity, duration, issuer, collateral. What happens to each of these risk descriptors drives price changes.

Once risk exposures are calculated for each asset class, the total passive and active risks of the whole portfolio can be estimated, considering each active and passive manager's risk components and their covariances with each other. Decisions can then be made regarding the size and granularity of the risks being taken—the extent to which the market is overvaluing or undervaluing certain assets relative to their expected return and risks.

How Much Risk Can You Take and Survive the Worst Case?

This is one of the most challenging and consequential questions faced by an institutional investor and its managers. Experience has taught me that if you have skills in asset allocation, asset-class structuring, and manager selection, it's reasonably safe to seek added value in a multi-asset-class portfolio by keeping a total active-risk (alpha) exposure of 120 to 200 basis points. Our information ratios (the value added over each asset-class benchmark, divided by the volatility of the value added) have been quite high in the more measurable marketable asset classes.

We took total active risk above 300 basis points in the late 1990s—and barely survived that stance in 1998 and 1999 by underweighting all stocks but particularly the grossly overvalued tech, media, and telecom sectors. Active risk of more than 300 basis points at the total portfolio level means that in a three-or-more-standard-deviation event—a market bubble or a crash—you could underperform your policy portfolio by 900-plus basis points in any year. If you have clients for which you have outperformed for three to five years by 150 or more basis points per year, 900 basis points of underperformance will wipe out many years of good performance, and your newer clients will lose faith quite rapidly regardless of the strength of your arguments. The pressures to change course will become intolerable. Those are the clients that fire managers at bottoms and hire new managers near the top of their markets. That's a risk you should not inflict on your clients or your firm. That's why I have come to believe total active risks relative to policy should be kept under 200 basis points.

18
Nonmarket Risks

THE MARKETS AREN'T your only yardsticks. Measuring risks relative to your peers, your own operations, and the client's internal structures may also be inevitable.

Peer Risks

Unfortunately, peers have become birds of quite different feathers and institutional peer benchmarks quite unreliable as performance yardsticks. For example, you can't compare an open defined benefit pension plan with large equity exposure to a closed DB plan with high, long-duration fixed income exposures. Similarly, you can't measure an endowment or foundation with low starting exposures to alternatives against a seasoned pool of high alternative exposures. But you ignore peer performance at your peril. Regardless of how convinced—and correct—a client is that it's different and its policies should be different from others, when the differences detract value relative to peer comparisons, the conviction will eventually be severely tested, most likely by newcomers on the investment committee or at the top of the governance pyramid. You may draw a really bad hand for an extended time, given the unpredictable behavior of markets. Your portfolio should deviate from peers' only to the extent that your skill and the governance structure can justify the deviation and withstand the jolts.

Making sure there is agreement on the most relevant peer group is critical. Active risks relative to peers should not exceed risks normally associated with the policy portfolio unless you are *very* certain the peers are wrong, *and* your skills are superior, so that you can make up with skill for the shortfalls bad luck might bring, or so that the investment committee will support the policy and your execution for as long as it takes to recover absolute or relative losses.

Operational Risks

Operational risks—those inherent in the *execution* of policy—have increased with the continuous development of global capital markets, high payouts for complex strategies, and the increasing diversity of alternative managers. Opportunity for fraud is a regular feature of capital markets. The higher the payout for outperformance and the higher the complexity of transactions, the higher the probability of error and fraud. Some markets are more vulnerable than others. Some of the emerging markets are still plagued by fraudulent accounting and lax or unfair regulations. Every year or two a hedge fund hits the press for some error or wrongdoing. The more diversified your selection of managers, the more likely one manager will shock you and the more vigilant you have to be, even if your losses are reasonably contained by manager diversification. Unavoidably, spending on supervision and fiduciary operational controls has increased significantly in the last 20 years.

Figure 18.1 illustrates a sample operational due diligence process to reduce the chances of manager error or fraud. The steps should be performed by professionals independently of the investment team's assessment.

Liquidity Risks

Clients must have access to sufficient liquidity to meet their spending and investment needs. Liquidity is generally available in the less volatile assets—cash equivalents and bonds—but even some of the more liquid assets may encounter extraordinary periods of restricted liquidity. In 2008, many bond mutual funds severely restricted their daily liquidity because they were

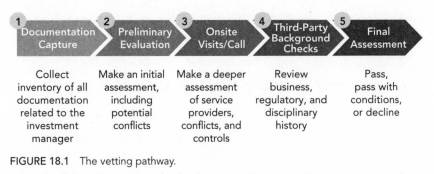

1 Documentation Capture	2 Preliminary Evaluation	3 Onsite Visits/Call	4 Third-Party Background Checks	5 Final Assessment
Collect inventory of all documentation related to the investment manager	Make an initial assessment, including potential conflicts	Make a deeper assessment of service providers, conflicts, and controls	Review business, regulatory, and disciplinary history	Pass, pass with conditions, or decline

FIGURE 18.1   The vetting pathway.

Operational due diligence is a process requiring judgment and experience, not a check-the-box exercise.

engaged in security lending and some loaned securities couldn't be retrieved in time to meet redemptions. Furthermore, there wasn't sufficient price certainty to trade some securities. Potential cybersecurity risks have also added to normal liquidity risks; any pricing or trading disruption can impede the normal functioning of markets. Imagine the ownership uncertainties that would ensue if the four major custodial banks were to be targeted for cyber disruption.

Sophisticated investors have put in place credit lines and futures trading capabilities to access loans or invest in leveraged futures if the securities in their portfolios face extreme illiquidity. Some institutions pay a modest amount to have credit lines with multiple banks available in extreme circumstances. In theory a 5 percent allocation to cash or bonds would allow you to buy almost 100 percent of your total portfolio value in any major marketable asset class through the futures markets, if those markets are functioning properly. During extreme market disruptions, however, regulators or exchanges may change margin requirements and restrict your access to futures and other hedging vehicles. Also, derivative prices might be so dislocated relative to theoretical values that their use may not be prudent. Therefore you might want to err on the side of caution. Other operational needs or governance restrictions might further limit your access to liquidity. Liquidity management and rebalancing needs may be especially complicated for investors that carry more than 50 percent of their assets in relatively blind, illiquid pools. Lack of visibility of the true risks embedded in those illiquid assets may make rebalancing and risk management at crisis times particularly challenging.

Coordinating Treasury and Investment Functions

An additional risk is the danger that institutions that have issued puttable debt can find it put back to them just as liquidity is vanishing in their investment portfolios. Quite surprisingly, many sophisticated institutional investors haven't optimally integrated their operational and financial functions—treasury assets, liabilities, liquidity, investments, revenues, expenses, and capital expenditures. Managers of those institutions should regularly assess the potential illiquidity of each asset class and total assets relative to the cash flows and other financial risks, to be sure they can meet their liquidity needs in extreme market circumstances.

In the last 35 years, the crisis of 2007–2008 was the one in which liquidity conditions were most stressed. Illiquidity was so severe that the U.S. and other governments had to intervene through a massive injection of liquidity to the banking and broker-dealer system. All major U.S. broker-dealers were forced to become banks regulated by the Federal Reserve System. A few broker-dealers went bankrupt, while others were forced to merge into healthier broker-dealers and banks.

Fortunately, we had anticipated that such an unlikely event as 2008 could happen and were able to manage the crisis and trade portfolios reasonably well. More important, we were able to rebalance back into the undervalued equity market in December 2008 and March 2009 to take advantage of the rebound in equity markets worldwide while meeting our clients' operational needs. As with hurricanes or earthquakes, you should be prepared to survive unlikely risks and rebuild. Risk comes from many sources, some obvious, some less obvious. Some risk management tools may never pay off because the risks don't materialize (consider yourself lucky). You manage for the probable but put in place minimum protections against improbable disasters, so you can rebuild the portfolio when markets steady. This is the functional equivalent of a spare tire.

PART VI

Built to Last: Leadership Attributes, Creative Management, Succession Planning, and Transitions

α

Uneasy lies the head that wears a crown.

—WILLIAM SHAKESPEARE, *HENRY IV, PART II*

19

The Wisdom
of Teams

WHETHER IN CENTURIES past, when kings could rely upon the ancient principle of *quod principi placuit, legis habet vigorem* (what pleases the prince has the force of law), or in the modern era, when statesmen like Churchill ruled with the sanction of the people, the image of the solitary leader looms large in the imagination. But monarchs have their ministers, and presidents their cabinets. Effective leadership is not a lone endeavor. And in the ever-complex world of investing, collaboration is key to success. The vast, roiling sea of economic and market data can be successfully navigated only with the help of many talented professionals with diverse skills and perspectives. The media image of the freestanding investment guru is misleading and leads to dangerous temptations. Vanishingly rare is the individual who can outperform the market consistently over the long run. *Investment excellence requires a team effort.*

Since its founding, Strategic has employed a collaborative approach to making investment decisions, drawing on multiple sources and testing to generate insights. This approach has been essential to fashioning a complete, integrated solution for each client. The group is devoted to optimizing the value of clients' assets and helping them achieve their core missions of educating the young, caring for the sick, or providing for those in retirement.

Facts, insights, pricing models, and news come regularly to investment professionals. Reading and listening broadly to opinion leaders, deep thinkers, academics, and other investors are key to staying informed, creative, and innovative. Information dots, like stars in heaven, need to be connected into constellations with better predictive powers than the signs in the zodiac. Every day we should read financial and other journals and academic research, and most important for those of us with access to valuable managers' and brokers' research, we should read all their reports. Identifying crowd-thinking and potential opportunities for dissent is as critical as identifying ignored opportunities. Develop your own models to confirm or deviate from crowd-thinking and to identify trends and extreme valuation anomalies.

To process the daily river of information, the investment manager may delegate fact- and insight-gathering responsibilities among the asset classes along which the investment world is currently organized. (See Figure 19.1.) This could change if the investment offerings change. What's important is to make sure facts and insights aren't lost through the cracks between asset classes. Cross-fertilizing ideas and checking opportunities against other specialists open the door to identifying market inefficiencies that can be exploited. For example, the emergence of online shopping has destroyed the outlook for retail malls. Identifying opportunities across the range of asset classes to "play" this trend and its eventual limits makes a difference in extracting value-added investments and avoiding securities that haven't adjusted to the trend. While retail real estate is a threatened sector in the United States, it's still doing well in emerging markets where internet shopping and delivery options are less available. But will that continue? Watch carefully for trends that may accelerate in the future but might not yet be reflected in prices.

Our decision-making team met regularly. Asset-class reviews took place monthly, but sometimes several times daily if markets were facing potential or actual disarray, as they were with the Brexit vote in the United Kingdom. At least quarterly the team would have an exhaustive capital markets review, joined by interested clients, support staff, and trainees. These reviews would

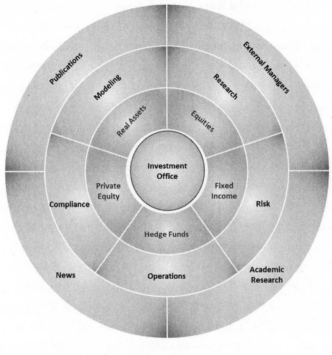

FIGURE 19.1 Structuring the flow of information.

cover all regions of the world and all asset classes and management styles, with insights from valuation and risk specialists. Emerging opportunities would be discussed but no decisions taken, to allow further development of ideas. More frequent meetings would follow in which decisions were made for each client, each asset class, and total portfolios. A cross section of investment professionals met regularly with potential or existing managers. All in the firm received a multipage summary of market performance to create a collective running memory of daily changes in prices, interest rates, and spreads for all marketable asset classes and regions of the world down to country, local currency, and dollar equivalent.

The classic experiments performed by Daniel Kahneman and Amos Tversky with Israeli pilots amply demonstrated that two (or more) informed minds and eyes are better than one sole decision maker.[1] Kahneman and

Tversky were able to reduce the number of pilot errors by allowing copilots to verify the decisions of the lead pilot rather than sit deferentially in silence. We had long been convinced that a single leadership voice is insufficient to construct a comprehensive investment solution encompassing all asset classes in all markets worldwide. The best decisions are made collaboratively in a diverse peer-reviewed process. As market sentiments are driven by millions of diverse perspectives and as complex data unceasingly flow from countless sources, it only makes sense that multiple well-informed and trained minds should work to process and make sense of it all. This is especially true during violent market upheavals when sound decision making is most critical. In crisis, cool heads must prevail. Therefore we have always had an office of the chief investment officer (CIO) composed of three or more highly experienced professionals, each with equal authority and expert knowledge of macroeconomic policies, qualitative modeling of risk, and portfolio management in normal and difficult trading conditions. Even the CEO has always been surrounded by an executive committee with oversight of all functional areas of the firm. Collaborative governance ensures that multiple, knowledgeable minds contribute to decision making.

Leadership Attributes

Managing portfolios teaches many lessons that apply to managing businesses, especially the critical leadership attributes that optimize the talents of others. Classic investment disciplines regarding operating philosophy, strategic planning, performance benchmarking, research, diversification, risk management, and delegation all come into play when managing talented professionals in a unified mission.

In any enterprise in which the assets of the firm leave the building each night, the ability to recruit, develop, organize, and motivate talented professionals within disciplined processes toward a common purpose is critical for superior results, especially in competitive marketplaces. Clearly these leadership skills extend beyond investment management firms, but they are most vital in an industry that creates alpha with nothing more than intellectual discipline and innovative insight. Investment management firms don't need large balance sheets, infrastructure, or brand awareness to produce excess returns that attract client capital. The industry model has long been the apocryphal example of two men and a dog in a garage in Greenwich, Connecticut, starting a hedge fund that grows exponentially and can still charge fees of "2 and 20" for the privilege of investing in the fund. The dog provides the warmth that may be lacking in a 24/7 emerging enterprise.

Admittedly there are levels of scale where more is required than just smart people working in concert to manage money, and where working capital, proprietary analytics, strong technology, and brand essence do drive growth to industrial levels. Think of this as the Disney model, in which an eminently creative firm can take ancient fairy tales, turn them into full-length feature films, and subsequently cross-sell those creations into coloring books, lunch boxes, fast-food action toys, and Broadway musicals.

Similarly, a few giant asset management firms invest with vast capital, deploy technology, and build global brands and distribution channels. They are similar to the Disney model, creating booming products by exploiting a free good such as access to capital markets—not entirely dissimilar to fairy tales! The core disciplines of the successful mega-scaled money management firms center on the management of talent and the discipline of investing. But these larger firms are more about beta (the markets) than alpha (excess returns relative to the markets); in markets that grow more slowly than the investment management industry, *the zero-sum nature of alpha ultimately constrains scalability.*

Leadership is critical to establishing and communicating a strategy to achieve a broadly understood goal, marshaling the talent to pursue the goal, and nurturing an adaptive culture that copes with change, a performance culture that is accountable for outcomes, and a collaborative culture that leverages talent for sustainable success. The extraordinary challenge of producing excess returns from capital markets requires creative, independent, disciplined thinking by talented people at all times. These people, like exceptional orchestras, must be well led.

When Strategy Comes to Work

Certain attributes are distinctive to superior leaders. In portfolio management it's always critical to set a policy framework aligned with investment goals. Since good fortune is the residue of design, this strategic framework is foundational in establishing business objectives that are clear to employees and clients alike.

The essence of strategy is setting priorities by agreeing on what will be done and in what order. *Prioritization* and *sequence* are the key elements of strategy because they reinforce the rationale of each other and by definition eliminate options no longer under consideration. A consistent point of strategy failure is attempting to undertake everything appealing to keep all options open. Options are necessary but expensive in business and in portfolios. Choosing which to preserve and prioritizing those options is the essence of strategy.

A simple way to think about strategy is to answer these three questions: Where do we compete, how do we win, and what are the risks? In portfolio management the sum of all market-weighted alpha equals a zero for a given market size, so to achieve excess returns an investor is competing to extract alpha from less capable others or from new assets being securitized. There are organic growth opportunities in business to "grow the size of the pie" where all participants can compete successfully; the expansion in global capital markets and new products and technologies such as Uber and Airbnb are examples of growth creating securitization of new assets. But ultimately sustainable success is predicated on outperforming your competition. If you can determine succinctly where you wish to compete and how to do so successfully, then you have a framework for winning, as long as you can execute that strategy.

Execution Excellence

Strategy is foundational to the chance of success. Execution is the source of success. Any athlete can attest to the difference between knowing what to do and actually achieving it. How can the probability of success be enhanced through execution discipline?

Investment philosophy and risk-budgeting discipline greatly enhance positive outcomes over time by increasing the probability of achieving your objective. Getting results requires focus and persistence applied in three ways:

- **Accountability.** People perform when they are held accountable. If results can be readily measured and constantly communicated, both individual and team ownership is the outcome. Lack of accountability enables bureaucracy (a "not my issue" attitude) or lack of ownership (no one washes a rental car). Look for competitiveness and accountability as key attributes in searching for talent. The best investors, like the best athletes, like to keep score to affirm their abilities and success.
- **Transparency.** Hierarchical organizations create layers of supervision to control employee activity, which in turn stifles creativity and initiative and ultimately discourages the most talented; this structure is the lifeblood of bureaucracies. All organizations need some oversight, or they cease to be organizations. In flat organizational structures such as those found in investment boutiques, however, decisions are devolved to the levels where they optimally take hold, empowering the most talented professionals to be creative, energized, and proprietary. For a flat organization with less supervisory intensity to work, employees must operate honestly and openly. Truth need not be brutal. It needs to be factual and gracefully insistent.
- **Collaboration.** Some quite accountable cultures are *not* collaborative. If the leadership tone is focused on teamwork rather than a star system, a powerful collaboration that leverages diverse human capital can thrive. As the organization grows, retaining the interdependency that holds teams together depends on implementing a structure that fosters excellence in each major functional area. However, a collaborative, trustworthy culture must be established first to achieve the teamwork that so many firms claim to practice.

Culture

I owe my early awareness of the unique value of organizational culture in developing successful societies and companies to my colleague and friend of over 35 years, Jack Meyer, former president and CEO of the Harvard Management Company (HMC) and founding CEO of Convexity. Jack is among the handful of people I have greatly admired throughout my career for his leadership and intellectual and human qualities. The governance structure and culture he developed at HMC, where I was a board member for 20 years, was among the best I have witnessed. But it was not to endure once Jack and a large portion of the board and the team turned over.

The key qualities of a strong culture are talent, trust, efficient allocation of resources, accountability, and the right incentives. But without constant communication to reinforce key cultural attributes, any culture will deteriorate over time because of turnover and complacency. To build trust, it's almost impossible to overcommunicate and hard to be too transparent in communication. If you are leading a firm of smart, ambitious professionals and your goal is to align their individual interests with the collective interests of the firm (which are presumably aligned with the clients'), the dots must be constantly connected and their emotions and intellects constantly engaged. Communication vacuums are typically filled with negativity and distrust. Absent facts, people will default to an unflattering conclusion. It's better to share adverse information correctly than to let employees fill an information gap with assumptions and rumors. This same communication style builds trusted relationships with clients and supervisory boards.

Talent Recruitment, Development, and Retention

The firm with the best cooperative talent wins over the long run, when good or bad luck washes out. Where creativity and intellect are the key components, the most enduring competitive advantage is always talent and how it is organized. Strong balance sheets, technology, and brands can all erode over time and sometimes suddenly.

However, *even investment firms with high staff turnover can succeed if the new talent is equal to or better than the departing talent.* Successful firms are talent-obsessed and seek to perpetually upgrade roles to create opportunities for distinctive talent even when those firms are not necessarily growing. This approach can seem ruthless at times and must be pursued in a balanced manner to preserve cultural values. Fear isn't a constructive leadership and governance attribute. However, the failure to be objective in assessing performance or ability always leads to long-term problems. A timely decision about individual performance usually leads to the best outcome for all.

Failing employees incubated for prolonged periods suffer the most career damage, while prolonging underperformance of the team and undermining the credibility of the enterprise.

Too often, leaders recruit to fill roles in tactical ways that result in retaining mediocre people who dilute the culture, productivity, and ultimately the ability to compete. Talent likes talent. The best athletes want to play on teams with other strong athletes who share their level of ability and desire to win. Talented employees attract and motivate other talented people, so winning organizations recognize the need to deploy strong talent throughout the organization and not just in some key roles.

Talent applies to leadership as well, because the most talented employees have the most choice about where they work. *People quit bosses more than they quit companies.* Weak leaders often ensconce themselves by hiring weak employees, so they can have more control. Strong leaders have the confidence to recruit talent that may even be stronger or smarter than they are, which further empowers the organization rather than just themselves. Of course, managing stronger, smarter people can create friction, particularly when the leader thinks he or she is right, but the discomfort is worthwhile. Airing informed disagreements leads to higher-quality decisions.

Commitment to talent requires the willingness to develop talent to retain it. Talent development can be organic in the form of heavy delegation and internal promotions complemented by lifelong training opportunities. Talented people are naturally curious and are constantly reading and learning; indeed, it's that curiosity and thirst for learning that best defines talent. Development can derive from people working within strong cultures with other skilled professionals who in turn make them better. It also can be formally cultivated through programs and specific investment in people's careers. For investment firms, the Chartered Financial Analyst (CFA) program, online executive training, and part-time MBA programs are good on-the-job training grounds.

Continuity of talent is valuable in client-facing firms where service and performance standards are high. Talented people need a reason to join, stay, and participate. Clearly, smart compensation policies that align short- and long-term interests are appropriate. But remuneration alone is insufficient.

Talented people want to work in rewarding environments that satisfy intellectual and emotional aspirations as well as financial expectations. Allowing some paid free time within work hours has been an enlightened practice at firms like Google, 3M, and Procter & Gamble. Free time to drift into new creative ideas can attract and motivate the most innovative employees. In any case, if you don't give it to them, creative types will take it anyway. You may as well get credit for it.

Awareness of the impact of talent and the need to nurture it leads to other positive leadership qualities, including avoidance of complacency; the courage to create opportunities for personal growth, which implies taking prudent chances; and strategic views about succession planning. The key to managing institutional and human transitions is disciplined succession planning. For each key position in a work group, there should be at least one or two people who could fill in some of the traits and abilities of the position holder.

Coping with Ambiguity

"Doubt is not an agreeable condition," said Voltaire, "but certainty is an absurd one." There are brilliant minds with binary approaches to problems. These people do not make good leaders even if they sometimes make good decisions. The sagacious leader understands the limits of any system or discipline. Structure provides guidelines for consistency but not the answers; the tool should never become the rule. The ability to be decisive under pressure can be informed by precedent or guidelines, but not always. Ultimately there is no substitute for the judgment of leaders and their ability and willingness to cope with ambiguity. Most people are uncomfortable with ambiguity, particularly when no action is the best action. That's why they look to leaders (or teachers, or parents) to sort out difficult choices. Movie and sports fans may favor unambiguously binary (winner-loser) resolution. But reality is less convenient and far less certain, especially at critical moments when decisions must be made in the face of hazy, evolving outcomes or incomplete information.

As an example, years ago we were confronting a difficult challenge to our investment strategy. After a period of relative overvaluation of U.S. equities, which we had handled by overweighting hedge funds and underweighting

U.S. equities, the equities fell significantly and were now relatively undervalued. There was no longer a justification for keeping them underweighted relative to other asset classes. The problem was that we had built up our hedge fund portfolio with some excellent managers we didn't want to terminate. They had demonstrated skill in delivering pure, uncorrelated alphas, and if we reduced our allocation to some of them, we might not be able to access that shelf space again, given how desirable these managers were to investors. For a moment we were thrown off our track. Ambiguity soon receded, however, because of our experience in combining disparate investments. The solution to the equity-versus-hedge-fund dilemma was simply to add 5 percent of total assets in equity futures as an overlay to the hedge funds. That was the amount we needed to increase our exposure to U.S. equities by a bit over the policy level while leaving our alpha-generating hedge fund structure intact. Our client agreements gave us authority to use futures for hedging purposes—we were hedging the risk of U.S. equities' missing their policy allocation—and our solution was within approved guidelines. We were increasing the beta (market) risk approximately up to policy and leaving our active-manager, alpha-generating risk untouched.

Strong leaders understand that choices don't come in discrete and obvious packages. Difficult decisions don't often lend themselves to rules or even complex algorithms. Difficult decision points typically arrive at inconvenient moments, and finding the right answers involves more than audacity. Most often it requires insights where there are no obvious answers and sometimes patience in gathering more facts. It requires knowledge that there may be more than one right answer or perhaps no good answers, but always the appreciation that the inability to decide is the larger problem. An adaptive GPS that adjusts to traffic patterns and acknowledges changing routes is the wiser guide.

So often, employees envy authority because they think it provides the power to resolve problems, never fully realizing that authority is a shared space that comes with even more challenges. *What many people lack is not the authority they seek, but rather the ability to cope with the ambiguity that they shrink from.* Remembering that some decisions are more reversible than others is the key to correcting course.

Smart leaders embrace ambiguity as a distinctive opportunity to apply their leadership expertise in a dynamic, flexible, adaptive way and to relieve anxiety for everyone else. Only after difficult decisions are made do outcomes become obvious to everyone. Coping gracefully with ambiguity, shifting gears, and taking responsibility where others dither because of uncertainty may be the most distinctive leadership attribute.

Embracing Change

As people don't like ambiguity, they resist change. A great deal of scientific evidence suggests that people will endure suboptimal situations indefinitely rather than risk the chance that any change may make their situation worse. Robert Kennedy famously remarked that "change has its enemies" because he so well understood both the obstacle of entrenched interests and the fear of the unknown. Humans seek comfort and the efficiencies that come from finding your groove, sticking to your knitting. Avoiding a rut requires mature insight or an external push. Diversity of cultures and experiences—and grooves—is a subtle but certain path to productive change and solution-driven innovation.

Life floats on a sea of change. Sometimes change is observed all at once in the form of some event, minor or cataclysmic. But absent acts of nature, most change is simply the product of forces in constant motion that go unobserved or ignored or sometimes even denied. Failing to think of change as a constant typically results in unwelcome events where changing reality "suddenly" becomes too obvious to ignore and choices are more limited and less nuanced.

Smart portfolio management requires keen awareness of constant change. The search for leading indicators of change at the margin paired with attractive valuations provides opportunities that can be exploited as possible market inefficiencies. The divergence between sentiment and fundamentals is the most reliable long-term source of alpha. Because the markets are a highly efficient discounting mechanism of change, markets are constantly absorbing new information that is reflected in prices. *Small changes at the margin can signal a new trend that can be exploited before it is more widely recognized in market prices, in many cases because investor sentiment is leading or lagging fundamental facts.* Only investment professionals alert to the opportunities of change can reliably exploit such inefficiencies.

This same necessity applies to leadership: alertness to change as both a constant and an opportunity. Leadership also requires the skill to convince others about the implications of new information and the need to alter or adapt behavior accordingly, rather than acceding to the desire to return to business as usual. To lead change effectively requires the application of the range of leadership attributes: a strategic framework to guide decisions and validate changes as they are being adopted; the acceptance of change as a means for achieving success; collaboration and communication skills to enlist the hearts and minds of the willing and unwilling to adapt to new realities; and the sagacity to identify important changes and cope with the ambiguity that attends uncertain new information.

Leadership also needs a "marketplace" in which those best qualified process facts, address options, and assign responsibilities. That management marketplace comes in the form of boards, committees, discussion groups, or task forces. The number and hierarchy of these groups and the quality of their analysis and decisions form the governance structure. Think of it as the organization's frontal cortex.

20
Governing
for Success

THE ORGANIZATIONS WE served are charged with the fiduciary responsibility of directing institutional or family savings to produce adequate returns within tolerable risks over the long run to meet the needs of pensioners, universities, foundations, corporations, and families. To discharge this obligation, they typically need to establish multiple decision-making hubs for different oversight functions and types of decisions. This is their governance structure.

Governance is the organizational ingredient bringing in the role of parenting in the growth and development of an institution. *At the root of good governance is usually a collective focus putting the organization's mission ahead of personal scores and selecting competent supporting staff who unambiguously share the mission.* Managing assets for both private and public institutions, we have seen a lot more good than bad investment governance. But the bad has been memorable.

Governance from Hell

One bad actor—a committee member, a staffer, an outside advisor—with some power to obstruct the open flow of information and discussion of facts, and how they affect the decision at hand, is enough to derail governance. We have been fortunate to encounter only a few bad actors. One in my memory was very smart, but impulsive and proud of being impulsive. Another was not so smart, insecure in his prospects, and deceptively malignant. We could never reach conclusions about his intent. Our intuition found him untrustworthy, but we had to maintain our professionalism and serve him as best we could. Much time and profitable opportunities were lost.

One source of ineffective investment governance is penny-wise, pound-foolish decisions. In our field, quite often the first action of a new senior executive is to cut management fees. It seems easy and shows immediate results that invite corporate praise. "I have cut expenditures by 10 percent," or even better 20 percent. The present-value impact of immediate savings is high in people's minds and positively affects year-end bonuses. The longer-term effects of cutting great managers and strategies likely to deliver superior returns net of fees can be devastating, but it might take a few years to become evident. It isn't easy to credibly compare what is with what could have been (the "null hypothesis" in academic parlance). Penny-wise, pound-foolish behavior is seldom punished, except through lower returns that can be shamelessly blamed on others.

Another short-term exercise of perceived discipline and clarity is to eliminate complex strategies for the sake of increasing simplicity. There's nothing wrong with simplifying unnecessary or contradictory bureaucratic structures, but risk management is generally not an exercise in simplicity. Diversification and expert knowledge of risk management tend to lead to more complex management structures. For example, years ago, an investment advisor was castigated by a board member for having a small allocation to commodities: "You should have either 10 percent or nothing at all; 2 to 5 percent is false precision." Wrong conclusion. A small allocation to commodities when commodities appeared grossly overpriced meant you were keeping your commodity manager in place to prime the pump when commodity prices became more attractive or inflation risk more prevalent.

Sometimes 1 to 2 percent was the maximum exposure you would add to the portfolio without damaging returns in a hostile commodity environment. It's the functional equivalent of dedicating a small portion of your portfolio to catastrophe insurance. It's the pinch of salt in a meal that you can increase or decrease depending on preference. The manager was right; the board member was wrong. Even smart, knowledgeable decision makers have trouble understanding second- and third-order effects: the law of unintended consequences.

While most successful executives find joy and share pride in a job well done, regardless of who is doing the job, some organizations and individuals find such sharing a tough pill to swallow. These individuals or cultures can bring havoc to a smooth, effective governance process. Their damage to performance is more severe the more powerful they are, but the damage can be quite severe even at lower levels of the governance structure, because they interrupt the efficient flow of information, innovation, and effective execution.

Luckily, we more often encountered good governance. In 1998 and 1999 we were seriously underweighting technology and large global stocks, which we deemed unsustainably inflated. Clients who patiently read our analysis and asked deep, pertinent questions about our conclusions, trying to clarify their doubts or test alternative interpretations, exemplified great governance. They felt the same discomfort we were feeling in trailing benchmarks or embarking on highly promising but uncertain new risk-hedging approaches, but they understood that is the price to pay for higher returns and lower risks over the long run. They have been generously rewarded for their discipline in the face of herd behavior.

A Word of Caution About Governance

The standard framework for institutional investment governance follows a decision-making fiduciary pyramid with a few variants depending on size, complexity of investment policy, and expertise. (See Figure 20.1.) At each of the decision hubs rests a set of responsibilities and capabilities that are summarized below.

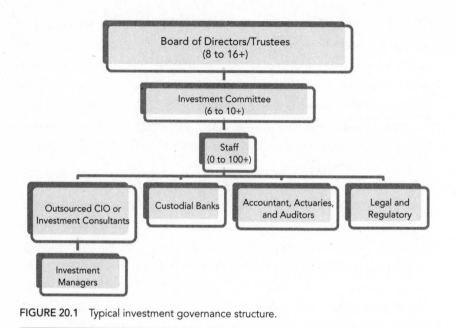

FIGURE 20.1   Typical investment governance structure.

Board of Directors or Trustees

This is the highest level of decision making at any institution. The board has
the authority and responsibility to approve or delegate approval of the investment policies that frame the types of investments and risks it is prepared to
take in pursuit of the mission its savings pool is supporting. The board is
broadly responsible for:

- Investment policy and choice of investable assets that respond to the needs
  and constraints of the institution
- Contractual arrangements and reporting frameworks for major service
  providers
- Quarterly or annual performance reviews
- Approval of budgets, contributions, and distributions policies for the savings pools, in close interaction with treasury and other internal functions
- Supervision, evaluation, and compensation policy of staff and other service
  providers

Any of these responsibilities, except the annual performance review, can be delegated to subcommittees of the board.

Meetings generally are quarterly in the absence of an investment committee or annual when there is an investment committee to which some oversight responsibilities have been delegated.

Investment Committee

The investment committee is a smaller subcommittee of the governing board, which may include non–board members and external experts with the experience and mandate to decide investment policy. The responsibilities of the investment committee are delegated by the board. The committee typically meets quarterly to formally review the performance, actions, and plans for the assets; to meet with staff and service providers who implement policy decisions and report on aspects of the management process and results; and to make most investment decisions on behalf of the board. The committee generally reports to the board of trustees or corporate board annually or sometimes quarterly. Additional phone or in-person meetings may be required when changing policies or handling special projects. Which decisions are delegated to an investment committee varies with the board's available time and comfort with the committee members.

Investment committee functions vary quite broadly. In some instances they are responsible for making decisions that could be best delegated to capable staff, such as selecting and terminating custodial banks, investment advisors, and legal, tax, actuarial, and other service providers. Selecting and terminating managers can be effectively delegated to experienced staff or external service providers. These functions may be appropriately left with the committee if the internal staff is inexperienced or untrustworthy, or if service providers able to properly exercise the role of co-fiduciary haven't been identified. In these cases, identifying appropriate external support should be a high priority of the committee.

Investment committees deeply involved in manager selection don't generally produce superior results. Part-time attention and shared, uncompensated responsibilities aren't conducive to responsible, timely decision making.

Even when the committee members are experienced capital market players, their expertise may not lend itself to managing multiple asset managers or asset classes. The board or committee does play a significant role in developing quality and performance standards by reviewing and approving the policies that will guide all these decisions and the manner and frequency in which performance will be measured.

Internal Staff

Investment staffs' qualities and capabilities range widely. Some provide simple secretarial and administrative support to a board or investment committee with a skeleton staff of one or two people handling a few external service providers. At the other extreme, some of the large pension funds, endowments, foundations, and family groups may employ 100 or more experienced investment specialists, modelers, analysts, portfolio managers, and administrators. The number, complexity, and cost are generally determined by the size and complexity of the asset pool, the complexity and competitive drive of the institution, the ability to attract, compensate, and retain talented staff in a tough recruitment environment, and the compatibility of the institution's mission with the asset management needs. Experience suggests that noninvestment institutions and the ability to sustain a talented internal investment staff are generally not very compatible.

The responsibilities of internal staff depend on its makeup and the functions it's expected to perform. Investment pools using external managers tend to have two to six investment professionals for a range of assets of $200 million to $5 billion, complemented by external service providers. The internal staff costs 5 to 10 basis points of assets under management, plus similar costs for external consulting and accounting services. An increasing number of institutions are opting for full or partial investment management outsourcing to specialized OCIOs such as our firm. Currently more than 100 firms provide such services, though only a few have proven track records and the organizational capabilities to fulfill a proper fiduciary role. As suggested by Figure 20.2, shown later in this chapter, institutions should expect different levels of value added (alpha), depending on the quality and sophistication of their staff and service providers.

Over the long run, an expert and highly experienced OCIO or internal team may be expected to deliver 100 basis points of alpha or more depending on the market environment and the stability of the governance structure— from balanced, globally diversified policy portfolios, net of all costs. One hundred basis points or more of greater-than-benchmark returns is highly significant value added, particularly in an environment of reduced returns, high volatility, and Knightian uncertainty. It may be the difference between meeting your operational objectives and exhausting the pool of assets over time. *An extra 100 basis points of annualized excess returns accrues to 20 percent higher terminal wealth in 10 years, given the average expected returns in stock and bond markets.*

Staff Compensation

From an enterprise perspective, compensation is fundamentally about the proper alignment of interests. The marketplace for investment talent is fairly efficient and transparent. The employer must determine where along the distribution curve of pay the firm wishes to compete (middle, high, or low) depending on the availability of talent in a particular locale, what the firm can afford, and the attractiveness of the workplace. Since talent is the key differentiator, and since the market sets the price relatively efficiently, employers hire cheap talent at their own peril.

Perhaps the bigger differentiator in pay is how compensation is structured. This is where there can be wide distinctions in pay practices and outcomes. The critical issue in setting compensation practice, beyond deciding on average, premium, or discounted pay levels, is to determine what organizational equation is being solved by compensation costs, which often represent over half the costs of operating investment firms.

The "Wall Street model" for top talent was composed for decades of low base salaries and high annual cash bonuses based upon either formulaic pay programs or a share of the profits. Although there was long-term compensation in the form of equity, deferred bonuses, and options, Wall Street assessed performance year to year in an effort to maximize results over a 12-month cycle and distribute the proceeds of that success to the persons who drove the results. This approach led to some regrettable behavior and amplified the cyclicality of the sales-centric culture of Wall Street. It ended badly in 2008, but there were certainly earlier examples of how this volatile short-term approach was flawed. The "sell side" of Wall Street (brokers and bankers) has undergone considerable change in compensation practices: somewhat higher base salaries, lower annual bonuses, and more and more restrictive long-term compensation with clawback provisions, as well as constraints on the percentage of compensation that can be paid annually in cash. However, the basic sales and trading culture of the Street persists in part because it maximizes short-term results and keeps sell-side businesses accountable. This culture is reinforced by the demands for steady earnings growth placed on public companies.

The buy-side asset management firms on Wall Street realized that they were solving for a different equation than their sell-side owners. Now that asset management firms mostly operate independently from financial "supermarket" firms, they have adjusted their approach to compensating their people to fit their mission of creating long-term value in client portfolios. If proper compensation practice is all about alignment of interests, the first thing asset management firms must recognize is that their interests must be aligned with client outcomes and that the results must be measured over much longer time frames than 12 months. This has typically led to the following compensation attributes:

- Higher base salaries than the sell-side firms as a percentage of annual compensation.
- Annual cash bonuses that are less volatile from year to year, to ensure retention and long-term focus. Even though financial results for buy-side firms can be volatile, cash bonus components are designed with limited annual "flex"—typically no more than 25 percent under normal conditions.
- More long-term compensation—deferred bonuses, equity and equity-linked components, and options—to align key talent to the value creation of the firm, which is highly correlated to value creation in client portfolios.

Optimal buy-side asset management compensation varies more with value added (alpha) than with growth. Of the three components, long-term equity is the most variable within the industry depending upon the structure, maturity, and size of each organization.

For-profit enterprises on the buy side compete for the best specialized talent with base salaries high enough that annual cash bonuses don't transform lifestyles; the hope is that this and a work atmosphere promoting professional excellence over political skill will encourage loyal, stable employees. Smoothing cash bonus payments year to year is intended to promote multi-year perspectives on success; investment results are measured over 3-, 5-, and 10-year horizons. The long-term equity interests are designed to retain and develop talent so clients can rely on sustainable results and relationships.

Are There Limits to Compensation?

In the best of times and the worst of times, there is never enough money to satisfy everyone's expectations. When the business is soaring, so are employee expectations of reward. When times are difficult, there isn't enough money to treat everyone fairly, at least in the short run. The combination of artful management of expectations and cultivation of career-oriented employees enables successful firms to transcend cyclical challenges and create long-term success for clients and employees alike.

Managing professionals toward mature expectations so that greed and fear don't provoke impulsive, destructive career shifts is both a science and an art. The science relies on reasonable transparency regarding what to expect and the realities of corporate earnings volatility, budgets, business opportunities, and challenges. Annual staff meetings that dig deeply into strategy and plans, followed by shorter meetings quarterly (or monthly if required by events), can go a long way toward making expectations converge on what needs to be addressed, managed, or overcome. With enough time to cover career development and prospects in the context of the evolution of the firm, individual performance reviews, annual or more frequent if needed, can help form realistic expectations of what you can do for the group and what support the firm is prepared to offer.

Buy-side compensation practices are more likely to avoid overpaying for talent in the short run or underpaying in the long run, because rewards are less episodic and more aligned with a long-term continuum that can and should be adjusted from year to year. Firms are discouraged from overpaying someone in any year since that level of reward establishes the baseline for the next year's award and subsequent payments. To balance that, employment continuity is harder to sustain with talented professionals in a competitive marketplace if employees are systematically undercompensated.

Compensation constraints often loom especially large in the nonprofit world. Thinking clearly about the implications of those constraints, however, leads to conclusions that apply beyond nonprofits.

Over the years, I've devoted thousands of pro bono hours to supporting and running nonprofits, including The Orchestra of the Americas, of which I am founder, chair, and donor. In my talks to competitively chosen groups of 35 talented young musicians from 15 to 20 countries across the world who are selected to join the orchestra's Global Leaders Program, I'm typically asked what to do when the financial resources of a new nonprofit social enterprise limit the ability to compensate the staff properly. I've developed a four-part response.

First, you should make every effort to hire people who truly believe in the nonprofit mission and would be willing to work for no pay if they did not need income to survive. An important part of your job as a leader and manager is to make sure you define and instill the importance of the mission so that no one forgets how meaningful it is. You have to understand if someone has to leave for a better-paying job. But as long as they are your colleagues, they should know and understand what your constraints are and stop complaining. Sometimes financial complaints can find an emerging voice in the supervisor. Watch that you're not doing that. Feeling yourself a victim of circumstances doesn't make your job easier, nor does it promote group creativity toward solving your financial constraints.

Second, be honest about your constraints with your staff. Let the staff members know that you understand the work they are doing should be paid better if that is the case, but you simply cannot do that because you don't have the funds. You're doing the best you can. You may want to facilitate their getting a second job.

Third, praise the people on your staff for the work they do when praise is deserved. Part of our compensation is the reward we get from knowing we are doing a good job. A large part of knowing how good a job you're doing comes from your supervisor's acknowledgment.

Fourth, see if there is some creative way to generate more income from new activities or fund-raising efforts. Elicit ideas from your colleagues and peers. There's always something that can be done to increase revenues, as frustrating as needing to find a new source of revenue might be. For-profit firms struggle as much as nonprofits to generate additional revenues, sometimes more. Think of the struggles that Apple or Samsung has to go through every year to come up with new successful products, revenues, and profits. It's a never-ending need. And there is never enough to make you comfortable. Never, ever. Sometimes, briefly, you feel you can breathe, until a new challenge comes up.

Being honest and creative and hiring *really* motivated people are an answer to your challenge. Sometimes volunteer workers are the most motivated— that is, until they have to earn their pay . . .

As experts on compensation tell you, how well compensated we are for our work is a subjective and objective question. Subjectively, job satisfaction and the respect and acknowledgment we get from our work are as important, sometimes more important, than the pay. Objectively, we want to keep progressing over time in knowledge and compensation, we want to improve the material well-being of our families, and we compare from time to time how we are doing relative to our friends and peers. All those factors influence the ideal blend of subjective and objective rewards for our work.

Despite Yale's success in managing its endowment over 25 years, the Yale staff members are not as highly compensated as those of some other endowments, and their total compensation may be significantly below what they could earn in the investment world. We don't know if they are happy, but they seem highly engaged with their profession and their jobs. And the university is most grateful for their contribution.

Nothing equals the total subjective and objective career satisfaction of getting the "full package": a job in which you find meaning, in the company of people who respect you and whom you respect; personal and professional growth day after day; and a fair financial reward for your efforts over time relative to your contribution, your peers, and the financial capabilities of your employer.

Service Providers

Multiple types of service providers support boards and staff in the discharge of their fiduciary duties. They range from simple balanced-portfolio managers to consultants with expertise in one type of institution or another and in some or all asset classes. What's critical in hiring any service provider is to distinguish between those who are highly experienced and conflict free in their advice and decision-making process and those who are inherently challenged by business conflicts.

Figure 20.2 presents the types of external support that can be found, depending on the level of control and insight an organization is prepared to bring to the investment process. Because the estimated net value added can't be sourced from independent industry data, the numbers shown are based on my own experience on boards and investment committees and my reading.

Selecting the Organizational Structure and Team and Handling Transitions

A governance structure is only as good as the people who populate it and how they relate to and complement each other in pursuit of a common mission. Governance models offer an almost infinite range of organizational alternatives. At one extreme stand the pyramidal, authoritarian, rule-driven, tightly controlled organizations, the best examples of which are military institutions, governments, and giant corporations. At the other extreme are flat organizations in which each level has significant autonomy, responsibility, and authority. We think of these structures as boutiques. Over the past two decades, investment boutiques have become the dominant sources of alpha, especially in equity and alternative-asset-class investing. This same organizational approach is sometimes deployed within larger businesses described as multi-boutiques or within academia using autonomous departments. In both cases the objective is to increase creativity and accountability by decentralizing decision making and devolving authority to the lowest level in which fact-based decision making is optimal.

Range of Services	Likely Quality Controls	Service Provided	Likely Net Value Added*
Traditional consultant, manager selection by beauty contest	Very Low	Consultant helps on policy and manager selection. Does not take strong positions; will go with the flow	Less than 0
Higher-fee, active consulting (a consultant provides strong guidance)	Low	Internal staff may implement decisions, generally with significant slippage in timeliness	Negative to 30 bp
Implemented consulting	Medium	Consultant/outsourcer implements at given quarterly/yearly intervals with no real attention to intraquarter pricing or market dynamics while implementing	Negative to 50 bp
Discretionary management with sponsor's staff/committee/board approval at each decision point	Medium High	Some delays created by approval process. Some slippage	Negative to 100 bp
Fully discretionary, experienced management working within preapproved guidelines/quarterly plans	High	Optimal control in timeliness and trading. Price and momentum sensitive	50–200 bp

FIGURE 20.2   Outsourced investment advisory services and likely outcomes.

*Based on a globally diversified balanced portfolio with likely average yearly value added increasing with higher use of less liquid alternatives such as hedge funds, private equity, real estate, and real return assets (up to 50 percent of the portfolio). Estimates based on the author's experience and "Universities Look to Yale for Investment Managers," *Wall Street Journal*, April 29, 2015.

Shelves of books have been written on the organizational structures that best fit different mission objectives. This is not one of them. For mission objectives that rely heavily on global open-market competitiveness, you need dynamic, innovative, flexible, and rapid response to market opportunities. That's why Cuba, Russia, and Iran can't compete with U.S. economic and human growth potential.

No factor determines the long-term success of a firm more than the culture on which it is anchored. In a nutshell, the culture of a firm is the manner in which we relate to each other and our clients in response to the changing dynamics of the environment and ourselves. A constructive culture respects the individual and the group, pursues knowledge and truth, and allows and promotes room for growth, change, differences of opinion, and creative solutions. In fact, a strong culture helps reconcile the tension between individual and group interests by defining success in a manner that no stakeholders will find mutually exclusive. Open, conflict-free environments keep the focus on satisfying the demands of the marketplace and our clients. Culture is in constant flux, but its basic qualities—ethical behavior, professional excellence, and commitment to the mission—should remain steady through all the challenges of the enterprise.

Not all enterprises share these values. Abusive, conflicted, and disrespectful cultures can survive and even appear to prosper for many years, but they won't create the best environment to survive the long-term competitive demands of the marketplace. These cultures may attract ambitious, hardworking staff, but they won't retain the best, most creative, committed professionals. Inferior cultures eventually succumb to conflicted agendas and less creative, less innovative solutions. They promote opportunistic, complacent responses, which will fail the test of market swings and changing competitors.

Market, client, and professional disruptions occur more frequently than we would like. We've witnessed professional and client turnover at all 13 firms we have incubated as capital providers, as well as in our own firm (which has low turnover), at service providers, and most frequently among our clients' own staffing. The arc of professional life is such that few people stay in the same job for more than three years, and even those who spend a lifetime in a company continue to develop new skills and interests that lead them into a changing set of responsibilities. So all institutions regularly or eventually face transitions of leadership at all levels. Capital markets tend to view corporate change and leadership transitions as a sign of competitiveness, innovativeness, and renewed potential, but investment boutiques have to persuade clients that the change is for the better. Changes in staff are always an opportunity to add or promote new and better skills, but not all firms take advantage of the openings.

Transitions in Strategic's life have made us stronger, because of the emphasis we have placed on building teams, doing succession planning, and developing and attracting new skilled professionals. The transition from founders to the succession team was effected over 15 years with no hiccups in our ability to deliver value added to clients. Staff satisfaction increased as we allowed more room for internal growth, higher responsibilities, and promotions. We all feel most proud of such a splendid accomplishment.

The Role of Diversity: Fact or Fantasy?

Every professional is a unique combination of personality traits, academic training, and experience. Everyone has strengths and weaknesses that should not replicate but complement others. Organizational vitality springs from diversity of strengths. The most interesting exercise we engage in regularly, especially during recruitment periods, is analyzing individual and group strengths and weaknesses to identify where additional resources are required. Some basic qualities we check for beyond the obvious ones—skills, intellect, experience, integrity—are the following:

- Accountability
- Selflessness and collaboration
- Creativity and flexibility
- Leadership potential
- Optimism and sense of humor
- Energy and work ethic
- Listening skills and the ability to learn and apply new skills
- Specialized expertise

Quantitative organizations tend to overlook communication skills, enthusiasm, and grace in personal relationships. In a business known for nerds, we sometimes tweaked our hiring to add more engaging personalities, if possible with analytical skills. Diversity has been pursued implicitly by avoiding discrimination and explicitly by recruiting from many countries, regions, and cultural backgrounds. Diversity is sought at every level of the organization as a necessary but not sufficient condition of success.

I will never forget the formidable lesson I learned outside the office about diversity and finding creative, lateral solutions to problems from an unexpected source. I had bought sneakers for our kids that turned out to be too small. The sneakers had to be exchanged at the shoe store. The problem was that while the kids were playing with the shoes, the shoelaces had been lost. We knew they were somewhere in the house but couldn't find them. Impatience became desperation. I had no time left to find the laces and exchange the shoes in the customer-unfriendly Caracas environment of those days. Our nanny, Catalina, didn't seem to understand the issue with the laces. She simply said, "Take the shoes in their boxes and ask for the larger size. When they bring them to you, take the laces off those larger shoes and place them with the smaller shoes you need to exchange." It worked like a charm. The shoe salesman was as impressed as I had been at such an obvious solution, and as expected, we did find the shoelaces later on, tied around the waists of Ken and Barbie dolls as stylish belts.

Why couldn't I have thought of that? There is a solution as simple as that to many, many problems. A mind open to unexpected ways of looking at problems and the innovative ideas that come from a diverse group have a way of producing surprising, charming, and winning strategies. Lateral, inductive thinkers are a great complement to sequential, deductive thinkers.

Every time we've compared our diversity numbers against financial industry averages, we've been pleasantly reassured by the plethora of nationalities, languages, ethnicities, and outstanding alma maters and the generational and women-to-men ratios at all levels of our organization. Diversity per se is not targeted; it's the outcome of searching for the most complementary, talented, independent, deep thinkers. A few examples as of early 2015 make the point: women made up nearly half our workforce, with more than 40 percent at director level or above, versus 18 percent of executive officers in U.S. finance and insurance industries.[1]

Work Environment and Work-Life Balance

I have experienced all kinds of work environments from linoleum floors, metal desks, and no personal space to beautifully appointed, light-filled spaces where you feel instant joy just being there. Clearly, a pleasant space helps our well-being, but much more important is for staff to feel relevant, engaged, and respected.

While any group or individual should be able to produce results under less-than-optimal conditions, a certain quality of life is essential for long-term professional excellence, motivation, engagement, and group cohesiveness. Flexible work schedules and work from home merit accommodation in certain cases. Vacations should be taken—no one should be irreplaceable. Time with family and friends and time for a healthy, well-balanced, community-engaged lifestyle recharge the batteries and increase efficiency, intellectual and personal roundedness, and creativity.

Closing Thoughts on Boards and Investment Committees

The most important quality to develop in the governance process is a culture of analysis of facts and forward-looking rather than reactive, impulsive, biased decisions. Among client institutions, uniquely well-run investment processes can be disrupted by high-level board appointees who are unfairly suspicious of results and cynical about the abilities of the staff and how decisions are made and implemented. Sometimes suspicions are well founded. Other times they arise from miscommunication, emotional reactions to comments, hidden—or open—agendas, and hubris. Suspicions based on facts can be easily addressed with factual, unemotional analysis. Suspicions that stem from personal agendas are difficult to properly address, short of engaging in some form of group therapy, which is seldom advisable or successful. Hubris and bad faith don't blend well with group therapy. The best cure for suspicion is one-on-one meetings with the questioning party to address the doubts. This approach works if the parties act in good faith and are reasonably open to learning.

All investment processes will encounter periods in which strategies don't work and even great performance weakens. Oversight bodies need to look deep into the reasons that strategies are failing and not be quick to blame the failure on incompetence. In a probabilistic, sometimes random world, rational assessments can encounter irrational markets. Joining the madness of crowds is not a winning response. A well-substantiated analysis shouldn't be taken lightly. Many times, a single vocal committee member may do just that, undermining sound decision making. Therefore, it's important to identify constructive fiduciary qualities that should be considered in selecting investment committee members. Open-mindedness, analytical ability, good faith, and intellectual humility are a good start.

Optimal Qualities of Investment Committee Members

The qualities and interpersonal dynamics of people charged with setting and overseeing policies for managing investment pools are at least as critical to the quality of governance as the qualities of portfolio managers selected for the daily management and trading of the assets. The following qualities are vital.

Professional Knowledge

Broad and deep knowledge of capital markets, portfolio theory, economics, and portfolio management is optimal. We have witnessed many investment committees where some members have deep expertise in some segments of capital markets—equities, debt, hedge funds, or private equity—but little knowledge of the other segments and even less experience with portfolio-construction processes that include multiple assets and managers. A competent hedge fund manager serving on a committee may share his or her view that the equity markets are extremely overvalued and that the fund should be holding more cash. That approach to portfolio construction might be appropriate for a hedge fund in search of opportunities that could yield 20 percent returns (there are a few of those from time to time) and prepared to hold abundant cash to pounce on those opportunities when they appear. For that fund manager, finding 10 such investments may be enough to deliver attractive risk-adjusted returns. But for a globally diversified institutional portfolio with multiple managers, and an unpaid, somewhat inexperienced committee that meets infrequently, the realistic expected return for equities should not be more than 5 to 7 percent in real terms. Missing those returns year in and year out while waiting for the 20 percent opportunities may be a fatally flawed approach to delivering sustainable returns. A profound understanding of what capital markets, not a specific investment style, can deliver is important to committee dynamics. A third of committee members with that understanding can help create a constructive consensus on a committee where others have more specialized skills.

Commitment to the Task

Regardless of professional qualifications, members should take their mission seriously. They should read all supporting materials and general trade journals with intellectual engagement and an open but also discriminating mind. For those situated far afield, allowing them to participate by conference call or video works quite well.

Ethical Standards

I've encountered prestigious corporate leaders, whose main apparent interest in joining an investment committee is to identify business opportunities for their firms that they can follow up with their internal staff or service providers, and who are otherwise quite unengaged. These committee members either are quiet, issuing no opinions during discussions, preferring to work their agenda outside committee meetings, or are surprisingly open about their biases in hopes of finding opportunistic supporters. It may be evident they haven't given full thought to the meeting material or absorbed the evidence presented with an open mind. Other members may acquiesce if the member is a generous donor to the foundation or endowment or is an authority figure they don't want to antagonize. The largesse of the member is seldom enough to counteract the damage inflicted on the fund's performance, and no single member's authority should preclude another's wisdom. Some of us have been forced to resign from committees in which our contribution would have been most valuable because performing well as a fiduciary stood in the way of civil relationships with the most powerful.

Personal agendas or conflicts of interest have no place in fiduciary committees. Where they appear, they should be disclosed and the member excused from discussion or voting. Public company boards generally have full disclosure rules regarding conflicts of interest. But we have sat in a few committee meetings in which conflicts are ignored, including meetings where members have blatantly tried to take advantage of their positions to generate business for their firms or friends. Worse, friends of consultants have proudly disclosed to me a clever but unethical quid pro quo by which the consultant sitting on a committee was voting to hire a manager who in turn was sitting on another committee voting to hire the consultant. Even an obvious lack of ethics may be condoned by members who choose to look the other way to retain their membership. If one can't change the culture, the best alternative may be to resign from the committee at a great loss for the organization.

Contributors to the Discussion and a Culture of Trust

Openness and serious goodwill should be present in reviewing, discussing, and deciding any course of action. Honest, constructive candor should be the tone of well-run meetings. Clients that have been most candid with us and with each other provide the best environment for innovation and dynamic responses to market developments. Many allowed us to interact in a culture of mutual trust, where doubts and uncertainty are fully disclosed. But with some clients, we can see seeds of mistrust being planted by their own staffs, competitors, or some committee members for their own purposes. A trust culture is quite evident to all and makes for sound discussions and superior decision making, but it can be stolen overnight.

Ability to Think Independently and Be Forward Looking

Here's where diversity plays the most critical role. Homogeneity usually creates rank-order, hierarchical behavior and identity politics. There seems to be a silent code by which homogeneous groups follow the leading voice. Those who dissent stay quiet. Competent independent thinkers are hard to find. Forcing a certain amount of diversity on committees brings at the least a diversified set of habits that may open the door to more nuanced thinking. We have often seen creative thought squashed because the group didn't assign sufficient authority to the independent-thinking committee members, exhibiting the "not one of us" outsider versus insider syndrome that can be so corrosive to creativity and competitiveness.

Finding and developing these qualities is the most important job of the committee and board chairs. A great chair seeks knowledge, independent thinking, and facts, and deflects conflicts and hidden agendas. If the chair lacks these qualities, there is little hope that committee decisions will produce good governance. Bad governance usually starts from the top and spreads geometrically through the next levels of command in an organization. Who is the chair of a committee or a board is one of the most important decisions in ensuring good governance.

Figure 20.3 summarizes the qualities of fiduciary boards and investment committees I have found most meaningful to performance. I have labeled them according to the way they may be experienced by the professionals

	Heaven	Hell	Purgatory
Longevity	• 75% or more of members are experienced fiduciaries who have shared committee responsibilities for over five years • Average duration more than seven years	• Few if any members have been on the committee for more than three years or a full market cycle • Average duration less than three years	• Committee members have an average tenure above five years with at least half the members above three years
Capacity to Learn	• High • Absolutely no axes to grind • Ranks wisdom above technical knowledge • Accepts benchmarks and peer comparisons in context, not as weapons of destruction	• Members push their friends as service providers. • Uses incomplete knowledge as weapon against wisdom • Uses benchmark comparisons destructively	• Wisdom prevails but insufficient technical knowledge threatens to derail initiatives at least once at each meeting • Can get confused about which performance benchmark is relevant at different times • Has a narrow grasp of financial theory; believes in dogma
Traits of Members	• Assume personal responsibility and read all materials sent to them • Committed to fiduciary role • Constructively seek enlightened consensus (iterate toward best practice)	• Fewer than half the members read all materials. Many do not read more than the performance charts • Limited understanding of fiduciary role	• All members read some of the policy material • A reasonably strong but still mixed bag of skills and fiduciary awareness

FIGURE 20.3   The choices for investment committees.

charged with the actual daily management of assets. (For a more comprehensive self-assessment form for fiduciaries, see the Appendix.)

Refreshing Board and Committee Membership

Some turnover on oversight boards, committees, staff, and asset managers is not just unavoidable; it is desirable. Renewing and updating the thought process is essential to innovation. But too much turnover can be destructive. Turnover may increase the influence of the least constructive and ethical members. Excessive turnover reduces trust, the glue that binds and strengthens good governance. The internal staff's reign is generally cemented by committee turnover, potentially reducing the level and quality of controls required by good governance. Agenda- and power-driven staffers sometimes take advantage of chairs who promote turnover.

In our experience, an *average* tenure for board and committee members of about six or seven years may be ideal. This implies that several valuable members may have tenure of fifteen or more years. Rotating and overlapping terms preserve institutional memory while refreshing the leadership dynamic of the committee. Renewable three- to five-year appointments can allow constructive turnover to occur without unduly offending anybody. An initial one-year period can be appropriate for new committee members.

The chair is crucial in promoting the right culture and group balance. A weak or uninsightful chair might ease out the most constructive, informed, independent committee members because they don't go with the flow of the majority, even if dysfunctional.

Delivering Alpha

Think carefully about your mission, your objectives, the environment in which you are operating, and your competitive advantages and disadvantages, and plan a flexible, reversible, but disciplined strategy to succeed incrementally. Remember the Piñata Strategy!

The capacity to deliver alpha will depend on the following qualities, *in this order:*

- Your governance structure and process.
- A frank assessment of your competitive advantage relative to the markets and your peers.
- The process by which you select and change your policy and service providers. Is it fact- and wisdom-based or more impulsively reactive?
- The state of the world and capital markets. Are markets providing the information you need to assess fair value?

And luck. But luck is random; the rest is not.

Acknowledgments

SOME MONTHS AGO I went to an event honoring chef José Andrés. The charismatic chef was wearing a red T-shirt with "IMMIGRANT" in big letters on his chest. In the currently charged political environment, I could readily identify with his source of pride. I wanted one of those T-shirts for myself!

My story is one more immigrant story. This one is of a woman from Venezuela who came to Harvard on a Fulbright Fellowship with a two-year-old child, Andres, in tow (arguably the first to do that), and years later left my country to join the World Bank. After a few months as a consultant in one of Robert McNamara's think tanks, I landed in a job in the bank's pension plan, a job no one else wanted at the time. The job was as far from glamorous as the linoleum floors were from the carpeted and marble floors in the bank's more elevated offices. The pension plan was not performing well in the aftermath of the oil and market turmoil of the seventies. I took the job because it fit my portfolio theory training at Harvard; I liked Bernie Holland and K. G. Gabriel, to whom I would be reporting; and I figured I could not inflict more damage on the assets than the markets already had.

I now take great joy in recalling with gratitude the role of the World Bank in Strategic Investment Group's beginnings. Not only did I learn as much as anyone could have in my 12 years at the bank, with outstanding and challenging colleagues, but quite unexpectedly the bank rewarded our performance of many years with a contract to manage its pension assets as an external service provider.

215

We began our journey as private entrepreneurs on November 1, 1987, at the worst and best of times, less than two weeks after the unforgettable world market crash of October 1987, which seemed to augur the possible end of capitalism. I felt comforted that the World Bank had allowed me to bring along any member of its staff who would agree to join Strategic. Initially I had invited just one senior bank employee, Antoine van Agtmael, to join me. Antoine was a kindred, creative, and entrepreneurial spirit I had worked with in developing a following for the emerging markets databases and developed-country funds being launched by the World Bank's private-sector affiliate, International Finance Corporation. My experience dealing with global assets as a pension investor nicely complemented Antoine's and IFC's interest in developing the capital markets of IFC's borrowers.

I had secured both working capital and a $300 million commitment from investors to manage European and U.S. institutional assets, and I could afford to bring a few more partners. The World Bank's offer to manage its pension assets and allow me to keep the pension team intact was something to be indeed grateful for—the best I could expect for an entrepreneurial journey launching into possibly the darkest capital market outlook. Our small band of six looked ahead into the worst of times. But adversity has a way of fostering innovative responses among the daring and able. It was precisely the sight of the abyss that led us to build a much-improved risk- and stress-testing model that would look not just at the downside but at the potential of such possibly undervalued markets.

Michael Duffy, Mary Choksi, Carol Grefenstette, and George Alvarez-Correa (who left the firm 20 years ago for health reasons, but is alive and well as of this writing) joined Antoine and me in what was to become an unforgettable journey of professional and personal growth—and great value creation for our clients. I could not have asked for a smarter, more resourceful, and more dedicated founding team. They were real partners and generous mentors to the two generations that have succeeded us, and I am moved daily by our loyalty to each other, our colleagues, our clients, and the firm we created and helped blossom over the last 30 years. They are beloved friends as well.

I am also profoundly thankful to our original and more recent capital partners, who have contributed insights, support, and liquidity to all our shareholders and allowed their gradual, seamless retirement and the engagement of a new generation of members.

Brian A. Murdock, who took my place as the CEO of Strategic in 2014, has been a better manager of the firm in a much more complex landscape than I could have ever been. I am indebted to his valuable direct contribution to this book, particularly in the last section dealing with the attributes of leadership and other governance issues. I only wish I could have met and brought along Brian 30 years ago; we could have been an even better firm. But it's never too late when you find exceptional management and investment talent.

The members of Strategic's senior investment and management team read and lent their insights to this book's story line, even when they might have disagreed with the way I describe certain topics. No great firm can reach high achievement levels without differences of opinions. Any errors left are my own. I am still learning and reserve the right to correct errors and get better in all I do. The book is not a prescription to be swallowed without serious questioning. It's a description of a way of thinking about many of the inputs that go into adding value to investment portfolios.

Some former Strategic colleagues deserve special mention because they helped put together analytical data, tables, graphs, and descriptions of processes, or offered useful comments on earlier drafts. They are, alphabetically, Eric Bendickson, Laurie Bonello, Jason Garelli, Paola Gomez-Erb, Dianna Gonzales-Burdin, Ken Grossfield, Taylor Henshall, Ted Joseph, Paul Kramer, Nikki Kraus, Markus Krygier, Jason Miller, Ted Mundy, Jeffrey Nasser, Victoria Nolan, Joshua O'Brien, Tim O'Hara, David Ordoobadi, Jason Rabineau, Ian Smith, Rafael Velásquez, Geoff Wilson, and Aksana Zabara.

Three people provided superb advice on early drafts: David Smick, who told me I should have at least 15 anecdotes, because that is all people remember (embarrassing as they may be, or just because of that). Joanne Leedom-Ackerman, novelist and vice president emeritus of PEN International, who insisted on the active voice and the *I* pronoun. David Nirenberg, of the University of Chicago, my intellectual if not my actual alma mater, who as an experienced history writer taught me the importance of the preface and introduction playing the role of overture to the rest of the piece.

My profound gratitude goes to my most talented, charming, and articulate editor, William S. Rukeyser, for having turned an almost illegible manuscript into a sensible, coherent text, while keeping the tenor of my voice. I have enjoyed every moment of our work together. And I am grateful to my agent James Levine, who has guided this effort to its successful publishing, and to Noah Schwartzberg of McGraw-Hill, who could not have been more insightful and graceful.

But the book would have never reached its deliverable form without the help of my husband, Arturo Brillembourg, who made sure the graphs and narrative supported each other. Without his knowledge of economics and finance, his modeling skills, and his patience, that task would have been near impossible. I never imagined how difficult it would be to come up with simple graphs that described complex issues. Now that I know, I might never write another book with graphs, ever again, despite how much I enjoyed working with Arturo and Bill on the wretched graphics. Arturo was a great fit for our modeling and graphic needs.

Friends and family devotedly read or snacked on the text and offered helpful professional and lay reader suggestions: our children, Andres, Clara, and Arturo; my partners, Mary, Mike, Carol, and Antoine; and dear friends Cristina and Pedro Mario Burelli, Gustavo Coronel, Leonor Filardo, Mirella Levinas, Jo Ann Mason, Nelson Ortiz, Robert Pozen, and the singularly relevant Charley Ellis, without whom I would have never found Bill Rukeyser. I am forever grateful to all. And finally, to Donna Lauderdale, who was my executive assistant, wise advisor, and alter ego for almost 20 years, without whom I would not have accomplished much in life or work.

There are financial industry firms and people—index developers, managers, and service providers—that have developed products, software services, and tools that allow us to manage assets in the most efficient, cost-effective way. Among them: Vanguard, BlackRock, State Street Bank, Mellon Bank, and all the ETF developers and distributors; S&P Global, MSCI, and FT; all the active managers in all asset classes that provide us with innovative security selection and trading strategies and the ethical and professional loyalty to serve their clients well; all the investment banks and broker-dealers that continue to securitize products that are indispensable to the investment and risk management needs of all investors; Harvard's Kennedy School, Department of Economics, and Business School Doctoral Program for their academic training and sharpening my curiosity and analytical skills; the academic community and the CFA Institute that encourage and sustain outstanding research and training to lend intellectual robustness to the investment process; and, of course, our magnificent clients, who have recognized real expertise in what we do and have entrusted us with their precious assets while demanding excellence of thought, process, and service.

To all of them my profound gratitude. You make us proud of our profession and its potential to make the world a better and safer place.

Appendix

Self-Assessment for Fiduciaries

GOVERNANCE IS THE set of policies, behavioral codes, procedures, modus operandi, and culture that frames the way decisions are made, implemented, and controlled to meet organizational objectives. Good governance, not good intentions or rules, leads to success more than any other factor. Good governance, while often overlooked, is more important than investment management skills in meeting investment objectives.

The following questions are designed to identify potential weaknesses in the governance process of investment fiduciaries. They provide a set of measurable yardsticks and simple diagnostic tools to identify weaknesses in the decision making, implementation process, and controls.

I have organized the survey around five categories:

- Mission awareness
- Governance structure
- Decision-making process
- Organizational culture and individual biases
- Controls

Instructions for the Short and Long Form

I have devised two self-evaluations.

A short survey form can be completed in five minutes, and a long survey form provides more information on the source of strengths and weaknesses in the five categories of governance. The longer survey takes 10–15 minutes to complete.

Short Quiz

Evaluating the Effectiveness of the Investment Committee

Circle the correct answer.

1. What is the average tenure of the committee members?
   a. Three years
   b. Five years
   c. Seven years

2. What statement best describes the majority of committee members?
   a. Rank wisdom above technical knowledge
   b. Use incomplete knowledge as a weapon against wisdom
   c. Struggle to prevent insufficient technical knowledge from derailing wisdom

3. How does the committee use benchmarks?
   a. Gets confused about which performance benchmark is relevant
   b. Accepts benchmarks and peer comparators in context, not as weapons of destruction
   c. Uses benchmark comparisons destructively

4. Do members read policy materials?
   a. All members read some of the policy material.
   b. Members read all materials sent to them.
   c. Less than half read all materials; many read only performance charts.

5. What is the committee's understanding of its fiduciary role?

a. Reasonably strong, but mixed bag of skills and fiduciary awareness

b. Very limited understanding of fiduciary role

c. Strong commitment to and knowledge of fiduciary role

6. How many manager terminations did you experience in the 24 months after the crash of 2008?

a. None

b. More than 10%

c. 10% or less

Question #	1	2	3	4	5	6
a	1	3	2	2	2	3
b	2	1	3	3	1	1
c	3	2	1	1	3	2

Scoring:

Committee from Hell	6–11 points
Committee in Purgatory	12–17 points
Committee from Heaven	18 points

Long Governance Survey

(15–20 minutes)

I. Mission Awareness

Circle the correct answer.

1. The committee has a clearly articulated, agreed understanding of the investment objectives and constraints, as they apply to both the short and the long run, and how they can impact the sponsoring organization and the beneficiaries.

Agree　　　　　　　　Undecided　　　　　　　　Disagree

2. After having read and analyzed reports on likely returns and risks embedded in the capital markets, I believe our objectives and constraints are realistic and achievable.

Agree　　　　　　　　Undecided　　　　　　　　Disagree

3. Our staff and service providers have a clear understanding of our objectives and constraints, and they believe they are realistic and achievable.

Agree   Undecided   Disagree

4. All decision makers have the appropriate training and work habits to help meet our mission.

Agree   Undecided   Disagree

5. Our mission is fully compatible with the way we make decisions. The horizon over which we make decisions that affect our investments is well understood, and the shorter horizon of corporate or sponsor decisions does not affect our ability to maintain our long-term perspective for investment decisions.

Agree   Undecided   Disagree

6. I believe that while diversification is important, it is also important to avoid entering a diversifying asset class at a historic high price.

Agree   Undecided   Disagree

II. Governance Structure

Circle the correct answer.

7. We have the right number of committee members that meet the right number of times to address appropriate policy issues.

Agree   Undecided   Disagree

8. The committee focuses strictly on policy issues and leaves implementation and operational decisions to the staff and service providers.

Agree   Undecided   Disagree

9. There is an appropriate division of responsibilities between policy initiatives, decisions, and implementation.

Agree   Undecided   Disagree

10. Our committee has all the information it needs to make appropriate decisions.

Agree   Undecided   Disagree

11. All committee members are sufficiently well trained and knowledgeable about investment and capital markets to properly discharge their responsibilities.

Agree   Undecided   Disagree

12. All committee members exercise their responsibilities without conflicts of interest. If there are any conflicts, they are fully disclosed, and the member in question recuses himself or herself from the discussion and decision.

Agree   Undecided   Disagree

13. While committee members seem to have high ethical and professional standards, they sometimes may push for service providers they like for reasons that are not openly disclosed or may be based more on sympathies than on full merit.

Agree   Undecided   Disagree

14. I go along with some group decisions more easily than I would go along on my own, because I do not feel comfortable standing out in an argument or letting the rest of the group know the extent of my discomfort.

Agree   Undecided   Disagree

15. I go along with the consensus if I do not fully understand the rationale or the true repercussions of a decision.

Agree   Undecided   Disagree

16. All decision makers participate in the discussion and give the impression of being properly prepared.

Agree   Undecided   Disagree

III. Decision-Making Process

Circle the correct answer.

17. Policy issues are always discussed with appropriate technical and professional support for the decisions, and appropriate time is given to read all the materials, as well as discussing them at the meetings, before decisions are made.

Agree   Undecided   Disagree

18. After a full discussion of the reasons behind a particular set of policy proposals, our group can decide and move to implementation promptly, and there is enough flexibility to address and resolve unexpected findings along the way without feeling either straitjacketed or confused about implementation plans.

    Agree   Undecided   Disagree

19. I feel comfortable raising doubts about a decision if I find new evidence leading me to question the expected outcome.

    Agree   Undecided   Disagree

20. I feel comfortable addressing, or finding someone to address, the doubts and informational needs of all my fellow committee members.

    Agree   Undecided   Disagree

21. All members' views are fully aired and properly discussed before making decisions.

    Agree   Undecided   Disagree

22. There is always appropriate information to allow me to make knowledgeable decisions.

    Agree   Undecided   Disagree

23. We know in advance the discussion and work schedule for each meeting during the year, and we have a full index of topics that as fiduciaries we should address on a regular basis.

    Agree   Undecided   Disagree

24. I wonder whether the committee is too involved in the day-to-day implementation issues (e.g., manager-specific issues) rather than policy.

    Agree   Undecided   Disagree

25. I feel we have a higher-than-average level of manager turnover in the portfolio. We tend to terminate managers for underperformance, as opposed to other issues.

    Agree   Undecided   Disagree

IV. Organizational Culture and Individual Biases

Circle the correct answer.

26. Trust but verify. I trust that investment service providers are generally well qualified to do their jobs, but I do like probing their rationales and methods to verify the depth of current knowledge and experience.

    Agree   Undecided   Disagree

27. I welcome investment policy innovation, because I know that is the only way to remain competitive, given the constant evolution of capital markets.

    Agree   Undecided   Disagree

28. While I see the benefits of financial innovation, I would rather wait until many others have tried it and proved the value added for a few years before we try it ourselves.

    Agree   Undecided   Disagree

29. There is a point at which I would rather accept market volatility than more illiquidity, even knowing that we do not really need liquidity for another 20 years.

    Agree   Undecided   Disagree

30. Even though I can see the benefits of leverage, under certain circumstances, I do not like it in any way, shape, or form. It makes me very uncomfortable.

    Agree   Undecided   Disagree

31. I know that past returns can be very alluring, but for me what is relevant is current valuations. If something looks cheap, I would buy it, even if the returns have been poor for a few years. I like to be price conscious.

    Agree   Undecided   Disagree

32. I can understand and be very tolerant of poor performance if I understand the environment in which it has occurred.

    Agree   Undecided   Disagree

33. The average tenure (average number of years on the committee) of our investment committee members is:

    Less than 3 years   3–5 years   5–10 years

34. The maximum numbers of years I think a manager should be allowed to underperform a benchmark is:

Less than 3 years   3–5 years   In the right context, does not matter

35. An investment advisor should be hired only if he or she has outperformed the market over the past three or more years.

Agree   Undecided   Disagree

36. While it feels right to outperform peers, I really only care about outperforming our own policy objectives in the context of market circumstances.

Agree   Undecided   Disagree

37. I have great respect and admiration for my colleagues in the investment committee, although I can disagree and be vocal about the reasons for my disagreement with them.

Agree   Undecided   Disagree

38. I feel great pride in the work we do on behalf of the pool beneficiaries and our sponsor.

Agree   Undecided   Disagree

39. I feel we could do much more to improve our discussions, decisions, and implementation.

Agree   Undecided   Disagree

40. I read all the material given to me in support of the discussions and decisions we need to take, and I come well prepared to the meetings.

Agree   Undecided   Disagree

41. I understand that one should never "buy high" and "sell low," but there is a point at which if you truly believe in investing for the long term, you should not be too concerned with the price you pay. Similarly, there is a limit to which you should absorb losses, even if you have sufficient resources to handle them for the foreseeable future.

Agree   Undecided   Disagree

42. You get what you pay for. I believe we should only pay high fees for demonstrable value added. Otherwise it is better to invest passively in indexed assets.

Agree   Undecided   Disagree

43. Timing is everything. While it is tempting to follow crowd behavior when markets are rising, one should avoid following crowds, even if you are being criticized for having missed a great opportunity.

Agree   Undecided   Disagree

44. I pay attention to most of the performance data and risk analysis I am provided with, and I like to look at it not as an instrument of reward and punishment, but as a description of market events and how they have affected our portfolio.

Agree   Undecided   Disagree

45. I believe that our committee is more a source of authority for decision making rather than being truly accountable for what happens in the portfolio, given that we have more service providers than one can keep pace with.

Agree   Undecided   Disagree

46. I like to learn more every day and welcome significant education in support of exercising our responsibilities as committee members. I want to stay ahead of the knowledge "power curve," whatever it takes.

Agree   Undecided   Disagree

47. While I believe in a clear delineation of responsibilities and in the importance of focusing our committee work on policy decisions, I think it is equally important to get involved in the process of selecting all managers. Probing the depth of knowledge through written material and the third-person references from our staff or service provider is not enough.

Agree   Undecided   Disagree

48. Wisdom is more important than technical knowledge.

Agree   Undecided   Disagree

49. I believe in simple rules of thumb over complex analytical explanations.

Agree   Undecided   Disagree

50. I trust an easy-to-explain process for managing risks much more than a more complex and nuanced understanding of opportunities and uncertainties.

Agree   Undecided   Disagree

V. Controls

Circle the correct answer.

51. We have an appropriate and easy-to-understand set of reports that regularly tell me all of our positions, the extent to which we are overweighted or underweighted relative to our policy and peers, and the full set of risks we are taking both absolutely and relative to policy.

Agree   Undecided   Disagree

52. We review performance in the short and long term, relative to appropriate comparators and expectations, and understand the context in which the performance is being delivered.

Agree   Undecided   Disagree

53. We review the policy portfolio at regular intervals (no less than every two to three years) to make sure it reflects our current needs and circumstances, given the capital markets outlook.

Agree   Undecided   Disagree

54. We review the appropriateness of asset class and manager benchmarks at least as often as we review the policy portfolio.

Agree   Undecided   Disagree

55. We review management succession plans to measure if we have sufficient depth of resources, institutional memory, and management capabilities over the long run.

Agree   Undecided   Disagree

56. We review our disaster recovery/business continuity provisions at least every two years.

Agree   Undecided   Disagree

57. We review management costs relative to expected value added at least every three years.

Agree   Undecided   Disagree

Ranking Your Committee

Long Governance Survey

Scoring Your Committee Along Five Key Governance Quartiles

Question	1–12	13–15	16–23	24–25	26–27	28	29	30
Agree	3	1	3	1	3	1	3	1
Undecided	2	2	2	2	2	2	2	2
Disagree	1	3	1	3	1	3	1	3

Question	31–32	33	34	35	36–38	39	40	41
Agree	3	3 (5–10)	1 (<3)	1	3	1	3	1
Undecided	2	2 (3–5)	2 (3–5)	2	2	2	2	2
Disagree	1	1 (<3)	3 (no matter)	3	1	3	1	3

Question	42–44	45	46	47	48	49–50	51–57
Agree	3	1	3	1	3	1	3
Undecided	2	2	2	2	2	2	2
Disagree	1	3	1	3	1	3	1

Questions	**Governance Factors**		**Section Scores**

Questions Governance Factors   **Section Scores**

1–6   Mission Awareness   _____/18 Max

6	9	18
Weak	Needs Improvement	Very Strong

7–16   Governance Structure   _____/30 Max

10	16	30
Weak	Needs Improvement	Very Strong

17–25   Decision-Making Process   _____/27 Max

9	15	27
Weak	Needs Improvement	Very Strong

26–50   Organizational Culture   _____/75 Max

25	37	75
Weak	Needs Improvement	Very Strong

51–57   Controls   _____/21 Max

7	10	21
Weak	Needs Improvement	Very Strong

Scoring

57–82:   Committee needs significant educational and fiduciary development support.

83–140:   Average committee—needs some improvement. Focus on areas where you could move from 1 to 3.

141–171:   Very mature and knowledgeable committee.

Glossary of Investment Terms

active strategy. The difference between current portfolio allocations and policy-benchmark weights.

alpha. A measure of the difference between a portfolio's actual returns and its expected performance, given its level of *risk* as measured by *beta*. A positive alpha figure indicates that the portfolio has performed better than its beta would predict. For actively managed funds, this can be a sign that the manager has added value to portfolio performance. A negative alpha indicates that the portfolio has underperformed, given the expectations established by the portfolio's beta.

alpha confidence interval (95 percent). The range within which the true quarterly alpha of the manager is estimated to fall with 95 percent probability.

annual return. The annualized return of the manager or index for the period.

annual value added. The value added by the manager in excess of the index.

annualized tracking error. The *standard deviation* of the annual value added by the manager. Another indicator of how well an index fits a manager's investment style. A tracking error below 2 percent indicates a close fit, and above 5 percent it indicates a loose fit.

arbitrage strategies. Attempts to exploit temporary price discrepancies between securities by buying the cheaper one and selling short the more expensive one. Investment managers use historical relationships between instruments in different markets to predict future trends of movements in price.

asset allocation. The distribution of assets among *asset classes*. Active asset allocation involves overweighting or underweighting a particular asset class relative to the target portfolio's allocation.

asset class. A broadly defined group of securities that have similar risk and return characteristics. For example, most large institutional investors such as endowment funds divide the universe of investable securities into the following categories (or asset classes): domestic equities, international equities, domestic fixed income, global fixed income, real estate, venture capital, alternative investments/special situations, and cash and equivalents.

batting average versus index. The percentage of quarters that the manager beat the index. For example, a batting average of 60 percent, which is good, means that the manager beat the index in 60 percent of the quarters.

benchmark. A reference market index that serves as a basis for performance comparison and, in the case of publicly traded investments, a passive alternative to active management.

beta. (1) A measure of a portfolio's sensitivity to market movements. By definition, the beta of the benchmark index is 1.00. A portfolio with a 1.50 beta can be expected to perform 50 percent better than the index in a rising market and 50 percent worse in a down market environment. (2) A *risk* measure derived from a regression of the manager's returns against the index's returns. For example, a beta of 1.0 means the manager's returns have been exactly as volatile as those of the index; a beta of 1.5 means the manager's returns have been 50 percent more volatile.

beta, alpha, and portable alpha. Beta and *alpha* have many meanings in statistics and finance. In the context of developing policy portfolios, beta is the market return in any given asset class, i.e., the S&P 500 for U.S. equities. Alpha is the expected excess return over the market benchmark from active management. Portable alpha involves transferring alpha from asset classes where confidence in active management is high to classes where it is low, while still retaining the beta returns of the receiving class.

beta confidence interval (95 percent). The range within which the true beta of the manager is estimated to fall with 95 percent probability.

carried interest. Expressed as a percentage of net portfolio profits, usually 20 percent in the case of straight private equity, but as much as 25 or 30 percent in the case of venture capital.

co-investments. Opportunities to be made available to limited partners, usually with certain restrictions.

commitment period. The period in years from the date of final closing during which investments will be made.

composite. A combination of two or more separate portfolios. For example, by treating all individual venture capital partnerships as a single consolidated portfolio, it is then possible to calculate performance statistics for a complete venture capital program. The same technique can be applied to any combination of portfolios or indexes for which consolidated results are desired.

convertible arbitrage. A strategy that generally consists of the purchase (or short sale) of a company's relatively undervalued (overvalued) convertible security, such as a convertible bond, convertible preferred stock, a warrant, or an option, as well as the short sale (or purchase) of the relatively overvalued (undervalued) underlying security for which the convertible security can be exchanged. There are a number of different styles of the strategy, but most managers aim to profit from (1) the yield return of the investments and (2) their relative *volatility*.

convexity. The rate of change of duration for a given change in yield. Convexity can be positive (for an option-free bond such as a Treasury security) or negative (for a mortgage security with an embedded "short" option position). In a rising interest rate environment, prices of bonds with negative convexity will drop by a greater amount than implied by a given rise in interest rates. For example, when interest rates decline suddenly or sharply, prices of mortgage-backed securities typically don't rise in the same proportion as option-free Treasury bonds, since the life of a mortgage-backed security may be suddenly shortened if homeowners prepay their mortgages, thus exercising their "long" prepayment option in a new lower interest rate environment. Changes in bond prices depend on a group of factors including the duration and the convexity effect.

correlation. A statistical measure used to express the relationship between two variables. The sign of the correlation coefficient indicates the direction of the relationship between two variables, while the absolute value indicates the extent of the relationship.

correlation coefficient. A measure (ranging in value from −1 to +1) of the association between two variables. If a variable is higher than its average value at the same time as another variable is higher than its average value, the two variables are said to be positively correlated. If a variable is lower than its average value at the same time as another variable is higher than its average value, the two variables are said to be negatively correlated. If there is no discernible relationship, the two variables are said to be uncorrelated. The closer the correlation coefficient is to +1, the more the two variables are positively correlated; the closer to −1, the more negatively correlated; and the closer to zero, the more uncorrelated. When considering adding an asset to a portfolio, the more it is negatively correlated or uncorrelated to the other assets in the portfolio, the greater the diversification the asset brings to the portfolio.

covariance. The extent to which two variables "vary together," used to determine the total *risk* associated with interrelated investments. A positive sign indicates a direct relationship, while a negative sign indicates an inverse relationship.

credit/distressed. These hedge fund strategies include investments in securities of companies that are experiencing a liquidity crisis, have defaulted on their debt obligations, have filed for Chapter 11 bankruptcy protection, or are otherwise financially distressed. A variety of strategies may be employed, including long credit, short selling, and capital structure arbitrage investing.

credit quality. Bonds issued by corporations and nonfederal government entities are rated by agencies such as Moody's or Standard & Poor's, with ratings descending from AAA to AA to A, etc. Issues rated BBB or higher are considered "investment grade," while unrated or lower-rated issues are often referred to as high-yield or "junk" bonds. The rating agencies assign ratings to a portfolio's securities based on their judgment regarding an issuer's ability to meet its obligations. U.S. Treasury securities are considered to have the highest credit quality.

disequilibrium real returns. The expected average annual real return after adjusting expected fixed income returns to reflect current disequilibrium conditions in yields.

down beta. A measure of a manager's *beta* to the benchmark. Here we isolate all time periods when the benchmark return was negative. The down beta is the slope coefficient in a regression of a return series during periods when the benchmark was negative against the negative benchmark returns, with both returns generally measured in excess of *risk*-free rates.

duration. The effect on price of a rise or fall of 1 percent in interest rates. For example, if the duration of a bond is five years, a 1 percent rise in interest rates will result in a 5 percent decline in the bond's price, all else being equal. The reverse is true for a decline in rates.

Durbin-Watson. A measure of serial *correlation* between regression residuals. A Durbin-Watson statistic of 2.0 indicates no serial correlation; near 1.0 means high serial correlation; near 3.0 means high inverse serial correlation. High serial correlation can mean that the R-squared of a regression is overstated because of a cyclical relationship between the manager's returns and those of the index.

equity long/short. These hedge fund strategies invest in equities and equity derivatives on both the long and short side. Here, the outcome is somewhat more correlated with movements in financial markets. Stock selection techniques are extremely varied and utilize fundamental analysis, technical analysis, quantitative programs, and macro and/or sector approaches, among others. The focus may be on global stock markets, country- or region-specific markets, individual industries, different capitalization classes within the same market, and other asset-class bets. The manager will often have a net-long bias (i.e., will generally have some market exposure).

equity market neutral. A hedge fund strategy that seeks to exploit temporary pricing anomalies. An inexpensive stock is purchased while a related expensive stock is simultaneously sold short. Many managers in this category look at fundamental variables using quantitative techniques and try to avoid style, industry, capitalization, and other non-stock-specific exposures.

equity/statistical arbitrage. A hedge fund strategy that seeks to exploit temporary price disparities among assets that have historically maintained a statistically significant, stable relationship. Unlike relative value, this strategy is more dependent on technical variables than fundamental analysis.

excess return. The annualized outperformance or underperformance of the manager versus the benchmark; *alpha*.

explained variance R^2. The fraction of total variance in the return series that is explained by the benchmark.

fat tails/kurtosis. A measure of whether a distribution curve is more or less sharply "peaked" than a normal distribution (and for this reason sometimes called "excess kurtosis"). Higher kurtosis means that more of the variance is due to infrequent extreme deviations (positive or negative) as opposed to frequent modest deviations. The normal distribution has a kurtosis of zero. Thus a positive kurtosis implies that a fund is more likely than predicted by the normal distribution to have large positive or negative return months, more commonly known as fat tails.

fixed income arbitrage. A hedge fund strategy that involves purchasing one fixed income security and simultaneously selling a similar fixed income security. The sale of the second security is done to hedge the underlying market risk contained in the first security. Typically, the two securities are related either mathematically or economically such that they move similarly with respect to market developments. Generally, the difference in pricing between the two securities is small, and this is what the fixed income arbitrageur hopes to gain.

foreign currency exposure. The percentage of the total portfolio that is not denominated in U.S. dollars and the corresponding contribution to *risk*.

general partner. The name of the legal entity sponsoring and performing the day-to-day operations of a fund organized as a limited partnership, which is often formed under Delaware or Cayman Island law.

geographic focus. Country or regional concentration of target transactions.

global macro. These hedge fund strategies speculate on the direction of currencies, commodities, equities, and/or bonds. They generally rely on both fundamental and technical analysis and combine long and/or short positions with leverage to optimize returns. *Correlation* with typical benchmarks is low except during exceptional *volatility* periods, when the manager might hold a directional bet in a particularly affected market (e.g., a long bet on Russian bonds when Russia defaulted).

hurdle rate. The rate compounded annually to be earned on capital drawn for investment or expenses before the *general partner* becomes entitled to carried interest.

immunization. Creating and maintaining a portfolio that will have a certain return over a specified horizon, irrespective of changes in interest rates. By matching the duration of assets and liabilities, along with periodic rebalancing procedures, investors can lock in rates and minimize the reinvestment *risk* that occurs with a simple maturity-matching strategy. Immunization balances the impact of capital gain or loss against reinvestment risk.

index. A number calculated by weighting a number of prices or rates according to a set of predetermined rules. A financial market index is a statistical construct that measures the relative or absolute price changes and/or returns in stock, fixed income, currencies, or futures markets. The purpose of the index calculation is usually to provide a single number whose behavior is representative of the movements of a variety of prices or rates indicative of a market. An investable index is one in which an investor can purchase securities and match the underlying market's performance, less transactions costs. For example, it is relatively easy to create an S&P 500 Index fund by purchasing all 500 stocks in the same weight as the index, but it is much more difficult to replicate certain emerging markets indexes.

information ratio. A measure of the likelihood that superior performance is the result of superior knowledge or judgment by an investment manager. The average excess return over benchmark (usually referred to as *alpha*) divided by its *standard deviation.*

leverage. The degree of indebtedness used to finance investment activity. For example, a leverage ratio of 2:1 indicates that $2 is borrowed against each dollar invested. Since leveraging enhances both positive and negative returns, it increases *volatility* but also profit potential.

liquidity premium. An extra component of yield or return required to compensate the investor for the possibility that an adequate resale market may not develop for a security.

liquidity score. A weighted average of the liquidity score of underlying assets. The liquidity scores for assets range from 0 percent for private equity to 100 percent for cash and represent our estimate of the percentage of assets that could be liquidated in one month without material market impact.

management fee. Expressed in basis points of committed capital during the investment period and of invested capital during the liquidation phase.

manager. The name of the legal entity managing the fund. Also can denote individual portfolio managers.

manager performance. The value added by the investment manager relative to an appropriate benchmark that reflects the manager's investment style. For example, although the entire U.S. equity sector is measured against the Dow Jones Wilshire 5000 Index, Strategic measures the individual managers against other benchmarks, such as the Russell 2000 (a small-cap index) or the S&P 500 equal-weighted index (a mid-cap benchmark).

manager structure. The value added by Strategic when it chooses a portfolio structure that differs from the portfolio structure of the asset class's benchmark. For example, in U.S. equities this is the value added by selecting managers that focus on small- or mid-cap stocks, when the benchmark for the asset class (i.e., the Dow Jones Wilshire 5000) has a much higher weighting to large-cap growth stocks and less exposure to small- and mid-cap stocks.

margin purchase. Using money borrowed from a broker-dealer to purchase securities.

minimum commitment. The minimum capital commitment accepted from each limited partner.

net asset value (NAV). The value of the investment pool calculated by taking the market value of all securities held in the portfolio and dividing by the total number of shares or units outstanding.

net long/net short. Net-long exposure occurs when a manager has more long exposure than short exposure. For example, if a portfolio is 100 percent long and 25 percent short, we say the manager is 75 percent net long. Conversely, if a portfolio is 100 percent long and 110 percent short, we say the manager is 10 percent net short.

nominal return. The expected average annual return of the portfolio before adjusting for inflation.

nominal tax efficiency. Estimates the percentage of pretax nominal returns that an investor could expect to retain after subtracting taxes.

objective. Target IRR, stated in specific terms but with appropriate qualifiers.

observations. The number of quarters or other periods used in the computations.

one-, two-, and three-standard-deviation losses. In any given year, assuming a normal distribution, returns equal to or lower than these losses would be experienced with a probability of 17.0 percent, 2.5 percent, and 0.5 percent, respectively.

policy benchmark risk. Estimated *volatility* of the current policy benchmark asset mix, assuming passive security selection.

policy portfolio. A long-term investment strategy that should achieve the objectives of the institution, provided markets deliver equilibrium returns consistent with the assumed rates of return for the asset classes selected for investment. The portfolio consists of a definition of each allowable asset class, a benchmark index for each asset class and the total portfolio, a strategic asset allocation, and a set of *risk* control ranges.

portable alpha. Portable alpha involves transferring alpha from asset classes where an investor believes there is a greater opportunity to create positive alpha to classes where the opportunity is low, while still retaining the beta returns of the receiving class.

portfolio risk. Considers benchmark, asset mix, and active security selection strategies.

quarterly alpha. The quarterly excess return of the manager, as estimated by a regression of the manager's returns against the index's returns.

rate of return. Three different return numbers are usually quoted. The average rate of return is the simple average of the periodic returns. It is used in statistical calculations like the *standard deviation*. The dollar-weighted rate of return (also referred to as the internal rate of return, or IRR) is the rate of return that discounts a portfolio's terminal value and interim cash flows back to its initial value. It is the true rate of return that an investor receives on her or his initial and other periodic investments. The dollar-weighted return is considered misleading for performance measurement purposes because the timing of periodic investment flows is considered outside the investment manager's control. The time-weighted rate of return adjusts for this by eliminating the effect of cash flows. It is the annualized compound rate of return achieved over a particular period irrespective of cash flows. When measuring results since inception, most managers will have higher time-weighted returns than dollar-weighted returns. This is because performance usually suffers as additional assets are added. The two returns should also be considered when measuring past results and considering commitments to private investments like venture capital. Historically, most of the good returns in these sectors have been achieved when the amount of capital committed has been small.

real geometric return. The compound growth rate in excess of inflation. The geometric return is often estimated by subtracting one-half the portfolio variance from the arithmetic return.

real return (arithmetic). The expected average annual return of the portfolio in excess of inflation.

real volatility. The expected annual *standard deviation* of returns.

return. (1) The YTD return is the NAV divided by the December 31 NAV, minus 1. (2) The one-year return is the current NAV divided by the NAV 12 months prior, minus 1. (3) The multiyear-and-since-inception return is the percent return such that if the beginning-period NAV were to be compounded annually by that rate of return, it would equal the current NAV.

return/beta. Annual return divided by the estimated *beta* of the manager or index. A measure indicating how much return has been generated per unit of risk as defined by beta.

return/standard deviation. A measure indicating how much return has been generated per unit of *risk* as defined by *standard deviation*.

risk. Exposure to uncertain change, either favorable or unfavorable. In popular usage, the focus is appropriately on adverse change. Annualized *standard deviation* is often used as a generic measurement of risk, but there are other more complicated statistical measures. There are also investment risks that do not lend themselves to mathematical calculation, such as political risk.

risk analysis. Estimates future annualized *standard deviation* of returns.

risk premium. An additional required rate of return due to the extra risk incurred from investing in an asset class. Often three-month U.S. Treasury bills are considered "risk-free" investments, and investors require no risk premium. Stocks are "risky" and investors require extra return above three-month T-bills to invest in them. This extra required return is the risk premium. Over time, the risk premium that investors require changes depending on the aggregate view of the market.

R-squared. (1) The percentage of a portfolio's movement that is explained by movements in its benchmark index. In a portfolio with an R-squared of 100, all of the portfolio's movements are completely explained by movements in the benchmark index. A portfolio must have an R-squared of 75 or higher for its *alpha* and *beta* to be considered reliable. (2) The proportion of the manager's return that can be explained by the index's return. A key indicator of how well an index fits a manager's investment style. For example, an R-squared of 0.93 means that 93 percent of the variation of the manager's return is explained by the index, and the rest is explained by other influences such as stock selection.

serial correlation (one month lagged). A measure of the *correlation* of a return series to itself over successive time intervals. In this case, how correlated the present month's return is to the prior month's. Less liquid strategies, and strategies that are marked to market infrequently or inaccurately, often exhibit serial correlation. Returns for relatively liquid strategies, such as those generated by investing in the S&P 500 or in equity market-neutral strategies, generally exhibit no serial correlation.

Sharpe ratio. A *risk*-adjusted measure of return. The average of the periodic portfolio returns minus the periodic risk-free rate divided by the portfolio's *standard deviation*.

short sales. The sale of borrowed securities considered overvalued in order to purchase them later at lower prices to make a profit. Short selling can be used as a hedging technique or for speculation.

skewness. A measure of symmetry in the distribution of returns. Positive skew implies that the right tail of the distribution is more pronounced than the left. In other words, relative to a symmetrical distribution, the return series has some extreme high values. For a positively skewed distribution, the mean is higher than the median. The distribution of wealth in the United States is an example of a positively skewed distribution. With regard to hedge fund returns, negative skew, a distribution where the mean is below the median, implies that while the fund may have generally exhibited consistent positive returns, outsize events have been to the downside.

Sortino ratio. A measure of excess return per unit of *risk* based on downside semivariance, instead of total risk. While similar to the *Sharpe ratio*, this ratio focuses only on downside *volatility* because investors are most concerned about the risk of loss.

standard deviation. A measurement of variation around a mean (the square root of the mean of the squared deviation of members of a population from the mean). The standard deviation is the most widely used proxy for *risk*. It is useful when the observations are normally distributed around the mean but can be misleading if they are not.

target fund size. Target amount of aggregate commitments given in round numbers, such as $100 million or $1 billion.

term. The period in years for which the fund is organized, usually 10 years, and the number of extensions at the discretion of the *general partner* or with the approval of the advisory committee.

total return. The time-weighted measure of performance that includes both capital appreciation (or depreciation) and dividends or other income received.

total volatility (standard deviation). The annualized *standard deviation* of the quarterly returns of the manager or index. A measure of the volatility of the returns of the portfolio. In any given year, there is a 68 percent chance that the manager's return will fall within plus or minus one standard deviation of the overall annual return.

tracking error. A measure of how much a portfolio deviates from its benchmark. Usually expressed as the *standard deviation* of the portfolio's excess return (*alpha*).

up beta. A measure of a manager's *beta* to the benchmark. Here we isolate all time periods when the benchmark return was positive. The up beta is the slope coefficient in a regression of a return series during periods when the benchmark was positive against the positive benchmark returns, with both returns generally measured in excess of *risk*-free rates.

volatility. A measure of the dispersion or spread of *observations* around the mean. Statistically, this is expressed by the *standard deviation*. The words "volatility" and "*risk*" are often used interchangeably, although strictly speaking volatility is only one of several investment risks.

volatility above-average return. The annualized *standard deviation* of the quarterly returns that fall above the average quarterly return. A measure of the upside volatility of the returns.

volatility below-average return. The annualized *standard deviation* of the quarterly returns that fall below the average quarterly return. A measure of the downside volatility of the returns.

win percent. The percentage of months with returns above the return to T-bills over the given time period.

worst four quarters. The lowest return over four consecutive quarters.

worst negative quarter. The lowest quarterly return of the manager or index.

Notes

Preface

1. The nineteenth century American humorist Josh Billings said, in a quote sometimes misattributed to Mark Twain, "It ain't so much the things we don't know that get us into trouble. It's the things we know that just ain't so." Ralph Keyes, *The Quote Verifier*. St Martin's Griffin, 2006.
2. SWOT analysis is credited to Albert Humphrey at the Stanford Research Institute in the sixties and seventies, but Humphrey did not claim the credit.

Introduction

1. McKinsey Global Institute.
2. World Bank Data Book.
3. World Bank. Poverty is measured by the percentage of people in the world living on less than $1.90 per day adjusted by cost of living standards and assuming purchasing parity across currencies, in real 2005 prices.
4. Albert-László Barabási, *Linked: The New Science of Networks*, Perseus Books Group, 2002.
5. Frank H. Knight, *Risk, Uncertainty and Profit*, Hart, Schaffner & Marx, 1921.
6. The SEI 100-Fund Universe.

7. Robert Shiller, "Relationship Between Cyclically Adjusted Price-to-Earnings Ratio (CAPE) and Average Annual Real Returns for the Subsequent 10 to 15 Years," Wikipedia.

8. "Robustness is a property that allows a system to maintain its function against internal and external perturbations . . . and uncertainties." Hiroaki Kitano, "Towards a Theory of Biological Robustness," *Molecular Systems Biology*, September 18, 2007.

9. Investors can be constrained by regulations, governance limits that may have been imposed without sufficient thought, and self-imposed rules to protect against criticism. Insurance companies are forbidden by state laws to invest their reserves in portfolios with less than acceptable ratings. These regulations constrain them from buying high-yield debt even if by their own analysis these instruments offer more attractive risk-adjusted returns. Many guidelines imposed by investment committees to limit specific risks prohibit certain investments (e.g., companies in bankruptcy or lower-quality debt) regardless of their investment merits. Certain endowments limit their fixed income to, say, 5 percent of total assets, but it can only go into government debt. These restrictions, while preserving something—culture, deniability, face, errors of inexperience—curtail the freedom to construct better portfolios. The unconstrained, experienced, undogmatic investor will have a competitive advantage.

10. A recent example of these opportunities is nonperforming bank loans, following regulators' requirement to increase banks' capital and shed bad loans. Banks are inclined to sell nonperforming loans because recovery is expensive for them. They aren't functionally equipped to collect from bad debtors, or they may not want to alienate the client and hurt future business. Managers that specialize in analyzing these loans and recovering a higher portion of the debt than is priced by the seller bank can find attractive risk-adjusted returns. These loans are a fixed income investment that does not fit in any of the rated debt ladders (they are unrated). They aren't in the high-yield bucket either, because they aren't marketable. They don't fit in unmarketable private equity because they are not equity. They could be in a new bucket, such as nonmarketable private debt, but the bucket doesn't exist because the market is relatively small and few managers specialize in the field.

11. Graham Allison, in "The Thucydides Trap," *Atlantic*, September 24, 2015, points to China's rising challenge to the United States as such a present risk.

12. Charles D. Ellis, *Winning the Loser's Game*, 5th ed., McGraw-Hill, 2010.

13. Andre Agassi, *Open: An Autobiography*, Knopf, 2014.

Chapter 1

1. Mandy Len Catron, "To Fall in Love with Anyone, Do This," *New York Times,* January 9, 2015.

2. Determining the price of an asset:

$$PA = PMR \times BA + e$$

where:

PA = price of an asset

PMR = price of market risk

BA = beta of the asset, where beta is the regression coefficient of that asset to the market

e = error term

3. Werner K. Heisenberg was a German theoretical physicist who said "what we observe is not nature itself but nature exposed to our method of questioning." Among countless contributors to theoretical physics, he demonstrated that there were not absolute states of the world that would not be altered by the momentum of the variable. The Heisenberg "uncertainty principle" states that the more precise the "position" of a particle, the more imprecise the "momentum" of the particle and vice versa.

4. Bridgewater Associates, "Daily Observations," February 2018.

5. Ibid.

Chapter 2

1. Edward I. Altman, "Financial Ratios, Discriminant Analysis and the Prediction of Corporate Bankruptcy," *Journal of Finance*, September 1968, p. 589.

Chapter 3

1. Ibbotson and Sinquefield, "Stocks, Bonds, Bills, and Inflation: Year by Year Historical Returns (1926–1974)," *Journal of Business,* vol. 49, no. 1, January 1976.
2. Antoine van Agtmael, "Emerging Securities Markets," *Euromoney,* 1984.
3. Roger G. Ibbotson and Gary Brinson, *Global Investing,* McGraw-Hill, 1993.

Chapter 6

1. During the 1998–1999 tech bubble, tech stocks traded at P/E multiples of 70 and higher. Many stocks had no earnings and quite a few no earnings prospects. Some stocks with earnings prospects were trading at P/E multiples of 100, which would have required 100-plus years to recover investment.

Chapter 7

1. *USA Today,* January 2, 2018.
2. David F. Swensen, *Pioneering Portfolio Management: An Unconventional Approach to Institutional Investment,* Free Press, 2009.
3. "The Yale Endowment 2015."

Chapter 8

1. The price per unit of risk in a globally diversified portfolio is also referred to as the slope of the capital market line (see Figure I.1). The price of 38 basis points per unit of risk (standard deviation) as of 2017 is derived from the expected 5.2 percent real return of and 11.5 percent standard deviation for a globally diversified balanced portfolio, using equilibrium assumptions.
2. The first academics to identify the risk-parity concept were the grandfather-granddaughter team of Franco Modigliani and Leah Modigliani in 1997 articles describing how securities should be compared and optimized by equalizing their risks. See Franco Modigliani, "Risk-Adjusted Performance," *Journal of Portfolio Management,* 1997, and Leah

Modigliani, "Yes, You Can Eat Your Risk-Adjusted Returns," Morgan Stanley U.S. Investment Research, March 1997. The first manager offering that used a 20-year duration bond future in its tactical asset allocation (TAA) product came from the former team at Wells Fargo Bank in the early eighties, made up of Bill Fouse, James Vertin, and Tom Loeb. Tom is currently chairman at Mellon Capital. More recent and successful proponents of the risk-parity approach are Bridgewater Associates and AQR.

Chapter 9

1. The NACUBO-Commonfund Study 2015.
2. "The Yale Endowment 2015."

Chapter 11

1. Dimitry Mindlin, "On the Relationship Between Arithmetic and Geometric Returns," CDI Advisors LLC, August 2011:

$$G = A - V/2$$

G = geometric (compound) return
A = arithmetic (average) return
V = variance (standard deviation squared)

This short and simple formula works well for normal returns around 10 percent and standard deviations under 20 percent. For higher returns and standard deviations, more complex approximations are needed.

The exact conversion of average annual returns to geometric compound returns can be calculated by the following formula:

$$R_{GN} = \sqrt[n]{(R_{A1} \times R_{A2} \times R_{A3} \times \ldots R_{An})}$$

That is the geometric return of a series of n years annual returns is the nth root of the product of n-year annual returns (Wikipedia offers a good number of alternative formulas and conversion tables for calculating geometric returns from annual series).

2. Warren Buffett, "Buy American. I Am," *New York Times*, October 16, 2008.

Chapter 13

1. BlackRock, 2011; Ryan Vlastelica, "ETFs Shattered Their Growth Records in 2017," MarketWatch, January 3, 2018.

2. Robert Arnott, Jason Hsu, Vitali Kalesnik, and Phil Tindal, "The Surprising Alpha from Malkiel's Monkey and Upside Down Strategies," *Journal of Portfolio Management*, Summer 2013.

3. $IR = IC^2 \text{ (breadth)}$

   where:

   IR = information ratio or value added per unit of risk
   IC = correlation between ex ante forecast and realized return
   Breadth = number of bets (signals) on which you have demonstrated skills to place a bet. Breadth is a function of how independent the bets are from each other.

4. "Career bets" is a term we first heard from Jeremy Grantham of Grantham Mayo Van Otterloo (GMO), touting the firm's heroic bets in several sectors.

Chapter 16

1. Amit Goyal and Sunil Wahal, "The Selection and Termination of Investment Management Firms by Plan Sponsors," *Journal of Finance*, vol. 63, no. 4, August 2008, 1805–1847.

Chapter 17

1. See Benoit Mandelbrot and Richard L. Hudson, *The (Mis)Behavior of Markets: A Fractal View of Financial Turbulence*, Basic Books, 2006.

Chapter 19

1. Michael Lewis, *The Undoing Project: A Friendship That Changed Our Minds*, Norton, 2016.

Chapter 20

1. Fortune 500 Women Executive Officers & Top Earners 2013.

Bibliography

Investment Strategy

Charles D. Ellis, *Winning the Loser's Game: Timeless Strategies for Successful Investing.*

Eugene Fama, *The Fama Portfolio: Selected Papers of Eugene Fama.*

Milton Friedman, *The Methodology of Positive Economics.*

Mark Gavagan and Warren Buffett, *Gems from Warren Buffett: Wit and Wisdom from 34 Years of Letters to Shareholders.*

Benjamin Graham and David L. Dodd, *Security Analysis.*

John L. Maginn, Donald L. Tuttle, Dennis W. McLeavey, and Jerald E. Pinto, *Managing Investment Portfolios: A Dynamic Process.*

William Sharpe, *Selected Works.*

Robert J. Shiller, *Irrational Exuberance.*

David F. Swensen, *Pioneering Portfolio Management: An Unconventional Approach to Institutional Investment.*

Richard H. Thaler, *Misbehaving: The Making of Behavioral Economics.*

Annette Thau, *The Bond Book.*

Risk Management

Peter L. Bernstein, *Against the Gods: The Remarkable Story of Risk.*

Gary L. Gastineau and Mark P. Kritzman, *Dictionary of Financial Risk Management.*

Benoit Mandelbrot and Richard L. Hudson, *The (Mis)Behavior of Markets: A Fractal View of Financial Turbulence.*

Innovation
Clayton M. Christensen, *The Innovator's Dilemma: The Revolutionary Book That Will Change the Way You Do Business.*

Adam Grant, *Originals: How Non-Conformists Move the World.*

Analytical
Mark P. Kritzman, *The Portable Financial Analyst: What Practitioners Need to Know.*

Behavioral and Governance
Daniel Ariely, *Predictably Irrational: The Hidden Forces That Shape Our Decisions.*

Albert-László Barabási, *Linked: How Everything Is Connected to Everything Else and What It Means for Business, Science, and Everyday Life*

Ray Dalio, *Principles: Life and Work.*

Charles Darwin, *On the Origin of Species.*

Milton Friedman, *The Methodology of Positive Economics.*

Ryan Holiday, *The Obstacle Is the Way: The Timeless Art of Turning Trials into Triumphs.*

Daniel Kahneman, *Thinking, Fast and Slow.*

Michael Lewis, *The Undoing Project: A Friendship That Changed Our Minds.*

Jim Loehr and Tony Schwartz, *The Power of Full Engagement: Managing Energy, Not Time, Is the Key to High Performance and Personal Renewal.*

Robert C. Pozen, *Extreme Productivity: Boost Your Results, Reduce Your Hours.*

Norman E. Rosenthal, *The Gift of Adversity: The Unexpected Benefits of Life's Difficulties, Setbacks, and Imperfections.*

Adam Smith, *The Wealth of Nations.*

Edward O. Wilson, *The Meaning of Human Existence.*

Index

Page numbers followed by *f* indicate figures.

About the Author

Hilda Ochoa-Brillembourg is the lead founder and chairman of Strategic Investment Group and co-founder of Emerging Markets Management and three affiliated asset management firms. A Fulbright Fellow and Fulbright Lifetime Achievement awardee, she completed doctoral studies (except dissertation) in Business Administration in Finance at Harvard Business School and received a Master of Public Administration from the Kennedy School of Government at Harvard and a Bachelor of Science in Economics from Universidad Andrés Bello, Caracas. She is a Chartered Financial Analyst.

Hilda was chief investment officer of the Pension Investment Division of the World Bank from 1976 to 1987 and continued as an external manager of the World Bank's pension assets until 1995. A native of Venezuela, she also served as asset and liability adviser to the World Bank, the Venezuelan government, Grupo Electricidad de Caracas, and others. She has been a lecturer at the Universidad Católica Andrés Bello and IESA in Venezuela, treasurer of the C.A. Luz Eléctrica de Venezuela in Caracas, and an independent consultant in economics and finance. She serves on the boards of directors of Strategic Investment Group; Cementos Pacasmayo, S.A.A.; the Asset Management Company (AMC), a World Bank affiliate; and the Atlantic Council of the United States. She is a former director of General Mills Inc., 2003–2016; S&P Global Inc. (formerly McGraw-Hill Financial, Inc.), 2004–2017; US Airways Group Inc., 2000–2004; Custodial Trust Company, 1988–1999; World Bank Group/IMF Credit Union, 1986–2008; Harvard Management Company, 1991–2010; Vassar College, 1988–

1998; Fulbright Association, 2007–2011; and Research Foundation of CFA Institute, 2009–2011, as well as an investment committee member of the Rockefeller Family Fund, 1982–2008.

Hilda is the founding chairman of the Youth Orchestra of the Americas and serves on the advisory committee of Harvard's David Rockefeller Center for Latin American Studies and the investment committee of the New England Conservatory. She is a lifetime member of the Council on Foreign Relations, a member of the American Enterprise Institute National Council, the Committee for Economic Development Board, Harvard's Kennedy School Dean's Executive Council and Dean's Alumni Leadership Council, and was a longtime member of the World Economic Forum. She was a trustee and in later years president of the executive committee of the Washington National Opera, 1998–2010, and of the executive committee of the National Symphony Orchestra, 1999–2007; vice chairman of the Group of Fifty (G-50) at the Carnegie Endowment for International Peace, 2000–2010, and an ad hoc member of the United Nations Secretary General's Joint Staff Pension Fund Investment Committee (2011–2012).

She has been featured in *Pensions & Investments*, *Fortune*, *Bloomberg Latin America*, *Investment News*, *Smart Money*, and *Money* magazine, as well as *Efecto Naím*, Fox News Latino, the *AIMR Exchange*, *Hispanic Business* magazine, and *PODER* magazine, where she was described as one of the "50 most successful women in the U.S." She has been quoted in the *New York Times*, *Wall Street Journal*, *Financial Times*, *Bloomberg*, and elsewhere. She received *aiCIO* magazine's Lifetime Achievement Award. She has published articles in the *Financial Analysts Journal*, *Pensions & Investments*, *The Atlantic*, and *International Economy*, and has been a guest lecturer at Columbia University, Georgetown, George Washington University, Johns Hopkins, The New School, and Yale.